The Politics of Bor

Borders sit at the center of global politics. Yet they are too often understood as thin lines, as they appear on maps, rather than as political institutions in their own right. This book takes a detailed look at the evolution of border security in the United States after 9/11. Far from the walls and fences that dominate the news, it reveals borders to be thick, multi-faceted and binational institutions that have evolved greatly in recent decades. The book contributes to debates within political science on sovereignty, citizenship, cosmopolitanism, human rights and global justice. In particular, the new politics of borders reveal a sovereignty that is not waning, but changing, expanding beyond the state carapace and engaging certain logics of empire.

Matthew Longo is Assistant Professor of Political Science at Leiden University. He received his PhD with distinction from Yale University in 2014 and was awarded the Leo Strauss Award for the Best Doctoral Dissertation in Political Philosophy, given by the American Political Science Association.

Problems Of International Politics

Series Editors
Keith Darden, *American University*
Ian Shapiro, *Yale University*

The series seeks manuscripts central to the understanding of international politics that will be empirically rich and conceptually innovative. It is interested in works that illuminate the evolving character of nation-states within the international system. It sets out three broad areas for investigation: (1) identity, security, and conflict; (2) democracy; and (3) justice and distribution.

The Politics of Borders

Sovereignty, Security, and the Citizen after 9/11

Matthew Longo

Leiden University

CAMBRIDGE
UNIVERSITY PRESS

CAMBRIDGE
UNIVERSITY PRESS

University Printing House, Cambridge CB2 8BS, United Kingdom

One Liberty Plaza, 20th Floor, New York, NY 10006, USA

477 Williamstown Road, Port Melbourne, VIC 3207, Australia

4843/24, 2nd Floor, Ansari Road, Daryaganj, Delhi – 110002, India

79 Anson Road, #06-04/06, Singapore 079906

Cambridge University Press is part of the University of Cambridge.

It furthers the University's mission by disseminating knowledge in the pursuit of education, learning, and research at the highest international levels of excellence.

www.cambridge.org
Information on this title: www.cambridge.org/9781316622933
DOI: 10.1017/9781316761663

First published 2018

Printed in the United States of America by Sheridan Books, Inc.

A catalogue record for this publication is available from the British Library.

ISBN 978-1-107-17178-7 Hardback
ISBN 978-1-316-62293-3 Paperback

For Nina

Contents

Preface: Anatomy of a Crossing

Imagine yourself at a border, or at the arrivals hall of an international airport. What do you see? It is a place swarming with activity. If you are in an airport, you have just walked past aisles of glimmering merchandise. If you are at a land border, you are accosted by touts calling out their wares – do you perhaps need a water as you wait in the sun, or umbrellas to defend against the rain? Then you come upon the queue of people waiting to cross into the country of their destination. Their faces reveal a medley of moods: excitement at coming home, fatigue from travel, anxiety about the impending interrogations. As you approach you wonder: what will they ask me? Have I filled out my forms properly? Will they search my belongings? What will they find? In fact, each border has two sides: one for each state. And within each border, two crossings: one for people (immigration), another for goods (customs). When you pass through these hoops – which cannot be taken for granted for many travelers – you breathe a sigh of relief. You are welcomed by flags and signs; a wall of gleaming faces. Perhaps this gaudy new horizon is a space of familiarity. Perhaps, trepidation. Either way, you are changed by the experience. Even if all you did was cross from one side of a line to another – an act that in the twenty-first century should be banal. You might wonder: what happened to have affected me so?

I

A border is a space of definition, of delineation. It is also an in-between place of heterogeneity and contradiction. A border can be like the wall of a fortress, fencing people out; like the wall of a prison, fencing other people in. The border is a palimpsest, signifying different things to different peoples at different times. It is a meaning-bearing space, meaning-generative too.

It is a place of absolution, of proving-one's-worth and proving one's not-worth-wasting-time-with. Of homogeneity-as-purity, security-as-omnipotence. And odd bedfellows: you should trust the system, but question your neighbor ("if you see something, say something").

It is a place where violence is most and least expected. Where the condition of its impossibility is also its allure.

The border is the definitive marker of the political, defining in and out, friend and enemy, us and them. It is also where all the paradoxes of modern politics come to the fore: the contest of *diversity* and *singularity*; *chaos* and *order*; *liberty* and *security*. And of course, power: power that is everywhere visible; that is invisible. That disciplines and directs; that saves some, as it punishes others. That watches and is watched, even when the lights turn off and the chamber empties of bodies. Power that lies in wait, that anticipates, which is, in itself, the antithesis of power.

For most of human history, the border was a peripheral thing, a dusty land of criminality and relegation, a haven for tax evasion and nonconformity. A forgotten, far-flung place. Today, it is the center of the political world.

II

This book draws inspiration from my own experiences at borders. Having traveled and lived for many years across the Middle East, border crossings have been particularly memorable – places I frequently felt uncomfortable as an American. What was I doing there, the officials wanted to know. Who was I working for? These were often spaces in which I came to feel unsafe, even though I was putatively in the hands of the state (including "friendly" ones), under the stewardship of my own government by means of the ceremonial blue-and-gold document in my hand. Yet just as frequently these encounters were banal, the giant flags and concrete towers excrescent from the sand bidding no process at all. In these cases, passage was automated, as through the turnstiles of a subway – my passport reduced to a glorified MetroCard. Either way, the border was an event. It was something to be anticipated, often the highlight of a long bus ride across a monotonous, lunar landscape.

But as much as these crossings abroad were formative, they paled beside my experiences returning home. Here, my passport – the very vehicle that protected me abroad and which guaranteed my re-entry home – became a liability. What were these foreign stamps – *Syria*, *Yemen*, *Egypt* – the port officials asked? Who did I speak to and what did we discuss? Because of my experiences abroad – as a student, an employee, a tourist – I have been escorted off planes, separated from my wife for interrogations, placed in vast databases (which continue to find me, unexpectedly). My documents have been taken away from me, placed in sealed plastic bags as though they – and thus, I – were a form of contagion. I was at home, but rather than feeling welcome, I felt *suspected*.

What these borders revealed to me was a discord between how borders appear on maps – simple, homogenous, uncomplicated lines – and how they were manifest on the ground. On maps, borders are defined by several attributes: thinness (they have no depth); external homogeneity (all borders look the same); internal homogeneity (all aspects of the border are the same); and moral neutrality (no history of violence, legitimacy). But these cartographic depictions do not align with our *experiences*. In fact borders vary mightily. Some are marked, others aren't. Some have long queues, others are untrafficked. Some feel secure, even though they are all, in different ways, vulnerable. On the map, the border is a line defining one monochrome state from another. They are taken to be simple, and given, which could not be further from the truth.

Embarking on this project, I took as my starting point the goal of identifying the border in all of its complexity – as a site of human interaction. Before we can appreciate why this is true, we need to change the way we see borders, away from *thin* jurisdictions, and toward *thick* institutions. The following vignettes and anecdotes of border crossings frame the discussion.

III

Salman Rushdie, in a talk entitled "Step Across This Line," describes his experiences at border crossings as follows:

At the frontier we can't avoid the truth; the comforting layers of the quotidian, which insulate us against the world's harsher realities, are stripped away, and, wide-eyed in the harsh fluorescent light of the frontier's windowless halls, we see things as they are ... At the frontier our liberty is stripped away – we hope temporarily – and we enter the universe of control. Even the freest of free societies is unfree at the edge, where things and people go out and other people and things come in; where only the right things and people must go in and out. Here, at the edge, we submit to scrutiny, to inspection, to judgment. These people, guarding these lines, must tell us who we are. We must be passive, docile. To be otherwise is to be suspect, and at the frontier to come under suspicion is the worst of all possible crimes ... We must present ourselves as simple, as obvious: I am coming home. I am on a business trip. I am visiting my girlfriend. In each case, what we mean when we reduce ourselves to these simple statements is, I'm not anything you need to bother about ... Truly. I am simple. Let me pass.[1]

In *Palestinian Identity*, historian Rashid Khalidi describes the Palestinian experience:

The quintessential Palestinian experience, which illustrates some of the most basic issues raised by Palestinian identity, takes place at a border, an airport, a checkpoint: in short, at any one of those many modern barriers where identities are checked and verified. What happens to Palestinians at these crossing points brings home to them how much they share in common as a people. For it is at these borders and barriers that the six million Palestinians are singled out for "special treatment," and they are forcibly reminded of their identity: of who they are, and of why they are different from others.[2]

Henk van Houtum, a geographer, remembers family trips as a child, crossing into Eastern Europe by car during the Cold War:

What particularly struck me during the passing of the Iron Curtain was the impressive sound of silence. On the way there, my parents were comforting and attentive. Games, music, eating, laughing – all was permitted up to this point. But the border stopped our childishness. When going through customs, my parents became surprisingly and impressively silent. We sensed they were no longer in control. Realizing that there was a bigger, overarching power other than our parents was frightening, unreal. The heavily armed men who checked our faces and passports made an intimidating impression on my sister and me. It was as if the making of sounds could lead to suspicion. We did not dare to look at each other. Our faces were motionless, without expression. We kept quiet. No laughter. No nothing. Passiveness. Tension. An atmosphere built out of machines, uniforms, domination, pressure and suspension. Not seldom this tension and containment turned into a joy of relief when we finally passed through. My father then would pedal the car a bit harder and we shouted things like "YEAH! We're through! Now our holiday can start!" It was if we had just passed a test.[3]

The power of these accounts derives from their commonality, despite radically different terms of encounter. For Rushdie, as for most first-world travelers, gates fling open. For the Palestinians, they slam shut. And yet, the same questions and anxieties obtain. The rollercoaster of emotions is captured masterfully by van Houtum, who describes breathlessness while awaiting judgment, anxiety at being watched, and euphoria at passing through to the other side. These emotions are familiar, despite taking place in an entirely different geopolitical era.

Interrogation has always occurred at international crossings. At the turn of the century, in the aftermath of the Haymarket Riot of 1886 and Immigration Act of 1903, US border officials asked questions like: "Are you a Polygamist?" or "Are you an Anarchist?" It's unclear the purchase of these queries except to prompt travelers to reflectively doubt their loyalties. Such was H. G. Wells' reaction upon reaching the US:

The questions seem impertinent. They are part of a long paper of interrogations I must answer satisfactorily if I am to be regarded as a desirable alien to enter the United States of America. I want very much to pass that great statue of Liberty ... [But it is] at the price of coming to a decision upon the (theoretically) open questions these two inquiries raise.[4]

Borders cultivate a sense of interiority and exteriority through their very presence (and practice). What is remarkable about this quotation is that the "other" created at the border has nothing to do with national differentiation – anarchists and polygamists are equally unwelcome, regardless of whether they hail from a friend nation or an enemy one, or *are themselves citizens*. The border is not home to anyone; it is a space of adjudication. One must prove one's worth to enter.

Border interrogation has evolved considerably since Wells' day and has come to include more invasive physical searches. Nowhere is this truer than at airport crossings. One contemporary social theorist, Gillian Fuller, describes these experiences as follows:

Visible to all, only our thoughts move in private. Our baggage, our bodies, and our movements are all part of an encompassing spectacle … On a recent trip through a "SARs scare," I was thermally scanned and appeared though the operator's windows interface as a series of roughly pixellated mauve, green, yellow, and orange blobs … Each of my movements, including the incorporeal ones, where my digital-double was being processed generated another abstraction of me.[5]

Fuller is not alone in feeling turned-inside-out by technology at the border. Much recent social criticism is dedicated to the dystopian aspects of new security protocols, with the border described as the interaction point between the human body "and the data-double," driven by biometrics that turn the human body into "readable text."[6] The border is a site of purging – a place "to cleanse of guilt, sin and impurities" – where everyone is a suspect, and everyone feels the imperative to self-categorize as non-risky.[7]

In any case, for the individual traveler, the border manifests as a moment of identification – a site where the rudimentary aspects of our political and social identities are called into question, scrutinized and judged; where we are forced to reconcile ourselves as *citizens* or *co-nationals* and understand the privileges and obligations of those commitments. At the border we distill ourselves and all our human complexity into our nation. We become our papers, no more, no less – the same identity that we might otherwise identify *against*. This experience changes us. Forced to *be* our nation, to *be* normal, we are compelled to reconsider ourselves (in all of our transgressive abnormality). Here the border is like a funhouse mirror: we are reduced to a self play-acting at normalcy, a normalcy that is itself revealed as artifice. To act "normal" means to vanish into the undifferentiated mass of what is expected of us – i.e. to be the antithesis of anything security would concern itself with (Rushdie's "I am simple, let me pass").

Foucault's distinction between discipline and law here is instructive: law leaves room for that which is unknown; for discipline, what is unknown is the least allowable.[8] At the border the citizen is risky until proven harmless, not innocent until proven guilty. It is for this reason that at the border the traveler feels *unfree*. Through its practice, the border turns individuals into *population*.[9] This sets up a paradox: through discipline, individuals are reduced to "population" at the precise moment they are, through increasingly advanced forms of identification, most individualized. Discipline at the border is thus a process of *de-individuation through regulated individuation*.

At the border we also encounter our own foreignness, as we are not-quite-in but not-quite-out. Although we are not "strangers" we nonetheless feel estrangement, as the border (even *our own*) is not yet home. The port of entry is, literally, a door – an "in-between" place between home and abroad. The ambiguous nature of the border makes it the site of a paradoxical, *inhospitable hospitality*.[10] When a citizen returns "home," she is in need of hospitality from her own state, thus she is "guest" in a house, where by dint of membership, she should be "host." This estrangement at the border is amplified by our encounters with foreigners. It is a common trope that in spaces of cultural interaction, differences and similarities are thrown into relief – we realize, as Julia Kristeva observed, "*nous sommes étrangers à nous même*."[11] This reaction is acute at the border, as we meet foreigners at a point of *mutual strangeness*.

The border is also a space of *state vulnerability*, as the border is its least defined point, the intersection of law and nothingness. In this way, we are also disciplined by the *force of ambiguity*. The border-crosser is the *subject* of discipline, to be protected by the state, and its *object*, that which the state must protect against. They are at risk from intruders and of being an intruder. For the traveler, this experience prompts ontological uncertainty. Part of why we respect state authority is because it provides cognitive stability. As Bourdieu argues, one of the central functions of states is to produce the "naturalization of its own arbitrariness."[12] Yet this "naturalness" fades at the periphery. It is an arresting space for the traveler, as the world's arbitrary underpinnings are laid bare.

The border is precisely this liminal zone, where self/other, distant/proximate, citizen/state are called into question. In such a climate, identities are not just filtered, but created, modified and destroyed. This is evermore the case now, in the age of expansive security protocols. Ironically, borders have become far more critical in light of today's globalized mobility – putative borderlessness – than they ever were during preceding eras of sovereign fixity. Why this is the case, and why it matters, is the subject of the chapters to follow.

IV

Not every project becomes a book; those that do, get help. This one would not have been possible without the assistance and support of many colleagues, friends and family along the way. I have had the immense fortune of working with two advisors that encouraged me in complementary ways. I first encountered Seyla Benhabib as an undergraduate at Yale. Her lectures introduced me to thinkers like Hannah Arendt, Michel Foucault and Jacques Derrida – figures I still engage with today, and without whom I probably never would have decided to pursue graduate education. As her doctoral student, she anchored me in critical theory, and refined my unruly ramblings into manageable and meaningful claims. At the same time, I became greatly moved by the writings and approach of Jim Scott, who encouraged me to go out into the field and test my intuitions; to see the border-world as it appeared to those that inhabited it, to abandon my comfortable perch many thousands of miles away. He gave me the courage to follow my passion for discovery, even though it fit uncomfortably in the rubric of the discipline. I am indebted to each in different ways.

Graduate education is a production with an ensemble cast; mine would not have reached its completion without Paulina Ochoa, Bryan Garsten and Andrew March, who coached me through the many stages that took this project from prospectus to dissertation to book. I also received support from a number of places, most notably the National Science Foundation Graduate Research Fellowship Program and the MacMillan Center at Yale. I feel particularly indebted to Ian Shapiro whose generosity helped propel the project at its outset; and later, kept it afloat. More recently, I feel very grateful to have had the opportunity to complete this work while as a postdoctoral fellow at St Anne's College, Oxford. A special word of thanks is due to Todd Hall, Neil MacFarlane, Ian Philips, Johannes Abeler and Terry O'Shaughnessy as well as to Michelle Clayman, without whom the fellowship would not be possible. Other colleagues who warrant a word of appreciation include Katharine Brooks, Daphna Canetti, Lucas Entel, Francesca Grandi, Nancy Hite, Humeira Iqtidar, Turku Isiksel, Leigh Jenco, Halbert Jones, Stathis Kalyvas, Willem Maas, Karuna Mantena, Lois McNay, Shmulik Nili, Erin Pineda, Ayelet Shachar, Steven Smith, Sarah Song, Luke Thompson, Peter Verovsek, Elisabeth Wood, participants at the Yale Political Theory workshop, the Oxford IR Colloquium, and the Comparative Political Theory Workshop at King's College, London and much earlier, to Ellen Lust, who helped pique my interest in scholarship long before this project ever took shape.

Finally, this book would not have been possible without the tireless, loving help of my wife, Nina. She has edited more drafts than I would like to admit, and her talent and dedication to craft has helped make this book what it is. Without her, this book may never have been written; it certainly wouldn't have been written as well.

Notes

1 Rushdie, Salman. *Step Across This Line: Collected Non-Fiction 1992–2002.* London: Vintage, 2003, at 412.
2 Khalidi, Rashid. *Palestinian Identity: The Construction of Modern National Consciousness.* New York: Columbia University Press, 1997, at 1.
3 van Houtum, Henk, and Anke Strüver. "Where Is the Border?" *you are here: the journal of creative geography,* 4, no. 1 (2002): 20–23, at 21.
4 Wells, H. G. *The Future in America: A Search after Realities.* Lexington, KY: Forgotten Books, 2014 [1906], at 3–4.
5 Fuller, Gillian. "Welcome to Windows 2.1: Motion Aesthetics at the Airport." In *Politics at the Airport,* edited by Mark B. Salter, 161–74. Minneapolis: University of Minneapolis Press, 2008, at 165–70.
6 Muller, Benjamin J. "Travelers, Borders, Dangers: Locating the Political at the Biometric Border." In *Politics at the Airport,* at 128; Ceyhan, Ayse. "Technologization of Security: Management of Uncertainty and Risk in the Age of Biometrics." *Surveillance & Society* 5, no. 2 (2008): 102–23, at 104.
7 Browne, Simone. "Digital Epidermalization: Race, Identity and Biometrics." *Critical Sociology* 36, no. 1 (2010): 131–50, at 145–6.
8 Foucault, Michel. *Security, Territory, Population: Lectures at the College De France, 1977–1978.* Translated by Graham Burchell. New York: Picador, 2007 at 46.
9 Ibid., at 57.
10 This follows Derrida's observation that every act of hospitality bears the potential for hostility. Derrida, Jacques. "Hostipitality." *Angelaki: Journal of the Theoretical Humanities* 5, no. 3, 2000: 3–18.
11 "We are strangers to ourselves." Cited in Benhabib, Seyla. *The Claims of Culture: Equality and Diversity in the Global Era.* Princeton: Princeton University Press, 2002, at 165.
12 Bourdieu, Pierre. *Outline of a Theory of Practice.* Translated by Richard Nice. Cambridge, UK: Cambridge University Press, 2003 [1972], at 164.

Notes on the Cover Image

Border Door, 1988

Site Specific Installation/Intervention Performance
Golden wooden door, nails, keys, door knob, blue wooden frame and hinges

Free standing workable door installed on the Mexico/USA border ¼ mile east of the Rodriguez International Airport. The performance extended to the neighborhood where the artist grew up in Tijuana. Where he gave out over 250 keys inviting the residents of La Colonia Roma and Altamira to use his Border Door.

Artist: Richard A. Lou

Photo Credit: James Elliott

Introduction

Inasmuch as the human world is political, it does not present an indefinite variability. It is structured and ordered ... If we decisively abandon the nation form, we shall have to enter another form for one cannot live politically in an undefined way.

– Pierre Manent[1]

A borderland is a vague and undetermined place created by the emotional residue of an unnatural boundary. It is in a constant state of transition.

– Gloria Anzeldua[2]

In the years since 9/11, two issues – terrorism and immigration – have dominated the global political imaginary. At the center of each, an institution: the border. Worldwide, states have responded to these challenges via the tightening of population controls within and without the territorial limit of the polity. The centrality of borders to these challenges is immediately manifest. What problem does immigration raise? It is the threat of *them* overwhelming *us*. And terrorism? Of *them* attacking *us*. Both problematics center on fantasies of exclusion and binary logics of interiority/exteriority, us/them, identity/difference. In short: borders.

This is understandable. The border is the defining institution of the nation-state. It is also the site of sovereign decisions over membership. Borders define *states*, as "bounded power containers,"[3] as well as *sovereignty* – territoriality, internal sovereignty (autonomy) and external sovereignty (mutual recognition) are all bounded concepts. Contrary to early prognostications, the relevance of borders has only grown with *globalization* or "de-bordering," and subsequent *securitization* or "re-bordering," with the proliferation of walls and fences worldwide after 9/11.[4] Indeed, the question of the *political unit* – the contours of the polity, as well as who is included or excluded from its ranks – is in many ways the soul of contemporary politics. It provides the stage on which all other politics is performed.

1

It would be no exaggeration to state that border security is a point of obsession of our times. The terrorism threat is well known, certainly after 9/11, but also more recently with attacks in urban centers across Europe, including Madrid, London, Brussels and Paris. The challenge of migration has exploded in recent years. At present, the number of estimated migrants – people living outside their country of origin – is up to 244 million people.[5] Most importantly, these two problems are increasingly seen as linked – the double-headed hydra of global mobility.[6] As with the prompt, we are familiar with the response. Worldwide there has been an increase in xenophobia and populism, with nativist backlash against newcomers and a return to bald forms of identity politics and nationalism, embodied by the desire for border walls.

Borders sit at the center of contemporary politics, but remain poorly understood, usually reduced to legal-topographical instantiations of sovereignty and placed as representative markers on the classic nation-state grid. They are jurisdictions without institutional existence – without "horizontal extent."[7] Like lines in the sand, they are thin and vertical as they appear on maps. This portrayal is misleading and problematic, as such two-dimensional entities can only vary along one axis – permeability – vastly delimiting the scope of debate. Empirical debates over globalization hinge on whether borders are more or less porous, with transnational flows more or less able to be stoppered.[8] Even in Wendy Brown's *Walled States, Waning Sovereignty*, new border walls are evidence of "the weakening of state sovereignty":[9] as borders become permeable, states become less sovereign. Normative writing focuses on whether borders should be open or closed, with scholars variously arguing that closed borders are incompatible with liberalism or that the state's ability to determine admission and exclusion suggests "the deepest meaning of self determination."[10] The same limitations beset debates over transnational justice, where scholars argue whether borders should be transcended in favor of a higher law.[11] In either case, they do not themselves have institutional existence.

This book takes a different approach. It takes as its subject the evolution of borders since 9/11 – i.e. *trends* in bordering – focusing in particular on the case of the United States. It begins with an empirical finding, that far from the walls and fences that dominate news coverage, in fact borders are *thick*, *multi-faceted* and *bi-national* institutions that have evolved greatly in recent decades. This point is illustrated by a detailed portrait of the US borders with Canada and Mexico since 9/11 and especially after several groundbreaking agreements in 2010–2012, such as the Beyond the Border Agreement with Canada and the 21st Century

Border Initiative with Mexico. Thereafter it builds out toward a discussion of how borders are changing worldwide.

The book takes as its warrant a series of extraordinary changes in thinking about borders after 9/11, which have been refined and expanded in subsequent years. The first is that after 9/11 border security and national security stopped being considered discrete domains. In the decades prior to the terrorist attacks, border security was primarily a response to illegal immigration and drug smuggling. After 9/11, the border became a central theatre of national security. An al-Qaeda press release in 2012 stoked this fear:

In 1996, 254 million persons, 75 million automobiles and 3.5 million trucks entered America from Mexico. At the 38 official border crossings only 5 percent of this huge total is inspected ... These are figures that call for contemplation.[12]

This shift in thinking about borders mirrors a change within the intelligence community. A leading intelligence expert explains: "We used to have a bright line between the domestic and the foreign. Now this is changing, such that the protection of the homeland is part of the same structure of information as foreign terrorism."[13] Blurring the distinction between home and abroad does not erase the border – quite the opposite, it situates the border at the center of information-sharing practice. Borders are the precise environment where transnational crime and terrorism intermingle, cohabitat and breed.

The second shift is that states increasingly do not believe they can secure their borders unilaterally. This thinking took time to take hold. In the immediate aftermath of 9/11, the breach of US soil mandated a large-scale security build up of manpower and infrastructure – Border Patrol more than doubled in size. It also led to the vast outpouring of support and funds for the fence on the border with Mexico. However, as discussed at length later, it became clear very quickly that by any measure, this strategy was insufficient to actually "seal" the border. As former DHS Secretary Janet Napolitano observed, "you show me a 50-foot wall and I'll show you a 51-foot ladder at the border."[14] The Government Accountability Office further criticizes our "poor record of accomplishment using technology to secure our borders."[15] Perhaps the most vocal skeptic of US border walls is Terry Goddard, former Attorney General of Arizona:

Much of the "secure the border" debate is nonsense ... Constructing any part of the wall wastes valuable time and resources. Worse, like a modern version of the Maginot Line, it provides a false sense of security, the illusion that we are doing something to remedy border problems.[16]

This shift in thinking about walling is pervasive. As a border technology engineer explained to me, our first approach after 9/11 was to address border security by saying "let's go with the big bang theory … let's build this virtual and physical fence;" it took a while before we came to the "understanding that you can't just build a wall around the United States."[17]

Third, border security came to be understood as a problem that could only be solved through the development of advanced data capabilities with an emphasis not merely on data accession, but also data-sharing. This move toward data-sharing portends a broader shift in security-strategy away from states and even sub-state actors and toward individuals. A US Department of Defense (DOD) biometrics specialist explained the evolution of our strategic environment as follows:

> The world as we have tried to secure it and thrive in it has made an evolutionary leap and continues to morph and amend at an incredibly rapid pace … [But] we have a national security culture that grew up facing and deterring threats from other nation-states, who operated within historically defined and well understood boundaries … [Today] we face complex and unpredictable threats that by their very nature, blur geographic, organizational and jurisdictional boundaries … [Our challenge is] to magnify our focus down to the individual person level. [To collect, analyze and manage] identity data and specifically the biologic, biographic, behavioral and reputational aspects of identity.[18]

The heightened focus on individual-level intelligence fuels the need for data – and for borders that can accommodate that data and international agreements that can produce this data – which, in turn, actually *necessitate* sharing. Robert Gilbert, former Chief of Border Patrol sums this up by explaining that their goal is: "to create a twenty-first century border … through information-sharing that has never occurred before … The reality is, while securing the border is upfront and personal, *you can't do it alone.*"[19]

These changes in thinking about border security form the empirical warrant for this book, which explores the evolution of borders, states and sovereignty. The research presented here highlights several trends, which can be disaggregated by the two central facets of the border – the *perimeter* and the *ports of entry*.[20] At perimeters, states are beginning to widen their border spaces, projecting surveillance far from the border itself in both directions and creating thick webs of infrastructure and law-enforcement that extend many miles inland. In addition, states are beginning to co-locate forces on either side of the line, creating a set of *de facto* overlapping jurisdictions. At ports of entry, states have moved toward risk-based adjudication of admission, with expansive technological infrastructure. The administration is fueled by vast quantities of data – so-called

Big Data – engendering a regime of cross-border data-sharing and even technological interoperability. The results are bi-national ports of entry that are cooperative, jointly managed spaces with co-located officials – mirroring relations at the perimeter.

These findings generate a number of significant conclusions. Beginning with the subject of *borders*, I argue that these sociological changes are evidence of a broader realization that in today's world, governments *cannot administer their borders alone*; instead, borders must be bilaterally managed and administered. These changes herald an epochal shift in border functionality. Under the early-Westphalian system of states, the border was conceived primarily as a buffer-line dividing states from each other, contra interstate war or invasion. By contrast, in the late-Westphalian period, borders became filtration-sites, protecting states from the movement of people – evermore so now with the explosion of global migration. However, this new phase of border-functionality we are entering – concomitant to the rise of securitization – is wholly different. It is one in which borders are not designed for states to oppose one another or to oppose migratory flows, but rather where states work together (co-locate, cross-designate) to regulate the movement of people – i.e. join forces in the *shared* fight against transnational migratory flows. The state is not simply reacting to de-bordering by re-bordering, it is forging a new path: *co-bordering*.

This implicates *sovereignty*. I argue that the dual management of border ports and overlapping perimeter patrols creates a heterogeneous form of sovereignty. These joint administrative and law enforcement structures present a challenge to our notion of sovereignty as indivisible rule over a territorial jurisdiction, or *territoriality*. In addition, sovereign decisions over entry/exit are now predicated on data gathered by non-national (frequently private or international) sources, whose origin can no longer be distinguished by border officials. This challenges the sovereign decision, as while border officials remain the ultimate arbiters, the predicates of their decision are increasingly obscure. In both cases, the sovereign control of borders is increasingly heterogeneous, paradoxically due to the very securitization mechanisms erected toward sovereign defense. In short: states are *ceding classic markers of sovereignty for the sake of security*.

This evolving geopolitical order raises a number of normative concerns. At first blush, this heterogeneous model of sovereignty has numerous attractive features, especially in its potential for multi-lateral institutional agreements between states – common in debates over global justice. However, there is also potential for harm in a system designed primarily to maximize states' abilities to organize against migratory flows. I argue that if left on it its own, co-bordering may metastasize into a form of *neo-imperial overreach*, with borders transforming into sites of asymmetrical co-optation. Indeed, on its face, joint sovereignty assumes *heterarchy*, but is here revealed to mask *hierarchy*. Instead, *heterarchy* is the model to which we aspire. The primacy of global data-sharing agreements adds another dimension here, as countries that agree to align their data security operations may increasingly form a union against those that don't – establishing a so-called data "firewall."

The purchase of this reconceptualization is considerable. The new politics of borders reveal a sovereignty that is not waning, but changing, expanding beyond the state carapace and engaging certain logics of empire. Wendy Brown was right to point out that our popular lust for walls is part of a fantasy of exclusion. But there is much more than this. New borders also embody fantasies of colonization, extraction, co-optation and control. These are *extra-mural* fantasies, to take the constitutive outside and make it our own; to catch the barbarians before they materialize. New border policies also demonstrate a need for distance, to push the outside farther away, where the threat can no longer get us. But there are *intra-mural* dynamics as well. New policies aim to perfect the control over the internal subject as well as the external one, thus engaging fantasies of entrapment, management and domestication. The dream of subjugation is especially prevalent with peripheral citizens, who embody not the threat to invade, but to secede.

We can here forge a connection between global subjects and domestic ones. By looking carefully at borders, we can see how new policies at the border collapse two forms of statecraft: *rationalization* (or the process by which the state uses technologies of security to monitor individuals within) and *securitization* (which includes the monitoring of all people, regardless of location or citizenship status). Across the globe, states are imposing ambiguous, imprecise and expansive security laws, especially as pertains data security. Increasingly, states monitor phone calls, texts and emails, collect "metadata" and geo-located data and track financial transactions – policies that affect citizens and non-citizens alike. This book diagnoses a number of harms associated with these new protocols and suggests models by which they may be alleviated.

The aim of this book is to unveil the many dynamics at play in the *politics of borders*. Its tenor is critical and cautionary, but also emancipatory. We must first understand the world as it is unfolding, before we can think through strategies by which it might change.

Through the Looking Glasses: Two Ways of Seeing

If you've seen one mile of the border, you've seen *one mile* of the border.
– US Border Patrol saying

What does it mean to *see* a border? How would we know if we succeeded? This book seeks to capture borders in all their complexity. This means inquiring into what border guards see when they are looking out into the borderlands – to peek through the looking glasses; to see like the state, at the state's edge. With this in mind, it is helpful to begin with a few words on method, focusing on two "ways of seeing." The first section makes a case for using methods common to anthropology and other forms of qualitative and interpretive social science to contribute to debates within political theory. The second discusses what it would mean to think about borders normatively and what kind of agenda such an empirical strategy would engender.

Dispatches from the Bazaar

The research strategy employed in this book is heterodox. It is *empirical* in that it establishes an argument from the ground up, starting with descriptive claims about the world – a type of sociological portraiture relatively absent in political theory. At the border, this research consisted of interviews with border guards and port officials, local and federal law enforcers and politicians (of various ranks and capacities).[21] This research *had* to be conducted in person, as many of the programs discussed here are in pilot form, created by Memoranda of Understanding between officials and thus no laws, acts of Congress or newspaper articles would be sufficient to inform.

But understanding the border is in no way limited to the periphery; most "bordering" takes place at the center – in the US case, Washington DC – where I interviewed engineers and tech developers who contribute to conceiving and designing the "twenty-first" century border. To this end, I attended conferences and expos where government officials and industry leaders meet.[22] These conferences were invaluable. They are sites where government officials outline what they consider to be the future concerns of the state and seek out new forms of technology to aid these agendas. In this way, it is a kind of *bazaar*, where government and industry form and express preferences in tandem. This window into the future of bordering is unique to this workshop-like setting: one does not get it at the border, where policies are applied, or in the news, where they get coverage. These conferences are also settings in which a researcher can engage directly with the technology – to look through new lenses that can focus miles across the border on a pair of *chonas* (undergarments) hanging from the window of a house in Juarez; to stand behind the screen of the newest airport scanners, observing modalities in heat representation and learning to read the contours. These experiences render border security tangible; they pull back the wizard's curtain, enabling a view from the other side.

This empirical course is at once *qualitative* and *interpretive*. It is *qualitative* by procedure, with field research dedicated to the goal of uncovering: it answers "what" questions, not "why" questions, more common to quantitative social science. What does a border do, what are its functions? What does it look like to border-designers; what about border-managers and technicians? What might a border look like in ten years time? It is *interpretive* in application: given this picture, what meaning can we extract about politics? What perspective do we gain?

Here the link to *theory* is clear, as with every act of uncovering comes reconsideration. This methodological cocktail is by no means new to political theory. I follow what Jean Cohen refers to as a two level approach, "empirical-diagnostic and normative-prescriptive," or what Paul Piccone calls "the discovery of systematically concealed interests."[23] In this vein, James Tully's work has been described as engaging "redescription with critical intent."[24] The goal is to tackle real world issues – here issues of power, authority and domination at the state's edge – and subject these findings to critical scrutiny.

Where I break ranks with most theorists is in the manner of performing empirical diagnostics. I consider it a weakness of contemporary theory that for its diagnostic component it relies almost exclusively on received wisdom – from print news sources or legal documents. As noted above, any scholar of borders that follows the news is subject to being swept into an unfortunate tide of hysterical and misleading information – even from the best available sources. Further, the lack of sociologically informed work greatly delimits the range of topics available to theorists, who avoid some of the most pressing issues in politics because they lack the empirical basis for argumentation. At the same time, immaculately crafted normative theories frequently seem out of place when set afield in the real world. Indeed, while theorists often pay lip service to the empirical world, they rarely engage it directly. And when they do, empirical methods are frequently relegated to a form of feasibility testing.[25] This is unfortunate, as diagnostic empirical work can also be theory *generative*. In fact, the tradition is filled with the works of great thinkers who also conducted empirical research: from Herodotus' emphasis on *kleos* or "what men say and hear"[26] to Tocqueville's gallivant across America. Many serious theoretical projects have engaged field-work; hopefully many more will follow.

The research detailed in this book begins with a microscopic view of particular policies in the US context, then expands out to increasingly large concentric circles of observation, from the local to the federal positions in the US, then finally to evidence from other sectors of the globe. With each expansive stroke, the picture becomes more appreciable: of a world that is changing before our eyes, in places most of us never deigned to look. In this way, it is a work of *speculative theory*: it portends changes on the horizon. Like any prognostication, this is risky. But only to a degree, as the sociological basis for these claims – the roots – are firmly planted in circumstances already observed.

Modes of Normativity

What would it mean to think normatively about borders? The answer to this question is not straightforward. For much of political theory, the problem with borders is that they won't go away. Thus normative solutions include superseding or erasing borders, cultivating transnational legal institutions or simply turning borders into administrative units. Instead, this book takes the *matter* of boundaries as given – it does not believe in a world without some forms of political delineation – but not their *form*. To this end, it analyzes various ways by which states have historically managed their peripheries (from city walls to imperial frontiers). The goal is not to question whether there should be boundaries, but rather whether they can be designed in such a way as to minimize harm.

This generates two kinds of normative agenda. The first is dedicated to understanding. It follows from the belief that by scrutinizing institutions we can uncover embedded forms of ideological distortion, or the ways in which our policies have been shaped by the operations of power. This calls to mind Bernard Williams' claim that political philosophy must focus on the interrelations between "power and its normative relative, legitimation."[27] It also invokes Foucault's conception of political philosophy, the role of which is to "keep watch over the excessive powers of political rationality."[28]

The second agenda is dedicated to change. Above all, this book aims at destabilizing our conventional view of borders and the justifications by which new security policies are enabled and perpetuated. This mirrors the agenda set forth by Judith Butler in her book *Frames of War*, in which she sets out to critique the narrative by which war is justified – the "frame." For her, the key is to disentangle strategic discourse from normative justification, enabling us to appreciate the grievability of the ungrievable. She calls this moment of realization a rupture in the frame that

provides the conditions for breaking out of the quotidian acceptance of war and for a more generalized horror and outrage that will support and impel calls for justice and an end to violence.[29]

With borders, as with war, we take a lot for granted. And we accept a lot as part of an instrumental discourse that might well be better placed in moral terms. The goal then is to provide the tools by which such a reconsideration is possible. We cannot eliminate borders, but we can shape them; we can't eliminate state rationalization, but we can alter its form. For new forms of political activism to emerge, we must better understand the modes of oppression as they develop: new binary logics engender new interstitial relationships, new sites of power mean new sites of resistance. The point of this book is to help identify points of power that seek redress. Although the bulk of this book is critical, it also offers constructive content – blueprints that others might use to design progressive social policies that are more inclusive, conscientious and egalitarian than those they replace.

Plan of the Book

Chapter 1 situates contemporary borders in their historical context, revealing how borders have come to take their present shape – a contingent outcome neither necessary nor irreversible. It asks how political units have historically managed their periphery, divided typologically between the three classic forms of political organization – city, empire and state – each of which offers insight into a particular aspect of bordering. This inquiry establishes several important conceptual distinctions. First, it challenges the classic dichotomy between frontiers, as *zonal* spaces and borders as *linear* ones, placing boundaries instead on a spectrum. Indeed, a central thesis of this book is that as borders move away from thin jurisdictional lines they also stop acting like borders: instead they start to resemble *frontiers*. Thus the border/state dyad is transforming into an empire/frontier dyad. As the border comes to resemble a frontier, sovereignty starts to resemble *imperium* – a Roman designation for authority, including over the management of the periphery.

Second, it distinguishes two forms of sovereignty present in peripheral spaces – authority (*de jure* rule) and control (*de facto*) – with an emphasis on the latter. Looking carefully at the ways in which peripheries have been (*de facto*) controlled in different periods offers insight into how and why sovereignty has evolved (and how it may again). As it is as likely that *de facto* changes drive *de jure* ones, it is imperative to analyze both. This is an important corrective to studies that only look at *de jure* sovereignty. In doing so, this chapter reveals how sovereignty has a spatial dynamic, with some swaths of territory under less control than others, including those beyond the juridical limit of the polity.

Two further points warrant mention. The first is that, as mentioned above, some form of boundary system is intrinsic to political orders. Insofar as this is true, this book encourages a rethinking of politics in terms of a dynamic set of *delineations* (boundaries), rather than any fixed *substance*. Second, whereas boundaries are necessary, this does not mean they engender homogeneous divisions. Borders by their nature culti-vate interiority and exteriority. But they also engender diverse modes of interiority: such as, between center and periphery. I refer to this as the *heterogeneous inside*. In fact, much of what is interesting about cross-border relations pertains to inter-peripheral engagements – between one peripheral group on one side (the *distant self*) and one on the other (the *proximate other*). A principal story of the border is the domination of the periphery by its own center.

This chapter opens the ground for discussion of *the politics of unit* – or the shape of polities – and lets us inquire into whether new forms of pol-ity are possible. In so doing, it paves the way for the in-depth empirical material on which the remainder of the book is based.

Part I – The Perimeter

Part I focuses on the *perimeter*. Chapter 2 provides a brief account of US border security leading up to the present and chronicles critical developments in technology, infrastructure, manpower and organiza-tional re-alignment – here looking solely at developments on the US side – toward the aim of making the perimeter *wider* and more akin to a *zone*. This new border area is first a *Zone of Surveillance*, as there is a broadening of physical infrastructure, with layered walls, roads, towers and surveillance installations – essentially a "net." It is second a *Zone of Heterogeneity*, as there are multiple forms of authority, including federal, state and local forces (as well as the military), the coordination of which includes information-sharing and inland checkpoints. Third, it is a *Zone of Vigilance*, given the increased role that citizens play in the monitor-ing of cross-border activity, amounting to the integration of local border communities in law enforcement.

This material raises a number of questions. The first regards the relationship between the state and its citizens. This chapter asks us to reconsider how authority is structured in the new borderlands. In many ways there is a blurring of security and law functions at the border, raising concerns of the *military acting like police* and the *police acting like military*. This feeds back into the discussion of vigilantism or individual *discretion* – a dangerous personalization of authority, that invokes pre-modern forms of statecraft. It also raises concerns about the nature of sovereign power in the borderlands. It asks: if authority is heterogeneous, who is sovereign in the periphery? The border is a space of great vulnerability, of sovereign *anxiety* – a space filled by the police. This raises Agamben's concern about the state of exception in which the sovereign assumes full powers and abrogates legal constraints. In doing so, the practice of sovereignty at the borderlands undercuts its normative basis.

Chapter 2 also raises questions about who is subject to sovereign rule. Broadly, sovereignty (*qua* control) is strongest in the center and wanes as it approaches the periphery; however, at the border, the state re-emerges. In this way, the border is the central state displaced at the periphery – it is an instrument of central control used as much to subjugate the periphery as to defend it. Indeed, the original challenge of statehood was to achieve homogenization within – essentially a local colonial project – not merely (and simplistically) to negate the world without. This fact is lost when we speak of democracy's edges in pure abstraction, as limits; but borders are physical spaces at which those originary acts of subjugation (including against the domestic periphery) are re-created daily.

This characterization raises important normative questions. What challenges do new security protocols place on the local peoples of the borderlands regions? Do we have a right not to live in a securitized zone, a place of constant surveillance? More importantly: *What is it about security that we find objectionable?* In part, we find it objectionable when it is not in the interests of the people it affects. In this case, the goal of security is not merely to protect the local populations against a threat, but also to condition their loyalty toward the center. Thus, as much as security is aimed at their protection, it is also aimed at their control. The people on the border have a double role: they are most *at risk* from outside threats, as well as *at risk of being a threat*. They are both the *subject* and *object* of security.

Chapter 3 takes this subject and expands it out to cross-border developments, including progressive forms of joint border management, such as co-location and cross-designation. The most comprehensive bilateral engagements are underway on the US–Canada border. This process began in maritime waters – via a program called Shiprider, with the placement of US border patrol officers on Canadian ships in Canadian waters and Canadian officers on US ships in US waters. This is expanding to include forces on land, enabling overlapping policing missions across the border and cooperation both in planning and management, establishing a de facto joint administration on the ground. It is also adjoined by tremendous political overtures. In 2012, DHS declared that its "vision for the northern border *cannot be accomplished unilaterally.*"[30] Similar plans are afoot on the US–Mexico border. One border guard explained the unfolding scheme as follows:

The concept of a 21st Century Border is having a border zone, a thicker area, if you will – not just that delineated judicial line – where we could cross and patrol together … It would be a dual-sovereign zone, almost like a Euro-zone … I can tell you, I have never seen greater strides, in the last three years. It is just incredible.[31]

Here too, the border is *widening*, both internally, as the border creeps inward, and externally, as the border becomes a cross-border zone of dual management.

Given this empirical material, this chapter makes a number of claims, centering on the notion of sovereignty qua *territoriality* or the idea that states are territorially defined, bounded political units. This form of sovereignty has been quite embattled throughout the period of globalization, although for the most part it has remained intact. Even supranational organizations (like the EU) and international organizations (like the UN) are comprised of member states which retain territorial authority. By contrast, the more radical move suggested here neither entails the spread of power within a state (horizontal) or a higher authority that transcends the state (vertical), but rather a territorial form of horizontality in which there is horizontal overlap *without any corollary vertical extent*. This challenge to sovereignty clearly exists on the *de facto* level; increasingly it exists on a *de jure* level as well.

So how might we go about understanding sovereignty without territory? We need a new conceptual vocabulary. Drawing on the idea of *de facto* sovereignty, we might first think of sovereignty not as binary – a state either is or isn't sovereign over a jurisdiction – but rather as *spectral*, with states more or less able to control their territories such that there are *degrees of sovereignty*. Under this rubric, sovereignty is not territorial but *spatial*, with the sovereign having power over as much space as it has capacity to control. Sovereignty that is *spectral* and *spatial*, starts to resemble authority familiar to empire – i.e. *imperium*, a designation for authority that is not territorially circumscribed. Thinking spatially also allows us to see adjoining states as *neighbors* – like Siamese twins, structurally conjoined. It also allows us to reconsider borderlands peoples – the *distant self* and the *proximate other* – as frequently subjects of artificial division, a harm that (re-)unification may rectify.

These marked changes in the nature of rule over the borderlands raise a number of concerns, but also opportunities for proactive change. With this in mind, the chapter closes with a blueprint for limited cross-border citizenship for border dwellers, who are increasingly subject to two sovereigns (and thus, uncertain rule). This model would entail some role in the decision-making process as regards border policies (and especially decisions that directly affect local communities), thereby enabling cross-border *representation*. Conceptually, this model is new in that it designs a form of citizenship geared not toward establishing a set of rights for members – i.e. a citizenship of interiority – but rather is aimed at establishing new kinds of membership that break down distinctions of interiority and exteriority. It is a form of *localization* – or the *turning local* of a community that was once geopolitical, by enabling and unifying practices of peoples on both sides.

Chapter 4 expands outward from the US case and engages examples of co-bordering worldwide. It shows how new perimeter-level bordering practices are re-structuring the international state system. As was evident in the US case, there is a clear understanding that problems threatening states – terrorism, illegal trade, immigration – threaten *all states alike*. This globalization of threats increasingly requires states to operate together. Far from the weakening of states, this results in their strengthening, through joint coordination. This chapter culls information from around the world, beginning with direct US involvement in global affairs, especially through technology transfers and regional modeling schemes. It also treats two cases carefully – the EU and South Africa – showing how co-bordering logics have taken root in extremely different contexts.

The chapter then addresses the question of global governance – a normative take on the *politics of unit* – asking whether co-bordering can approximate some form of territorial ideal. Certainly, the concept of jointly managed borders has normative allure. Indeed, this form of bi- and multilateral institutionalism is immediately promising for the global project of cosmopolitanism. For example, co-bordering might facilitate federalism, or the repooling of sovereignty between states, providing building blocks to a regional schema and a framework for how states can form political institutions in tandem. In this way, co-bordering could provide the glue, adhering member states, compatible with a supranational constitutional structure. At an advanced level, co-bordering could pave the way for the synching of laws between neighboring polities, planting the seeds for an enduring form of *heterarchy*. This said, there are also myriad potential harms to co-bordering. Borders as institutions can help protect weak states from strong ones. Once the black box of mono-sovereign borders is opened, this protection falls away. Co-bordering might enable forms of imperialism between *neighbors* that we normally associate with the more distant abroad – a form of *proximate colonialism or occupation*. In this regard, looking at the contemporary US, the wall is perhaps the least normatively concerning aspect of the border. Instead, the fear is that joint borders may enable neo-imperial overreach.

In concluding this discussion, I offer another citizenship model – raising the question of whether co-borders could become fruitful zones for engaging the problem of *migrants*, expanding upon the cross-border citizenship concept introduced in Chapter 3. Such a model could offer an institutional basis whereby certain human rights could be protected and state institutions might be checked by international powers.

Part II – The Ports of Entry

Part II follows the same model – starting with the evolution of border practice in the United States and then expanding globally – but focuses on *ports of entry*. US ports are undergoing considerable physical and organizational changes. Most importantly, they are transforming to accommodate a strategic shift from "deterrence" to "risk assessment." This means policy initiatives focused on the process of filtration, such that ports "let in the good" and "keep out the bad" at the same time. This is achieved by improving the quality of checks – via "smart" checks – such that the *good* is let in more quickly and the *risky* are slowed down. Obtaining this balance requires effective risk management, which in turn depends heavily on data – both biometric and biographic – captured at or in advance of border ports and used to verify identities at the gate. As a result, port security has undergone a major transition from "minimal security checks" to, immediately after 9/11, "more security checks for all" to today's variant, "security checks for some more than others," via risk-based filtration.

Chapter 5 unpacks the basics of data usage in governance – the parallel processes of *classification, filtration* and *capture* – and establishes the relationship between these data protocols and border security. In addition, it raises large questions about the nature of state and citizen, especially as part of the expanding project of *rationalization* – or the management of a state by scientific principles, designed to maximize the state's capacity to control the *totality* of its subjects and to distinguish between them as *individuals* – to which Big Data can be added as its most recent and in some sense most perfect variant. Following Foucault, governments are interested primarily in the guiding and shaping of individuals according to their interests. This is the essence of the state's power – turning rough, ungainly subjects into malleable ones.

This raises a host of concerns. One harm of data rationalization is *normalization*. By filtering and categorizing subjects the state polices normal behavior and penalizes deviance. This conditioning of the "normal" traveler is precisely the mechanism by which the individual is obliged to "disappear" into population (de-individuated individuation). Another harm of this system can be expressed as a form of invasion, *the permeation of our innermost boundaries*, as data collapses the boundary between state and subject. In the creation of many data worlds and data-doubles that reside within and constitute the person, there is no form of meaningful escape from the experience of being monitored by the state. Such state rationalization engenders a world of totalizing institutions, which can have a dampening effect on human agency.

New data security protocols represent bureaucracy in its distilled form. We live now in a society in which evermore institutions and state officials enjoy authority over citizens. With data we are constrained by an invisible hand of information – a hidden text – that can be leveled at any time, including at moments we could never have predicted and, without warrant, can never understand. We sometimes have to plead with officials to let us past borders, to recognize our papers, thus forcing us into positions of humiliation and defense. Put back into the logic of data, one might say that there is an inversion of security: to become *secure* vis-à-vis physical threats, we have to surrender security-qua-domination. And since the threat may never materialize, we are actually submitting to domination – i.e., we are *insecure*-qua-domination – even though on any lived dimension, we are just as physically secure as we ever were. This is a Faustian bargain.

Chapter 6 advances this discussion by looking at cross-border practice at the ports. Here, a growing bi-national and multi-national strategy is only natural as, for pre-detection and data-centric strategies to be effective, these strategies need data in advance of the border as well as at the border itself – thereby necessitating data standardization and sharing. The filtration mechanism is only as good as the data coming in: for the data to be good, as much information as possible must be known about travelers before they arrive. At the physical ports, there is increasing interest in the creation of "bi-national" or "shared" ports of entry that look very similar to the co-location at the perimeter. This type of joint planning and management solves one of the principal shortcomings of most ports, which is that while ports are capable of monitoring *entry* into the country, they are not equipped to monitor *exit*.

At the US–Canada border these changes are already beginning to take effect. The White House goes so far as to envision future ports as shared spaces. This collaboration solves the problem of negotiating across jurisdiction – as achieved at the perimeter with Shiprider. While less advanced, the same types of policies are being pursued on the US–Mexico border – consolidated entry/exit program, standardization and even co-location. Additionally, there are already US and Mexican officers working "shoulder by shoulder" at major ports, collaborating and sharing information if trouble arises.[32]

Drawing upon this empirical baseline, the principle arguments of this chapter are about sovereignty and what I call the *politics of trust*. Changes at the ports primarily challenge the sovereign decision. This claim has three parts. First, ports are filtration devices drawing on information from national security databases. These databases produce risk evaluations based on algorithms, combining the many sources of data available on travelers to determine whether the individual should be admitted or rejected. Second, we are increasingly sharing information with other nations and deriving our own data from non-sovereign sources. Third, once entered into the system and transferred into a risk-reading, most information about data (its origins, linkages) becomes obscure to users at the point of decision. Therefore, as far as the official at the border port is concerned, these decisions are made based on information that increasingly may not be derived from sovereign sources and cannot be disaggregated or traced. Thus while the choice occurs at the port, the predicates of that choice are based on information that is increasingly in heterogeneous state control. In relying on heterogeneous sources, the sovereign is not stripped of choice, but the choice is stripped of sovereign exclusivity.

A second challenge to sovereignty comes from private or corporate sources. This means data that comes from the private sector – such as from mobile phone providers, credit card companies or internet browsers – but also data that is *stored* and *processed* by the myriad tech companies that have contracts for government work. In these cases, the data is *national* but not *sovereign*. Thus the same concerns about veracity, context and use arise. This issue will only grow in importance due to collective concerns over cybersecurity, which requires that the state work more with private companies, not less. This is further concerning, as the state is delimited in ways that corporations are not. This gives undue power to private entities, not just over individuals, but over law enforcement, which is forced to rely on data they cannot themselves collect or regulate.

This raises a host of normative concerns. If data is shared between countries, how is it to be protected and maintained? Does it bother us that another country might have access to information about us? Will states privilege gathering information on others, over protecting information of its own citizens? This chapter approaches these questions through the lens of citizenship. New technologies of filtration used at ports of entry segment people not based on citizenship – membership in a polity – but on risk scores. These data protocols force a distinction *between citizens* and between wanted and unwanted travelers *irrespective of citizenship*. Put otherwise: data filtration turns people into *de facto* non-citizens, even if they are *de jure* citizens. In doing so, it severs the political meaning of citizenship from its legal basis, further depleting the normative core of popular sovereignty.

In a world of devalued citizenship, vast classes of travelers considered undesirable, such as immigrants and travelers from other states (Third Country Nationals or TCNs) are left without protection. With this in mind, the chapter sketches a new model of citizenship designed specifically for border-crossers, suggesting that overlapping borders create not merely bilateral management and enforcement structures, but also an adjudicative wing situated at ports of entry through which border crossers can seek and obtain representation against human rights infringement. As TCNs are by definition without representation this is precisely the population that a strictly territorial law is poorly equipped to address (and which a world governance structure would be too bloated to manage).

Chapter 7 looks at the problem of data as a global concern. Global politics is dominated by the movement of people and goods. The principle solution to this glut of mobility is for states to collaborate through the sharing of data. The empirical portion of this chapter chronicles collaborative port security and data sharing worldwide. Thereafter, it turns toward a more careful exploration of data sharing and the politics of trust in the EU. Data sharing is an obvious solution to matters of cross-border concern and agreements are proliferating, but remain de-centralized, operating mostly on a bilateral basis. How this expanding web of relations takes shape will greatly inform the future of global governance.

Normative questions abound. This chapter focuses on the problem of global polarity, offering a vision of a new kind of imperial relationship between those on the inside and those on the outside – or the bifurcation of the globe along the lines of data capacity. This is what one analyst I interviewed refers to as the global *firewall* – the virtual "wall" erected between the community of nations that shares data at the exclusion of those that don't. Those about whom nothing is known (i.e. without data trails) would fall into a state of perpetual risk and exclusion – a digital dark, so to speak. Such a scheme maximizes data-security, but at the expense of a new stratification of the world. This raises concerns about dehumanization, as the firewall gives substance to the concern that modernity has an "exterior" – a form of permanent dispossessed. As such, people without data trails might come to no longer count really *as people*. Human Rights would then become a limited concept: where there is no data, there are no rights. With this polarization, and heightened inequalities, comes the perpetuation of *distance* – exacerbating what Butler called inequalities of grievability. Such authority also revisits the specter of neo-imperialism.

The chapter closes by calling attention to threats that loom on the horizon. There are a lot of critical sub-trends intrinsic to the rise of data – trends within trends – that we should take care to observe. The first concern pertains to the "digital land grab." More data is being collected today than at any point in human history, a trend that will likely continue. This raises complicated rights claims – vis-à-vis storage and the quasi-permanence of records – and greatly changes the relations between individuals, as well as notions like *consent* and *privacy*. A second concern is that people will lose the will to resist forms of data encroachment due to the banality of data. A potentially damning outcome of this trend is that, as we become inured to data, we will become unable to see the kinds of discrimination embedded in new data policies. A final point pertains to what I call *pixilation* – a natural outcome of individuation and targeted data collection. A central aim of this book has been to identify the grand strategic shift away from a focus on nation-states and toward individuals. But what if this foretells the end of the individual too, now at the expense of the sub-individual, a subject composed of data points? The implications here are far-reaching.

By way of closing, it is worth revisiting the remit of the book. This study uses an in-depth look at the border as a launching off point to enter broader discussions about some of our most cherished political ideas, such as sovereignty, citizenship and justice, in the age of enhanced security. This timely subject matter lends the book a speculative air – it asks a lot more questions than it answers. But it also engenders a strong normative agenda. Looking closely at institutions helps us unlock their emancipatory potential. In this regard, the inchoate and moveable nature of the material studied is an advantage: it is at precisely this point that critical engagement is most meaningful.

Notes

1 Manent, Pierre. *A World Beyond Politics A Defense of the Nation-State.* Princeton: Princeton University Press, 2006, at 44.
2 Anzaldúa, Gloria. *Borderlands: The New Mestiza.* San Francisco: Aunt Lute Books, 2007, at 25.
3 Giddens, Anthony. *The Nation-State and Violence: Volume Two of A Contemporary Critique of Historical Materialism.* Berkeley, CA: University of California Press, 1987.
4 For writing on de-bordering and the weakening of the classic Westphalian nation-state, see Andreas, Peter. "The Mexicanization of the US–Canada Border: Asymmetrical Interdependence in a Changing Security Context." *International Journal* 60, no. 2 (2008); Benhabib, Seyla. *Dignity in Adversity: Human Rights in Troubled Times.* Cambridge, UK: Polity Press, 2011. For writing on securitization, see Huysmans, Jef. "The European Union and the Securitization of Migration." *Journal of Common Market Studies* 38, no. 5 (2000): 751–77; Bigo, Didier. "Frontier Controls in the European Union: Who Is in Control?" In *Controlling Frontiers: Free Movement into and within Europe,* edited by Didier Bigo and Elspeth Guild, 49–99. Chippenham, Wiltshire: Ashgate Publishing Company, 2005; Brown, Wendy. *Walled States, Waning Sovereignty.* Cambridge, MA: Zone Books, 2010.
5 "244 Million International Migrants Living Abroad Worldwide, New UN Statistics Reveal." United Nations Sustainable Development Report, 2016, www.un.org/sustainabledevelopment/blog/2016/01/244-million-international-migrants-living-abroad-worldwide-new-un-statistics-reveal/.
6 "Risk Analysis for 2016." Frontex Press Release, March 26, 2016, Frontex .europa.eu/assets/Publications/Risk_Analysis/Annula_Risk_Analysis_2016 .pdf.
7 For example, see this classic definition: "[International boundaries] occur where the vertical interfaces between state sovereignties intersect the surface of the earth … As vertical interfaces, boundaries have no horizontal extent." Muir, Richard. *Modern Political Geography.* New York: Palgrave Macmillan, 1975.
8 See for example, Ohmae, Kenichi. *The End of the Nation State: The Rise of Regional Economies.* New York: Free Press Paperbacks, 1995; Castells, Manuel. *The Rise of the Network Society.* Malden, MA: Blackwell, 2000; Bauman, Zygmunt. *Globalization: The Human Consequences.* New York: Columbia University Press, 1998.

9 Brown, *Walled States, Waning Sovereignty*, at 24.
10 For the former position, see Carens, Joseph H. "Aliens and Citizens: The Case for Open Borders." *Review of Politics* 49, no. 2 (1987): 251–73; for the latter, see Walzer, Michael. *Spheres of Justice: A Defense of Pluralism and Equality*. New York: Basic Books, 1983, at 62.
11 This creates a division between *sovereigntists* and *cosmopolitans* or between an *affirmative approach* and a *transformative approach*. For the former, see Cohen, Jean L. "Sovereign Equality vs. Imperial Right: The Battle over the 'New World Order'" *Constellations* 13, no. 4 (2006): 485–505, at 485; for the latter, see Fraser, Nancy. *Scales of Justice: Reimagining Political Space in a Globalizing World*. New York: Columbia University Press, 2009, at 22.
12 Cited in Patrick, J. Michael. "The Economic Cost of Border Security: The Case of the Texas-Mexico Border and the US VISIT Program." In *Borderlands: Comparing Border Security in North America and Europe*, edited by Emmanuel Brunet-Jailly, 197–230. Ottawa: University of Ottawa Press, 2007, at 209.
13 Allen, Charles E. Keynote Address by Allen, Principal, Chertoff Group. Counter Terror Expo Conference, Washington DC, May 17, 2012.
14 Cited in Lacey, Marc. "Arizona Officials, Fed Up with U.S. Efforts, Seek Donations to Build Border Fence." *The New York Times*, July 20 2011.
15 Cited in Hovsepian, Marcel. "Frontlines: Border Security Strategy Remains Myopic." *Homeland Security Today*, January 2, 2011.
16 Goddard, Terry. "How to Fix a Broken Border: A Three Part Series." In *Perspectives*, Immigration Policy Center Report, 2012.
17 Jay Kalath, CEO, Allied Mission Group LLC. Personal interview, Washington, DC, May 16, 2012.
18 Munn, Christopher. "Developing Human Domain Awareness." Remarks by Munn, Program Manager, Biometrics, Office of the Under-Secretary of Defense for Intelligence (OUSDI). Biometrics for National Security and Law Enforcement Conference, Alexandria, VA, January 31, 2013.
19 Gilbert, Robert. "Cooperative Efforts between Mexico, Canada and the U.S. in Law Enforcement and Prosecution." Remarks by Gilbert, former DHS Attache, Mexico City and Former Chief, US Border Patrol. Border Security Expo, Phoenix, AZ, 2012, (italics mine).
20 The term *port of entry* refers to all forms of ports – air, land or maritime. This is the nomenclature used by the US Department of Homeland Security, which refers to ports as part of a "network of nodes," through which "persons and cargo transit [across the border] by air, land and sea." See for example, "Northern Border Strategy." United States Department of Homeland Security, 2012: 1–20.
21 Because of the sensitive nature of this subject matter, some of my interviewees asked to be unnamed. In these cases, the material from the interviews is quoted anonymously.
22 These include the Border Security Expo & Conference in Phoenix, AZ (2012, 2013), the Counter Terror Expo & Conference, Washington, DC (2012), the Border Management Conference & Technology Expo in El Paso, TX (2012), the Canadian Association of Defence and Security Industries SecureTech Conference, Ottawa, Canada (2012), the Homeland

Security Conference and Expo, Washington, DC (2013) Conference on Biometrics for National Security and Law Enforcement, Washington, DC (2013, 2014), Big Data for Defense and Government, Washington, DC (2014), as well as Border Management Southern Africa, Pretoria, South Africa (2013).

23 Cohen, Jean L. *Globalization and Sovereignty: Rethinking Legality, Legitimacy and Constitutionalism.* Cambridge: Cambridge University Press, 2012, at 7; Piccone, Paul. "General Introduction." In *The Essential Frankfurt School Reader,* edited by Andrew Arato and Eike Gebhardt, *ix-xxi.* New York: Continuum Publishing, 2000, at *x.*

24 Owen, David. "Editor's Note." In *On Global Citizenship: James Tully in Dialogue.* London, UK: Bloomsbury Academic, 2014, x–xi.

25 See e.g. Miller, David. "Political Philosophy for Earthlings." In *Political Theory: Methods and Approaches,* edited by David Leopold and Marc Stears, 29–48. Oxford: Oxford University Press, 2008, 47–8.

26 Grene, David. "Introduction" to *Herodotus: The History.* Chicago: University of Chicago Press, 1987, at 14.

27 Williams, *In the Beginning Was the Deed,* at 77.

28 Foucault, Michel. "The Subject and Power." In *Power,* edited by James D. Faubion, 326–48. New York: The New Press, 2000, at 328.

29 Butler, Judith. *Frames of War: When Is Life Grievable?* London: Verso Books, 2010, at 10–11.

30 "Northern Border Strategy," at 8–9; 20 (italics mine).

31 Interview, El Paso, Texas, October 16, 2012.

32 Gilbert, "Cooperative Efforts between Mexico, Canada and the U.S. in Law Enforcement and Prosecution."

1 Borders: *Thick* and *Thin*

A space is something that has been made room for, something that is cleared and free, namely within a boundary, Greek *peras*. A boundary is not that at which something stops but, as the Greeks recognized, the boundary is that from which something *begins its presencing*.
— Martin Heidegger[1]

The border is perhaps our oldest political institution. In Greek mythology, Zeus was afforded the appellation *Herkios*, or "the fence," for his role in protecting Greece from the outside and determining the boundaries between estates.[2] Thucydides, in his history of the Peloponnese, defines boundaries between peoples and cities, a systemic antecedent to the current constellation of states. In the *Republic*, Plato differentiates between enemies abroad (*hostis*) along the demarcation of Hellenes and Barbarians and those at home (*inimicus*) within the Hellenic community.[3] In the Bible, land was divided by God's decree (Ezekiel, Bk 47).

At base, the border is a line of jurisdiction – a legal-topographical instantiation of authority. This conception has deep roots. In ancient Greek thought, the border was synonymous with law or demarcated jurisdiction. In *The Human Condition*, Hannah Arendt explains:

The Greek word for law, *nomos*, derives from *nemein*, which means to distribute, to possess (what has been distributed) and to dwell. The combination of law and hedge in the word *nomos* is quite manifest in a fragment of Heraclitus: *machesthai chre ton demon hyper tou nomou hokosper teicheos* ("the people should fight for the law as for a wall") ... The law of the city state [was] quite literally a wall, without which there might have been an agglomeration of houses, a town (*asty*), but not a city ... Without it a public realm could no more exist than a piece of property without a fence to hedge it in.[4]

The boundary is the law, and the law, the assertion of boundaries. Arendt expands upon this illuminating exposition in a footnote: "The word *polis* originally connoted something like a 'ring-wall,' and it seems the Latin *urbs* also expressed the notion of a 'circle' and was derived from the same roots as *orbis*. We find the same connection in our word 'town,' which originally, like the German *Zaun*, meant a surrounding fence."[5]

Carl Schmitt, in *The Nomos of the Earth*, offers a similar account by placing territorial delineation at the origin of all legal and political spatial orders:

> In some form, the constitutive process of land-appropriation is found at the beginning of the history of every settled people, every commonwealth, every empire ... Not only logically, but also historically, land-appropriation precedes the order that follows from it. It constitutes the original spatial order, the source of all further concrete order and all further law.[6]

The link between borders and linear division carries through into modern political philosophy. For Locke, the delineation of territory (and property, thus enabled) forms the basis of the legal and political order. In his *Second Treatise on Government* he writes:

> At the beginning, Cain might take as much ground as he could till and make it his own land and yet leave enough to Abel's sheep to feed on; a few acres would serve for both their possessions. But as families increased and industry inlarged their stocks, their *possessions inlarged* with the need of them; but yet it was commonly *without any fixed property in the ground* they made use of, till they incorporated, settled themselves together and built cities; and then, by consent, they came in time, to set out the *bounds of their distinct territories* and agreed on limits between them and their neighbours; and by laws within themselves, settled the properties of those of the same society.[7]

In his *Discourse on Inequality*, Rousseau places boundaries at the root of the entire social order: "The first person who, having enclosed a plot of land, took it into his head to say *this is mine* and found people simple enough to believe him, was the true founder of civil society."[8]

These classic renderings are familiar, as this *thin* notion of borders as *jurisdictions* remains prevalent today. But a central aim of this book is to recast our understanding by using a *thick* notion of borders as *institutions*. After all, borders are not just legal limits; they have material embodiment, history and context. They are not merely sites of *authority*, but also *control*. To omit these characteristics of borders is to mischaracterize the state system. It is also to place borders as secondary to states – temporally and conceptually *derivative* – when in fact, borders and states are *co-constitutive*.

The border, following Heidegger, is where the state starts its *presencing*. The border is generative of political space; it is also the site of politics – of violence, of technologies of control and the architecture of state. Foucault's definition of discipline is here instructive: "Discipline works in an empty, artificial space that is to be completely constructed."[9] By creating the border, the state has disciplined the land; generated meaning out of barren, empty space. The same can be said of territory: borders transform land into territory, itself a "juridico-political [notion]: the area controlled by a certain kind of power."[10] Indeed, etymologically *territory* is linked to *terror* – it is land terrorized by power.[11]

What purchase does this viewpoint offer? It makes possible discussion on *the politics of unit* – or the shape of polities – and lets us inquire into whether and how new forms of polity are possible. In particular it asks how different political units have defined and controlled their peripheries through history. The focus will be on three forms of polity most prevalent in the West: city, empire and state. In doing so it helps restructure our thinking about borders by challenging that there is anything natural or inevitable about the linear borders of the contemporary nation-state. Showing how they came to be helps us to see how they might come to change shape again. Indeed, we far too quickly accept the givenness of states and in particular the state-sovereignty-territory nexus, as though this were the natural and thus only legitimate, form of political order. This is not a new problem. Lucien Febvre, writing in 1925, remarked:

> The great nations of the modern world [appear to us] ... like actual historic and moral personalities. They have their inner life and their own character, but also their physical individualities, their exterior shape and their material figure, which is so distinct and familiar that we never think of them under any other aspect than the present one; their shapes seem to us to-day to have a sort of external necessity ... The whole problem [is] a question of boundaries. Within us, so deeply implanted that we no longer notice its hold on us, there is a certain idea of the "natural limits" of the great States which causes us to think of their boundaries as things in themselves, having an actual value, a kind of mechanical virtue and a compulsory and at the same time a creative power.[12]

This is reminiscent of Nietzsche's critique of "monumental history": the pursuit of similarities blinds us toward dissimilarities and surrenders causes to effects.[13] Instead, we might question, as Bernard Williams does, whether a state must inevitably take the form of a bounded unit: "There is no general answer to what are the boundaries of the state and I suppose that there can in principle be a spongiform state."[14] What might a "spongiform" political unit look like? This is an essential question of the *politics of unit*.

This historical review also provides a frame through which the principal arguments – about new overlapping or "zonal" border spaces – can be understood. As borders move away from thin jurisdictional lines, they also stop acting like borders; instead they start to resemble *frontiers*, thereby rendering states more akin to empires. In this way, different forms of periphery management are better understood as existing on a *spectrum of linearity*. As the border comes to resemble a frontier, sovereignty starts to resemble *imperium* – a Roman designation for authority that is not territorial bounded.

The chapter closes by highlighting three arguments about how we might think about borders and boundaries going forward. The first is that some form of boundary system is intrinsic to political order. These boundaries do not need to be antagonistic; they are simply a feature of human engagement. Our objective should thus be to craft boundaries in a way that is normatively affirming – rather than simply accept them as given or attempt to do without them. Second, whereas boundaries are necessary, this does not engender homogeneous divisions. Borders by their nature cultivate forms of interiority and exteriority, but also distinct modes of interiority: namely, between center and periphery. I refer to this as the *heterogeneous inside*. Indeed, a principal story of the border is the domination of the periphery at the hands of the center. The third point pertains to sovereignty – namely that it shouldn't simply be understood vis-à-vis authority (*de jure*) but also as a matter of control (*de facto*). Thinking in this way allows us to imagine a form of sovereignty that is not limited to the territory within a border – bringing us back to *imperium*.

The Politics of Unit

City

Cities, or city-states, have always existed as political units. They occupy an outsized place in the Western canon due to the historical importance of the Greek *polis*. They are idiosyncratic in that they tend not to be geographically conjoined and thus remark little on the modern state system in which land is essentially exhausted. For this reason, the subject is treated only in brief. This said, cities reveal a tremendous amount about the nature of bordering – and city-walls are illustrative forebears to contemporary fortified borders.

The image we have of the Greek *polis* is a city ringed by a wall – the archetypal linear border. But this only represents a small portion of what we mean when we talk about *bordering* or the way that a polity maintains and controls its periphery. Indeed, as much as the *polis* was a circumscribed urban space, the city itself controlled and maintained territory that was outside the city walls, but which was nonetheless part of the constitution of the polity. Territory was understood not as "the land *of* the *polis*, but that surrounding it … The idea of modern territory as politically and geographically bounded *space* belonging to or under the control of, a *state* would seem to be alien to the discussion."[15] In short, the Greek polis was comprised of two conjoined parts: an urban center and surrounding agricultural lands to feed the city's inhabitants.

This understanding of territory as possession outside the city also finds its place in the *Oxford English Dictionary*, which until 1494, and the beginnings of the modern state system, defined territory as: "the land or district lying round a city or town and under its jurisdiction."[16] This conceptualization of territory is an important differentiator from the state. The state *is* territory; the city *has* territory. For the former, territory is enclosed within the bounded unit; for the latter, the territory is held outside the bounded unit.

The question then is how this territory held outside the city walls was regulated – i.e. what was the city's strategy of peripheral management? This question was heavily debated. In his *Laws*, Plato suggested that extramural territory be included in the polity's defenses – creating a form of radiated, multi-layered defense, similar to present day "defense-in-depth" strategies. Indeed, Plato was against walling, as it encouraged laziness amongst the citizens – unless the wall consisted of parts of private houses, in which case citizens would be vigilant in its protection (these points are revisited in Chapter 2). Instead, the fortifications and ditches built in the countryside were to be considerable enough to deter invasion. In this rendering, the classic *polis* is turned inside out. In fact, the bounded city has little role in defense, whereas the zonal extramural countryside is essential. This point is seconded by Machiavelli in the *Prince*. No wall ever stopped an invasion, he argues, because material will eventually be broken through. On the inside, the wall promotes a false sense of empowerment among defenders, promoting laziness. On the outside it invigorates offenders bent on its destruction.

In contrast to Plato, in *The Politics*, Aristotle defends walling: "As to walls, those who say that cities making any pretension to military virtue should not have them, are quite out of date in their notions ... Those who have their cities surrounded by walls may either take advantage of them or not, but cities which are unwalled have no choice."[17] But the model itself is not tremendously different. Aristotle too articulates concerns over the thinning of loyalties on the outskirts of the territory, thereby suggesting a form of radiated defenses (in addition to walling the center). Moreover, he discusses the importance of civilians having a stake in the center and in the periphery (and even taking part in central politics and peripheral defense):

The land must therefore be divided into two parts, one public and the other private ... of the private land, part should be near the border and the other near the city, so that, each citizen, having two lots, they may all of them have land in both places.[18]

The concern that there are differential layers of commitment within the citizenry to border defense recurs in our contemporary setting. As does the idea that citizens at the center must be incentivized to care about the periphery through their own holdings.

The question of city defenses was not unique to ancient Greece. Independent city-states persisted throughout the Roman Empire, but most cities remained on the fringe of the Empire. In fact the Imperial frontier created strong states and alliances on its edges, which maintained even after the Empire itself fell to pieces.[19] This gets at a core thesis on power in pre-modern Europe: power gets weaker the farther it emanates from the center, but these emanating radii of affiliation nonetheless serve an important function as buffer-zones protecting the center (true for cities, as for empires).

The medieval city-state system that developed out of the shadow of Rome is also elucidating. While the cities of antiquity did have a clear notion of territory (even if it was outside of the city-walls), the medieval "system" was more heterodox. Due to conditions of considerably lesser population density in central Europe, medieval cities possessed territories that were quite distant from the loci of authority, enabling a system of overlapping, mixed rule. Feudal lands were frequently not contiguous and towns were the dependencies of more than one lord. Rather than field their own armies, rulers frequently bought off mercenary forces with shifting loyalties. This meant that while cities remained securely territorial entities with walled exteriors, their defense in a broader sense was part of an overlapping web of interrelations.

Rule in this period has two principle components: a vertical relation of power with the Holy Roman Empire and the Church, as well as horizontal relations of power between and among city-centers. This system of overlapping dominions meant that there could be no one-to-one relationship between land and sovereignty. Additionally, this system of overlapping domains meant that there could be no clear interiority or exteriority outside of the city-center itself. In the medieval period it is impossible to "distinguish domestic from international politics," feudal kingdoms had "border regions – we cannot speak of borders yet."[20] To be sure, linear boundaries existed in the medieval period, just as in the ancient period and were marked by "stones, rivers, trees and sometimes man-made trenches."[21] But linear borders at this point remained largely ceremonial due to problems of enforcement. This medieval system of overlapping rule came about in part because polities were unable to control the territories over which they putatively had authority – further evidence of the mismatch between *de jure* and *de facto* forms of rule.

Several themes emerge from this discussion that play a role in later chapters. Most importantly it introduces the concept of layered defense systems, with linear borders appearing as *internal* to the polity – a line of last resort, of sorts – and zonal boundaries forming the external face of the polity. These layers of boundaries were themselves varied: some created zones of homogenous sovereign control, others created zones of heterogeneous control. The former type of boundary, reminiscent of borders, creates spaces more akin to states; the latter, reminiscent of frontiers, cultivates nebulous zones of interaction, akin to empires *writ small*. Further, the city introduces the fact that boundaries can at once have zonal and linear properties – thereby placing borders and frontiers on a spectrum.

Empire

Michael Doyle defines empires as "relationships of political control imposed by some political societies over the effective sovereignty of other political societies."[22] Empires have frontiers, frequently taken to be *zonal* spaces of "osmotic communication."[23] While broadly true, this definition masks a great amount of variation. Was the frontier populated or empty? Was it established for defense or taxation? What kinds of threat did it anticipate? This section unpacks these questions, focusing on the case of Rome. Here I follow Edward Luttwak's tripartite classification of Roman imperial strategy: the "Julio-Claudian" system (27 BCE – 68 CE), a period of expansion; the "Antonine" system (70 – 180 CE), which focused on territorial security; and the "Diocletian" system (180 – 305 CE), a period of decline.

Caesar Augustus (27 BCE – 14 CE) oversaw massive imperial advance, which brought Roman troops out of the center and toward the periphery. This was a period of expansion, consolidation, and the cultivation of client states in the periphery. The frontier in this period was not clearly demarcated. In fact, because of internal troubles, the border was maintained only with small auxiliary units, rather than legions. Far from being placed on the frontier, at this point, the legions were situated on roads between the frontier and the interior as "mobile striking forces" and were "not tied down to territorial defense."[24]

During this period the central diplomatic means of peripheral management came through the manipulation of the so-called client states that amounted to a soft edge of empire, an "invisible frontier."[25] These client states share affinity with what today might be called "buffer states," but they were more active. They granted depth to the frontier and a cushion against attacks, assuming the burden of incursions until Roman defenses could arrive. This is a common feature of empires. For example, the Chinese empires formed extensive tributary systems to co-opt nomadic peoples at their frontiers, creating a buffer force against the "real" barbarians outside:

> The method [of neutralization] that worked best was one of enlisting the services of the very tribes that were supposedly excluded by the boundary, thus turning them about so that they faced away from the boundary instead of toward it.[26]

These concepts of the "invisible frontier" and "depth" are central to discussions about contemporary *thick* borders. Further, presaging a recurring theme, the lack of linear borders made surveillance indispensible: "Inherently dynamic and unstable, client states and client tribes required the constant management of a specialized diplomacy: Roman control and surveillance had to be continuous."[27]

The complexity of the frontier is brought forth by Machiavelli, who comments in his *Discourses on Livy* on the importance of co-opting the periphery: "in a new province [the Roman authorities] always sought for some friend who should be to them as a ladder whereby to climb, a door through which to pass or an instrument wherewith to keep their hold."[28] In the *Prince*, Machiavelli lauds Roman tactics in their outer provinces, as when they "sent out colonies, indulged the lesser powers without increasing their power, put down the powerful and did not allow foreign powers to gain reputation there."[29] He also remarks on Rome's strategy for conquered territories:

> When those states that are acquired ... are accustomed to living by their own laws and in liberty, there are three modes for those who want to hold them: first, ruin them; second, go there to live personally; third, let them live by their laws, taking tribute from them and creating within them an oligarchical state which keeps them friendly to you.[30]

Such co-optation is a central aspect of contemporary co-bordering strategies too.

Frontiers in this period have both *zonal* and *linear* attributes – although zonal aspects were predominant. This is a direct outgrowth of the Roman notion of territory, which was based more on radii of control emanating from the center, than any logic of circumference. Rome measured its extent by way of the roads that emanated from the capital. The importance of the road to establishing control is evident in the meaning of the word *limes*, which originally derives from the highway that reaches out from the center to the periphery. It only later came to embody fortifications along this line:

> [In this period *limes* referred to the] access road *perpendicular* to the border of secured imperial territory; *limes* thus described a route of penetration cut through hostile territory rather than a "horizontal" frontier and certainly not a fortified defensive perimeter ... It is the *absence* of a perimeter defense that is the key to the entire system.[31]

The idea of *limes* being definitive of the extent of the empire, measured by the reach of these roads, accords precisely with our idea of frontiers as zones. Unlike a perimeter – lines of definition – roads represent an extent of control that reaches as far as it can, but loses strength as it does. Thus, empire fades into its extremity – into a space of non-definition. Otherwise put, there was no sense that the frontier behaved like a container, enclosing the polity. Even where the perimeter was defined it was not continuous, with long swaths of land simply without designation. Being non-continuous made frontiers eminently permeable. Thus while they had a juridical purpose, distinguishing citizen from non-citizen, there was no expectation of enforcement.[32]

That Rome did not define itself by area is unimaginable today – driving home the difference between states as bounded political units and empires as unbounded ones. This is a common feature of empires. For example, in the Mughal Empire, frontiers were not a "defensive line keeping people out, but lines of communication penetrating deeply into areas beyond direct imperial control."[33] In this way, empires are not too different from cities. More generally, for most of human history, political units were just walled centers and long marches of empty land and nominally loyal peoples.[34]

Before closing this discussion it is worth adding that while so far the focus has been on frontiers – a type of *perimeter* – it is also important to say a few words on *ports of entry*. In a Roman system that privileged roads, the *ports were the perimeter* – the main protection against attacks came not from strong perimeter fencing, but the road system that radiated back and forth from the center. This said, entry points did not exist in empires in the same clear way they exist in modern states, due to problems of non-contiguity and permeability. As such, compared to the city, the empire was exceedingly permissive: freedom of movement was the norm. Indeed, most empires were open to new members in the polity out of a desire for tax revenue. Ports of entry were discrete places where such tax collection became possible. In this way, our causal understanding should be reversed: the need for taxation at ports was one of the driving forces of the formation of the modern perimeter.

The second period of imperial strategy was the "Antonine" System (roughly 70 CE – 180 CE). This window was dominated by the principle of territorial security and is considered to have given birth to the idea of "scientific" frontiers and preclusive defense. This meant having clearly defined perimeter areas, defended by more stable troops. It also meant the phasing out of the client system, which had become a liability. Weak client states could not contain strong incursions and strong ones had become a threat to the empire. The solution was to move troops from the interior out to the frontier – toward the ideal of a perfectly rationalized, "scientific" perimeter, "designed not to encompass as much territory as possible, but to encompass the *optimal* amount of territory – in other words, the area that it is profitable to enclose on political, economic or strategic grounds."[35] The meaning of *limes* also shifted at this point to accommodate the fixed perimeter.

The most famous delineation during this period was Hadrian's Wall, in Britain. But even these frontiers were not strictly linear. They were part of a complicated system, predicated on a network of forts and roads, as well as watchtowers and outpost forts, designed to provide surveillance throughout the region. Importantly these posts extended not merely up to the barrier but past it. In one case, in the *Fossatum Africae* in modern Algeria, "an outer zone of surveillance" extended "to a depth of sixty to eighty kilometers beyond the border line."[36] Further, these linear elements were not strictly defensive: when they wanted to launch off beyond the line, they could. As Maier explains, outposts frequently served as "springboards for further expansion."[37] This feature is a common aspect of empire. Like the Romans, the Qin Empire (221–206 BCE) saw the Great Wall as a launching-off point: "Build and move on was the principle of the wall, not setting up a fixed border for all time."[38] Indeed, the Wall was part of a layered system of defense against nomadic tribes.

Further, even when the *limes* did look like lines, this was based on an elaborate scheme of coordination on both sides. This is most clearly captured in the case where the *limes* were rivers:

> The *limes* are not simple lines of zero width, but areas or zones ... The Romans secured the land on both sides of these notional lines: the far banks of rivers or lands beyond fortifications. It was therefore more a case of controlling, rather than preventing, passage. But in this way they were able to force passage through specific sites and to extract taxes.[39]

Even with linear boundaries, Rome settled and performed operations on both sides – precisely what we see with co-bordering today. Moreover, we see here an early version of ports and perimeters acting as part of a coordinated system.

In sum, linear defenses provided a trip-wire to slow down invasion and enabled a thick region of surveillance to better inform the Roman legions. The challenge was to try and resolve the two types of security threats at the frontier – large-scale ones that threatened the center and small-scale ones that ravaged the peripheral lands. How do you protect both? By placing linear fortifications within a zonal defense: a preclusive defense against low-intensity threats and mobile forces deployed against high-intensity threats. The purchase of the new system was that it protected civil security, even in frontier zones. But the cost of this system is readily apparent – with "scientific frontiers" came fixed boundaries, which eliminated the possibility of new tax revenue derived from expansion.

The third imperial system was "Diocletian" (roughly 180–305 CE). This was a period of extreme vulnerability and conflict. The elastic defenses of preceding eras were replaced by defense-in-depth – a purely defensive version of the system above, incapable of engaging enemies beyond the periphery. The logic behind defense-in-depth is simple: like a spider, ensnare the enemy into your web. In sum, Roman strategy went from being offensive (forward) to defensive (rearward):

Meeting only static guardposts and weak patrol forces on the frontier, the enemy could frequently cross the line virtually unopposed, but [then would] find itself in a peripheral combat zone of varying depth, within which strongholds large and small as well as walled cities, fortified farmhouses, fortified granaries and fortified refugees would remain ... The general character of Roman defense-in-depth strategies was that of a "rearward" defense, as opposed to the "forward" defense characteristic of the earlier frontier strategy. In both, the enemy must ultimately be intercepted, but while forward defense demands that he be intercepted *in advance* of the frontier so that peaceful life may continue unimpaired within, rearward defense provides for his interception only inside imperial territory.[40]

Defense-in-depth was adept militarily, but a hazard for citizens, especially peripheral ones, as the borderlands became protracted sites of battle. This point is important, as the relationship between the defense of *some* citizens (especially those in the center) and *all* citizens is contentious – another theme revisited in Chapter 2. Where it could, Rome attempted a compromise, with a shallow defense-in-depth, basically a thick border.[41] This amounted to a system with broad frontier zones that went deep into Roman soil that required new and enduring form of physical infrastructure. This thick, refortified line shares affinity with the system being designed today. Our contemporary model is an attempt once again to merge the purchase of a preclusive frontier (for civilians) and defense-in-depth (for security).

Two further points warrant mention. The first is that during this period, as perimeters became less defended cities began to take on firm walls. Thus, a dialectic of walling became evident: when there were clear walled borders, internal cities didn't need walls. But when the frontier was open, cities walled themselves. Townsfolk became soldiers and citizens had to self-police. A second point regards state power and space. As the empire weakened, the connection between center and periphery thinned. This meant that colonial loyalties were frequently with local barbarians rather than the distant center. As a result, the tides had been reversed: peripheral populations were not buying their peace from Rome; rather, Romans were buying their peace from barbarians. These conditions on the frontier give lie to any clear notion of interiority/exteriority; rather, peripheral peoples were besieged from both sides, with weak, heterogeneous loyalties to each. In this way, the center is like a magnet: when it has the strongest pull, the periphery stays in its orbit; once the pull wanes or a countervailing pull emerges, the periphery either dissolves, flips loyalty or takes off on its own. Such is a classic weakness of frontiers: if interiority and exteriority are not defined, the periphery defines itself as it chooses. This establishes a principle difference between borders and frontiers: frontiers have to be *maintained* because they are otherwise not *defined*. Borders, in being *delineated*, do not. Thus a border will always be peripheral; a frontier, by contrast, can become the center.

State

The final political form of interest is the state. Why do states have borders and how did they adopt their function? By most accounts, the modern state system formed in the interstices of the two reigning empires of Western Europe in the Middle Ages: the Holy Roman Empire and the Church. This relationship was not seamless, and in the crevices of their rule new polities formed, independent of these macro-units. The system that formed would come to entail the exclusive authority of the state upon its own territory with no allegiance to a higher authority, whether Emperor or Pope. State power rose from the shackles of feudal networks through the rise of small kingdoms. This entailed a form of feudal Darwinism, with large power centers defeating smaller ones and eventually consolidating territory and power. With the formation of larger territories came a primordial form of the international state system, known as the polity of estates, *Standestaat*. It is through this consolidation of power that we see states embark on the road toward a one-to-one relationship with territory, constitutive of sovereignty.

States, even in their earliest form, tended to favor clear, permanent boundaries, rather than zones of heterodox dominion – although it took a while before this became the norm. This transformation began in the thirteenth century, prior to which exterior and interior boundaries were indistinguishable – i.e., external boundaries "were fundamentally similar in kind to feudal limits within the kingdom."[42] Border formation at this point was a direct outcome of population growth, as the expansion of medieval towns meant that clear delineations had to be forged between them, many of which were meted out through conflict. By one account, the critical years were 1212–1221, during which period "the notion itself of boundaries was established."[43] This window also saw the first steps toward the development of ports of entry, as the gateway to the territory could be a site of taxation. In thirteenth-century France, it was Philippe le Bel who first understood that frontiers could be a tool in extracting customs – although this process remained rudimentary as points of entry could not be established with precision.

The aggrandizement of competing units set the stage for boundaries as truce-lines between polities. However, the transformation of boundaries into truly *linear* entities did not occur until the sixteenth century, at which point, the frontier took on the meaning as a place with an "othering" capacity:

The word "frontier" dates precisely from the moment when a new insistence on royal territory gave to the boundary a political, fiscal and military significance different from its internal limits. The "frontier" was that which "stood face to" an enemy. This military frontier, connoting a defensive zone, stood opposed to the linear boundary or line of demarcation separating two jurisdictions or territories.[44]

In their initial manifestation, borders were places where states defended against each other (i.e. where one state "stood face to" its enemy). The linear boundary also acquired symbolic purchase at this time and became a locus of royal concern. In 1564–1566, Charles IX of France did a two-year tour of the frontiers of France as a means of both identifying the limits of their authority and solidifying their dominion.

The idea of the linear boundary also caught on in later manifestations of empire, especially as the Spanish and Portuguese crowns rose in the fifteenth century to have significant overseas holdings. In the Treaty of Tordesillas of 1494, Spain and Portugal divided the western hemisphere, such that "A boundary or straight line [*una rraya o linea derecha*] be determined and drawn, from pole to pole ... [Marks] shall separate those portions of such lands belonging to each one of the said parties; and the subjects of the said parties shall not dare, on either side, to enter the part of the other, by crossing the said mark."[45] The push for linear distinction derived in part from technological developments and especially the astrolabe, which determined lines of latitude. This is a recurring theme: it is through technological advances in boundary-making that the state and border co-evolved.

Shifts in the logic of boundaries went hand in hand with thinking about territory – and specifically that states possessed sole authority over tracts of land or what we now refer to as *territoriality*. This process began with the Great Schism (1378–1417) diminishing the authority of the pope, which enabled kings to contend that they were essentially emperors over their territory – i.e. sovereign. This process solidified in the sixteenth century, during the Reformation, especially in England and France – as with Henry VIII's Act of Supremacy (1534). This was consecrated in several peace accords of note, including the Peace of Passau (1552) and the Diet of Augsburg (1555), at which the principle *cuius regio, eius religio* ("to whom the region, the religion") was introduced.

Given this evolution in thought, most scholarly accounts trace the formation of the modern state system to the sixteenth and seventeenth centuries in Europe, roughly with the end of the Thirty Years' War (1618–1648) and the peace agreement that resulted in the Treaty of Westphalia. This agreement is important first and foremost in establishing sovereignty over territory as an organizing principle of the system of states – i.e. the "territorialization" of space.[46] The treaty of Westphalia significantly weakened the Holy Roman Empire and created a political space for over 300 political units to become actors on the international stage. Paradoxically, while it let many units in the door, it also created the terms for the contraction of most of these units. In 1500 Europe had over 150 discrete political units; by 1900 this number had fallen to twenty-five, due in large part to the hegemonic expansion of states.[47]

From the very beginning, sovereign authority was situated in a bounded territory. This is manifest in the quotation from Locke used in the introduction to this chapter, as it is in Bodin and Hobbes. But while these texts provide ample discussion of jurisdiction, at no point is there any discussion of what the boundaries to the polity look like or how they are maintained.[48] This omission is puzzling. Earlier philosophers – notably Aristotle and Machiavelli – took great pains to articulate the means by which territory was *controlled* by the state. Yet this is absent from modern accounts. This section pieces this narrative together with historical materials.

France is held up as a model for state making and border-delineation, largely due to the work in the late seventeenth century of Marquis de Vauban, a central figure in Louis XIV's statecraft. After the Treaty of Westphalia there was a scramble to define territory – i.e. to solidify sovereignty, thus established. In a memorandum in 1673, Vauban wrote: "The king ought to think a little of squaring his field. This confusion of friendly and enemy fortresses mixed together does not please me at all." Peter Sahlins explains that the Nijmegen Treaty (1678) was a watershed moment in rethinking the frontier:

> The "politics of open doors on neighboring countries" gave way to the "politics of the barrier." The idea was Vauban's, the architect of France's new frontier. Long before the Maginot Line, Vauban had built his "iron frontier" consisting of two lines of fortified sites. The idea was to abandon the most advanced fortresses and towns, relinquishing more distant outposts in the interests of a more enclosed space ... [In addition] the new military frontier required the "purging" of enclaves within France ... For almost thirty years, Vauban directed the construction of a barrier system ... "The enemy," writes Vauban, "will almost never know what is going on behind our backs."[49]

This passage reveals just how revolutionary the concept of a strict linear border was. Previously, interweaving territories – the enemy behind one's back – were the norm.

Going a step further, it is clear that *territorial sovereignty* was not fully established until more than a century after Westphalia. This was finally brought about through an appreciation of the need for clear territorial mutual exclusivity (which has as much to do with fencing *in* as fencing *out*). In 1775, the French Ministry of Foreign Affairs developed a strategy for "establishing and fixing the limits of the kingdom," which included the creation of a Topographical Bureau for the Demarcation of Limits. During the subsequent decade, France negotiated almost two dozen "treaties of limits" with their neighbors as a means of fixing finally the boundaries of the state. Notable geographer Vidal de la Blache saw this as the expression of France's need to "carefully close its territory, as a peasant would enclose its field."[50]

At the macro level, this process of border delineation was well on its way. But the view at the micro level was more complicated, as rendered by Sahlins' seminal study on a small tract of the Pyrenees, the Cerdanya, which forms the border between France and Spain. The official claims of each country to the lands in question were meted out by the Treaty of the Pyrenees (1659–1660), but the exact location of the border was not fixed until centuries later, at the Treaties of Bayonne (1866–1868). A couple of points are illustrative here. First, while there was a territorial logic to the seventeenth century border, this was not true in practice. In fact there was no visible evidence of the territorial boundary (markers, customs officials). As a result, in practice the border was distinguished along jurisdictional grounds – i.e. privileging persons over territory – until the nineteenth century:

The history of the boundary between 1659 and 1868 [can] hardly be summarized as the simple evolution from an empty zone to a precise line, but rather as the complex interplay of two notions of boundary – zonal and linear – and two ideas of sovereignty – jurisdictional and territorial.[51]

Until very recently, people rather than territory remained the source of political loyalty – a link to the medieval bonds whence the early state arose.

Second, borders during this period remained permeable. With this permeability came trade and transit between the two peripheries. This brought unity *across* the line, with both peripheral communities more fearful of raiding from the central state. This concept, of periphery-periphery loyalties that are sometimes created and maintained in opposition to (each) center, is an important one that will recur through this book. As a consequence, the seventeenth century border took on many of the properties of the Imperial frontier, in the sense that it was a site of political declaration and demonstration, with loyalty to the state continually affirmed and re-negotiated. In this way, the state's border-creation was reflexively engaged with the border's state-creation.

Consequently, Westphalia was essential in the formation of the Western state system, but it was not a watershed moment *on the ground*. In fact, the real changes we associate with the modern state and linear borders are later developments – more associated with the eighteenth and nineteenth centuries, especially the years between the French Revolution and World War I. This period brought the rise of bureaucracy and the increased administrative capacity of the centralized state. This has several ramifications for bordering.

A paradigmatic case of bureaucratic development is Prussia under the Hohenzollern dynasty. This is a model administrative state, in large part because of the rise of police activities – designed in principle toward the population's welfare. This *Polizeystaat* came to connote "coercion, imperiousness and surveillance,"[52] but is of particular interest for our purposes, as it introduced for the first time clear, tight controls of its bounded territorial domain. This led to the paradox of civil society revisited throughout these pages: popular freedoms expanded alongside fortifications externally and surveillance internally. Indeed, alongside the rise of *administration* came population control, especially via statistics – an important forebear to contemporary data protocols – which enable the "coding of information," toward "the supervision of human activities."[53] James C. Scott explains how by contrast the pre-modern state: "knew precious little about its subjects, their wealth, their landholdings and yields, their location, their very identity ... It lacked, for the most part, a measure, a metric, that would allow it to 'translate' what it knew into a common standard necessary for a synoptic view."[54] This rise in administrative capacity also enabled the depersonalization of power.

As a result of this spread of administration, in the nineteenth century the state was for the first time able to cover the whole territory of a state – and thus control the rough and unstable periphery. It is this capacity that made the modern state uniquely *territorial*. Suddenly the periphery was integral to policy-making, not merely territory-making. Indeed, for much of Europe, democratization and the formation of mass, territory-wide parties was enabled by a tightly monitored periphery, which became the cite of extreme control and violence. As the state grew administratively, this disproportionately affected the periphery, now under state control for the first time, as this was where crooks and tax-dodgers went to evade the law. In fact, the periphery is the site alone of a double-violence: the violence of interiority (population management) and the violence of exteriority (war).

These two components, of an expansive administrative state interested in monitoring a population and increasingly capacious enough to control its periphery, led most radically to changes at the ports of entry. Indeed, it was only in the nineteenth century that states were able to exhibit any uniform control over their ports. Ports of entry became the nexus of surveillance for the expanding modern state, as it was only through "documents such as passports and identity cards, along with elaborate registration and information systems" that states could effectively distinguish "who is who" and "what is what."[55] It was this process of documentation that finally let external borders replace internal ones. This evolution from sovereignty over territory to government over people is part of what Foucault terms "governmentality," or the situation such that population becomes the "object of government manipulation."[56] It is this precise evolution I identify at the border and which provides the baseline for the historical shift in border functionality I articulate in these pages (and treated at length in Chapter 5).

At this point the modern state – and the state system we refer to as "Westphalian" – comes into view. A few points about the modern state warrant mention. First, it is in the modern state that we appreciate the intertwining of law and politics – a subject that will recur in my later discussion of sovereignty at the border.[57] Second, in addition to the rise of the centralized administrative state and controlled borders, there also became a more regulated and legally ordained international arena, in which borders became consecrated as the defining lines of polities. This was true at the inception of international law, which was *pluralist* in that it was based on the coexistence of independent and legally equal states within the European state system and the mutual recognition of sovereignty. Borders constitute the essential foundation of this system, in which states were the only units and no protection was offered to individuals. Thus it was at the same time constraining to states vis-à-vis other states, but empowering of states vis-à-vis individuals. In both ways, international law was an instrument of sovereignty. The Paris Conference of 1919 followed the Congress of Vienna in 1815 in cementing these norms; as did the UN Charter (1945). The state system adopted its final form in the 1950s and 60s with decolonization, as the postcolonial states became independent and affirmed the system.

It was in this window, 1950–1990, that the border became the most border-like, coinciding greatly with the Cold War: the border as a "wall" was associated originally with communist nations or the "police state." True control of the perimeter was in most cases apocryphal. However, extreme control did become a reality at ports of entry, where the monitoring of passage was aided by the advance of technology, engendering an increased capacity of the state to regulate movement. These restrictions also followed the tide of immigrants created by the great wars, with states uniformly concluding that freedom of movement was disadvantageous and thus restricted the flow of immigrants, refugees and asylum seekers.

With the end of the Cold War and bi-polarity, came a refashioning of the concept of "invasion" – no longer by Russian tanks, but by migrants. At this point it is clear that borders generally stopped being places where states faced off against each other and rather places where states controlled migration. With the disappearance of the threat from the USSR, European states turned their concerns toward migration and the fear of being "flooded" by immigrants.[58] Didier Bigo makes this point that the border has changed from being a military space (concerned with armies) to a police space (concerned with migration):

For a long time the enemy – the "natural" enemy – was the territorial neighbor; the frontier served as a protection against the neighbor ... [But] States are now less and less "containers" which are clearly defined and only have a thin but tough line between them (a no man's land) ... If the border function of security is to survive, it will be more along its second function, the police function.[59]

The picture is now complete. Such is the modern state-system in its finished form. It is the model against which the remainder of the book will articulate deviations.

Through the Looking Glasses, *Revisited*

This discussion raises a number of points regarding how we might go about seeing borders. The first pertains to the persistence of boundaries in politics. There is always some form of boundary between polities, just as identity requires a constitutive outside. These boundaries do not need to be antagonistic, nor must they be linear. Insofar as this is true, this book encourages a rethinking of politics in terms of a dynamic set of *delineations* (boundaries), rather than any fixed notion of *substance*. This idea that there is something intrinsic to boundaries recalls the position of Carl Schmitt, that the essence of politics is the determination of friend and enemy. But, the categories of "friend" and "enemy" are here without content; what is essential is the distinction itself. The question of politics is not whether to have boundaries, but what they should look like and where they should lie. Limits determine what matters and what doesn't, who wins and who loses (not to mention the nature of who is "who" and what it means to "win"). It is for this reason that understanding the nature and shape of borders is so essential.

A second point pertains to the relationship between center and periphery. While borders forge binaries, they also cultivate sites of contestation between binaries and within them. I refer to this as the *heterogeneous inside*. This fact of internal heterogeneity is present even at the initial drawing of the border. In cultivating interiority and exteriority, borders contain some and expel others. Those expelled are made into barbarians. The border is thus there to defend against the barbarians it at the same time creates. Those on the inside are domesticated, brought under control. As Sheldon Wolin describes it, the "native country" (*domus*) is the site of *domitus* or "taming."[60] The border is thus a mask, covering over concealed distinctions. William Connolly remarks: "most historically established systems of identity veil the element of arbitrary conquest in the differences they create and negate."[61]

A third point pertains to sovereignty – namely that it shouldn't simply be understood legally (*de jure*) but must also be understood as a matter of control (*de facto*). Doing so allows us to see that sovereignty has a spatial dynamic – with some swaths of territory within a polity under less control than others – thereby placing it in concert with *imperium*. This point will be revisited at length in Chapter 3.

The border is commonly thought of as a great tectonic plate where states and nations clash; the location of the pomp and circumstance of the state. In this rendition, the border is a locus of power. But precisely the opposite is also true. It is the place where states lose definition, where the signal from the center is weakest and power is most precarious. Here one is reminded of Benedict Anderson's claim in *Imagined Communities* that the way to conceive of the state is as a light bulb that dims as it radiates from the center. Anderson examines this push-and-pull from a historical lens: "In the modern conception, state sovereignty is fully, flatly and evenly operative over each square centimeter of a legally demarcated territory. But in the older imagining, where states were defined by centers, borders were porous and indistinct and sovereignties faded imperceptibly into one another."[62] Anderson exposes a central paradox of the modern state: the periphery is at once its weakest yet defining point.

This warrants unpacking. Our assumption is that centers draw boundaries at their peripheries to define themselves vis-à-vis other states. But if states were truly conceived as we now imagine them (such that sovereignty and identity are leveled smoothly across the territory), such self-definition would be unnecessary. In fact, we draw boundaries because precisely the opposite is true: the center defines itself by drawing a boundary to make up for the periphery, which does a poor job of such definition. Center A draws the boundary, not because of its similarity to Periphery A, but because of its differences. This statement re-imagines border conflicts as a paradoxical dialectic: clashes between people occur at the peripheries, not because of irreconcilable differences between those peripheral peoples themselves, but rather due to their similarities. Therein the ecological fallacy intrinsic to studying boundaries once they have been erected and differences reified, rather than tracing them to their roots. This is a general fallacy of group logics – i.e. any sort of "us"/"them" or friend/enemy distinction, in which we presume that the differences within groups pale in relevance to those between groups. This in turn engenders a second fallacy, whereby we reify the boundary between known identities, thus asserting that the master cleavage (i.e. the familiar inter-group boundary) is the relevant one, rather than alternatives that remain invisible to us.

This brings us back to the first claims, earlier, about the over-reliance on *substantive* differentiation and (fatuous) assumptions of in-group loyalty, as well as the reliance on the logic of *antagonism*, as when Schmitt takes us too far toward a totalizing binary of self/other, in which all others bear the potential for enemyhood. Rather than take as assumption any us/them dichotomy proffered by borders, we should question the internal homogeneity of these categories.

Conclusion

This chapter has been structured around a typology of political forms – city, empire, state. Its purpose was to provide some context for the changes in border management we see today and to challenge the strict dyads – empire/frontier and state/border – we take for granted when we speak of political boundaries. In fact, all systems employ linear and zonal aspects of peripheral management. To this point, boundaries are scalar – i.e. they exist on a *scale of linearity*, starting from a line (i.e. a boundary with no horizontal extent), or what we commonly call a border, to a wider area, or what we think of as a frontier. Additionally, all peripheries to states are parts of *frontier-systems*. Thus, borders that appear more linear are *minimal* renderings of the frontier system, built up borders that extend inland are more *maximal* renderings of the same. In this rendering, the classic modern border is simply the frontier's visual manifestation, the real contours of the frontier are invisible on the map.

With this frame in place, the remainder of the book is divided into two parts. Part I looks at contemporary trends in bordering at the perimeter, starting with the case of the United States and expanding outwards toward the rest of the world. It treats a number of the subjects discussed here, including the question of central management of the periphery, strategies of defense-in-depth and a new form of rule that mirrors the Roman concept of *imperium*. Part II follows from this and examines ports of entry in the same way beginning with the case of the United States and expanding outward. Although much of this discussion focuses on so-called Big Data, a hypermodern phenomenon, it nonetheless takes a lot from this chapter, including the idea of the "scientific" frontier, rationalization and new logics of polarity and division.

Notes

1 Heidegger, Martin. "Building, Dwelling, Thinking." Translated by Albert Hofstadter. In *Basic Writings: From Being and Time (1927) to the Task of Thinking (1964)*, London: Routledge, 1993, 343–63 at 154.
2 Plato. *Complete Works*. Indianapolis: Hackett Publishing Company, 1997, at *Laws* VIII: 842e.
3 Ibid., at *Republic* V: 470b–d.
4 Arendt, Hannah. *The Human Condition*. Chicago: University of Chicago Press, 1998 [1958], at 63ff; 64.
5 Ibid., at 64ff.
6 Schmitt, Carl. *The Nomos of the Earth in the International Law of the Jus Publicum Europaeum*. Translated by G. L. Ulmen. New York: Telos Press Publishing, 2006 [1950], at 45–8.
7 Locke, John. *Two Treatises of Government*. Cambridge: Cambridge University Press, 2014 [1689].
8 Rousseau, Jean-Jacques. *The Basic Political Writings*. Translated by Donald A. Cress. Indianapolis: Hackett, 1987 [1757], at 60.
9 Foucault, *Security, Territory, Population*, at 19.

10 Foucault, Michel. *Power/Knowledge: Selected Interviews & Other Writings 1972–1977.* Translated by Colin Gordon, Leo Marshall, John Mepham and Kate Soper. New York: Pantheon Books, 1980, at 68.

11 Elden, Stuart. *The Birth of Territory.* Chicago: University of Chicago Press, 2013, at 222.

12 Febvre, Lucien. *A Geographical Introduction to History.* Westport, CT: Greenwood Press, 1974 [1925], at 296–7.

13 Nietzsche, Friedrich. *Untimely Meditations.* Edited by Daniel Breazeale Cambridge: Cambridge University Press, 1999 [1876], at 70.

14 Williams, *In the Beginning Was the Deed,* at 6.

15 Elden, *The Birth of Territory,* at 39.

16 Cited in Sassen, Saskia. *Territory, Authority, Rights: From Medieval to Global Assemblages.* Princeton: Princeton University Press, 2006, at 33ff.

17 Aristotle. *The Politics and the Constitution of Athens.* Cambridge: Cambridge University Press, 1996, at [1330b30–1331a10].

18 Ibid., at [1330a10–15].

19 Anderson, Malcolm. *Frontiers: Territory and State Formation in the Modern World.* Cambridge: Polity Press, 1996, at 14.

20 Spruyt, Hendrik. *The Sovereign State and Its Competitors: An Analysis of Systems Change.* Princeton: Princeton University Press, 1994, at 36, 51.

21 Sahlins, Peter. *Boundaries: The Making of France and Spain in the Pyrenees.* Berkeley: University of California Press, 1989, at 5–6.

22 Doyle, Michael. *Empires.* Ithaca: Cornell University Press, 1986, at 19.

23 Maier, Charles S. "Once Within Borders: The Space of Empires and the Space of States." Talk delivered at Yale University, November 1, 2011.

24 Luttwak, Edward. *The Grand Strategy of the Roman Empire: From the First Century A.D. To the Third.* London: Weidenfeld & Nicholson, 1976, at 18.

25 Ibid., at 19.

26 Lattimore, Owen. *Inner Asian Frontiers of China.* Boston: Beacon Press, 1951 [1940], at 245–6.

27 Luttwak, *The Grand Strategy of the Roman Empire,* at 30–1.

28 Machiavelli, Niccolo. *Discourses on Livy.* Translated by Ninian Hill. Mineola, NY: Dover Publications, 2007 [1531], [II:I], at 151.

29 Machiavelli, Niccolo. *The Prince.* Edited by Harvey C. Mansfield. Chicago: University of Chicago Press, 1996 [1513], [III] at 12.

30 Ibid., [V] at 20.

31 Luttwak, *The Grand Strategy of the Roman Empire,* at 19.

32 Stemming from this point, asserting frontiers also didn't necessarily mean that the area contained within them was actually under control. By one account, "control of enclosed areas seems to have been a second-stage of each expansionary thrust ... First came the roads and march routes radiating from settled regions, then gradually the fortified lines of enclosure." Maier, Charles S. *Among Empires: American Ascendancy and its Predecessors.* Cambridge, MA: Harvard University Press, 2006, at 85–6.

33 Jos Gommans, cited in Maier, *Among Empires,* at 92.

34 Scott, James C. *The Art of Not Being Governed.* New Haven: Yale University Press, 2009, at 8.

35 Luttwak, *The Grand Strategy of the Roman Empire*, at 86–8.
36 Ibid., at 66.
37 Maier, *Among Empires*, at 84–5.
38 Burbank, Jane and Frederick Cooper. *Empires in World History: Power and the Politics of Difference*. Princeton: Princeton University Press, 2010, at 43–5.
39 Elden, *The Birth of Territory*, at 88–9; 92.
40 Luttwak, *The Grand Strategy of the Roman Empire*, at 132; 6.
41 Ibid., at 176–8.
42 Sahlins, *Boundaries*, at 6.
43 Sassen, *Territory, Authority, Rights*, at 44.
44 Sahlins, *Boundaries*, at 6.
45 Cited in Elden, *The Birth of Territory*, at 242–3.
46 Benhabib, *Dignity in Adversity*, at 99.
47 Poggi, Giovanni. *The State: Its Nature, Development and Prospects*. Stanford: Stanford University Press, 1990, at 22.
48 Anderson concurs: "For Rousseau, as for Hobbes and Locke, the frontiers of polities were unproblematic – they were defined by the territories occupied by the people who participated in the original contract." Anderson, *Frontiers*, at 38.
49 Sahlins, *Boundaries*, at 68–9.
50 Ibid., at 93–5.
51 Ibid., at 6–7.
52 Poggi, *The State*, at 51.
53 Giddens, *The Nation-State and Violence*.
54 Scott, James C. *Seeing Like a State: How Certain Schemes to Improve the Human Condition Have Failed*. New Haven, CT: Yale University Press, 1998, at 2.
55 Torpey, John. *The Invention of the Passport: Surveillance, Citizenship, and the State*. Cambridge, UK: Cambridge University Press, 2000, at 37.
56 Foucault, *Security, Territory, Population*, at 105.
57 Poggi pinpoints the development of the modern state-as-law: "The balance between, so to put it, the *juridicisation of politics* and the *politicization of law*, is an unstable and variable one; but whatever its vicissitudes, clearly the mutual involvement of those two phenomena, politics and law, becomes deep (particularly in the nineteenth century)." Poggi, *The State*, at 29–30.
58 Anderson, *Frontiers*, at 35.
59 Bigo, "Frontier Controls in the European Union," in *Controlling Frontiers*, at 55–6.
60 Wolin, Sheldon. "Fugitive Democracy." In *Democracy and Difference: Contesting the Boundaries of the Political*, edited by Seyla Benhabib, 31–45. Princeton: Princeton University Press, 1996, at 33.
61 Connolly, William. *Identity/Difference: Democratic Negotiations of Political Paradox*. Minneapolis: University of Minnesota Press, 2002 [1991], at 68.
62 Anderson, Benedict. *Imagined Communities: Reflections on the Origin and Spread of Nationalism*. New York: Verso. Original edition, 1983, at 19.

Part I

The Perimeter

2   The *Wall* and Its Shadow: Security in the Borderlands

Every border is different. Every perimeter, unique. Which means that to meet security needs, we need to integrate a range of capabilities. Mobile and fixed towers. Vehicle and hand-held solutions. Infrared and daylight capabilities. Surveillance radar and motion detection.
        – DRS Technologies, Advertisement, 2012[1]

Fixed fortifications are monuments to the stupidity of man. If anything made by God can be overcome, anything made by man can be overcome.
        – George S. Patton[2]

If the border is a line, it is also a zone. The *spectral* conception of borders was introduced in the previous chapter, stipulating that even the most linear borders have zonal elements or catchment areas that extend far inland. But what do these look like? In one sense, they are like everywhere else, populated by cities and towns, highways and minimarts. But they differ too: they are the sites of extensive security presence, the center, repositioned at the periphery. This is not the *wall* – the material instantiation of the linear border – but *sprawl*, a process by which border areas are becoming "wider." Metaphorically, changes at the perimeter have turned *walls* into *moats*. As one official explains, the new US strategy toward border security entails a "layered detection system that focuses on risk-based screening, enhanced targeting and information sharing."[3] Another remarks: "The wider we make our borders ... the more effective we are going to be."[4]

This chapter investigates the evolution of security in border zones, exclusively within the territorial US. Three features of the border area coalesce into meaningful trends. It is first a *Zone of Surveillance*, as there is a broadening of physical infrastructure, with layered walls, roads, towers and surveillance installations. This includes a new move in technology toward the creation of a "net" – using long distance radars, sensors and UAVs to make the perimeter double-sided. It is second a *Zone of Heterogeneity*, as there are multiple forms of authority, including federal, state and local forces – and increasingly military involvement – the coordination of which includes information-sharing and expanded border networks, replete with inland checkpoints. Third, it is a *Zone of Vigilance*, given the increased role that citizens play in the monitoring of cross-border activity (or questionable behavior, subjectively defined), amounting to the integration of local border communities in law enforcement.

This material raises a number of questions. We are familiar with the idea that the state watches its populations. But *who watches*? It is too easy to characterize the state as puppet master of the citizenry. In fact, there are several states, and the people act as police too. This chapter asks us to reconsider how authority is structured in the new borderlands. A number of questions obtain: what happens when citizens cross the line between *vigilance* and *vigilantism*? And what is the impact of the overlap between *security* and *defense*? In many ways there is a blurring of security and law functions at the border, raising concerns of the *military acting like police* and the *police acting like military*. This feeds back into the discussion of vigilantism or individual *discretion* – the personalization of authority, reminiscent of pre-modern forms of governance.

This chapter also gives a first look at the complex nature of sovereignty in the borderlands. If authority is heterogeneous, who is sovereign in the periphery? The border brings out the vulnerability of the sovereign at the border – its point of definition – as the border is the site where the exception arrives constantly at the doorstep of the state; where border-guards (or the national guard or the local police) react to a case that could not have been anticipated and for which, while there may be protocol, there can be no precedent. In this way, the border is less a site of sovereignty, than sovereign *anxiety*. This fact erodes the normative basis of sovereignty – precisely because the border is in a perpetual state of exception. This echoes Agamben's critique that in the state of exception the sovereign assumes full powers and abrogates legal constraints.

Drawing on this, the chapter raises questions about who is subject to sovereign rule. Unlike *nation*, which we take to be an amorphous, border-transgressive phenomenon, we expect *state* to be a uniform, bounded concept. In fact, state power – or sovereignty-as-control – is uneven and heterogeneous. In general, it is strongest in the center and wanes as it approaches the periphery; however, at the periphery, the state re-emerges. With or without security installation, the border is a site of central presence and national iconography. Revisting points raised in Chapter 1, to focus only on state policies vis-à-vis the "other" – the barbarians outside – is to miss out on the function this projection of power has internally. Flags are part of this inculcation, this *domestication*. They are there to remind the people on their own side of the border who they really are, to garner loyalty from the state's most *distant* self. Indeed, in a significant sense, the border is itself the center displaced at the periphery – i.e. it is an instrument of central control used as much to subjugate the periphery as to defend it. I suggest this is best understood as a *local* colonial project. Indeed, if any space embodies the violence of founding it is the border. Borders embody this history of violence, like scars.

This characterization raises important normative questions. What challenges does securitization place on the local peoples of the borderlands regions (hereafter: border dwellers)? How much security is too much? But also, *what is it about security that we find objectionable*? In part, we find it objectionable when it is not in the interests of the people it affects. In this case, the goal of new security initiatives is not merely to protect the local populations against a threat, but also to condition their loyalty. In this way, there is a displacement of burden – a weight not necessarily of their choosing. As much as security is aimed at their protection, it is also aimed at their control.

Border Security *at the Perimeter* in the United States: 1986–2016

After 9/11 the US pursued a "big bang theory" of border security,[5] which entailed building a hi-tech fence and placing tens of thousands of additional law enforcement personnel, as well as the National Guard, at the border. Today, more than a decade removed from the attacks, a new consciousness about border securitization is forming, borne of the knowledge that "you can't just build a wall around the United States."[6] This evolution in thinking is detailed below.

Walling, 9/11 and the First Border Patrol Strategy

In the United States, the move toward fences and walls[7] began with the Immigration Reform and Control Act of 1986 (IRCA), which doubled the size of Border Patrol (USBP) and introduced numerous laws related to migration enforcement or border security – part of a general policy known as "prevention through deterrence."[8] This immigration reform, signed into law by President Ronald Reagan, enabled the legalization of more than 2.5 million illegal aliens. It also marked the beginning of raised consciousness in the US toward the importance of border security. This in turn produced the first stretch of fence at the US–Mexico border, in the San Diego sector in 1990.

This pilot initiative was expanded in 1994 with the National Security Plan (NSP), which began a more concerted deployment of resources to the border, including "Operation Hold the Line" in El Paso and "Operation Gatekeeper" in San Diego, which produced two stretches of fence. This meant putting more boots "on the line" and using landing-mat fencing, stadium lighting, cameras and sensors. However, support for walling at this point was still in its nascent stage; in fact, fencing was placed last on the list of policy imperatives in the NSP, which were, in descending order: personnel, equipment, technology and tactical infra-structure. This policy was generally considered effective and in 1996, through the Illegal Immigration Reform and Immigrant Responsibility Act (IIRIRA), the use of fencing was extended, especially in San Diego, where a triple-layered fence was installed. In 1997, the NSP unveiled a second phase of fence deployment, with "Operation Rio Grande" in McAllen and Laredo, Texas and then again with "Operation Safeguard" (1999) in Tucson, Arizona.

The terror attacks of 9/11 prompting renewed interest in the border, especially with the creation of the Department of Homeland Security in 2003. US Customs and Border Protection (CBP) was formed in 2003 under the DHS umbrella. A new focus on the apprehension of terror-ists and calls for new investments in technology produced a compre-hensive border security plan in 2005 called the Secure Border Initiative (SBI), which emphasized a comprehensive surveillance technology sys-tem – SBI*net* – which included sensors, night vision, remote video sur-veillance, light towers and unmanned aerial vehicles (UAVs). Defending the new focus on technology, Chief of US Border Patrol, Michael Fisher critiqued earlier strategies as essentially brute force: "We said 'get eve-rything we can and get it to the line' … more Border Patrol agents came on, more technology, more fence, more roads." The strategy was called "terrain denial."[9]

But alongside this technological deployment came a major increase in tactical infrastructure with the Secure Fence Act of 2006, which amended IIRIRA with a requirement for double-layered fencing along the Southwest border, totaling 850 miles – thereby radically expanding the infrastructural developments of the 1990s. The amount of financial appropriation for border fencing increased markedly in these years, from $25 million in 1996, to $298 million in 2006 and then again to $1.5 billion in 2007. In addition to this move toward walling, there was an enormous increase in personnel – as with Operation Jump Start (2006–2008), which sent 6,000 National Guard troops to the southwest border – a controversial deviation from the norm, discussed below. Funding for walling increased steadily over the next years, culminating in 2010 in the Supplemental Border Appropriations Bill (HR 6080), after which, CBP became the single largest law enforcement agency in the US. On the northern border, the number of border patrol agents climbed from 340 in 2001 to over 2,200 in 2012. On the southwest border, the increase was from roughly 9,100 in 2001 to more than 17,900 in 2012.

Speaking in 2012, Jayson Ahern, former CBP Acting Commissioner, declared that the border was better staffed than at any point in its eighty-year history.

Walling and Its Discontents

The post-9/11 window witnessed an enormous effort toward the securing of the border through manpower and walling. But what success did this really bring? There have been some palpable returns – but nothing conclusive. For example, illegal immigration, as measured by Border Patrol apprehensions, dropped precipitously. From 1999 to 2004, apprehensions fluctuated around 1 million per year, but in the years after the 2004 National Strategy (NS) they dropped precipitously, by more than 60 percent, from 1,139,300 in 2004 to 447,500 in 2010. This said, there is no way to accurately account for whether walling had any positive impact. For example, while the numbers of undocumented migrants attempting to cross US borders illegally have decreased, this period correlates with the slowing of the US economy. Moreover, the project remains incomplete. For example, as late as 2011 the Government Accountability Office disclosed that of the 873 miles along the southwest border that BP claimed to have under operational control, only about 129 miles (15 percent) were classified as "controlled;" the remaining 85 percent were classified as "managed," meaning that while there were some interdictions, this only could be achieved *after* illegal entry into the US was detected. If you include the northern border, only 69 miles or 1.7 percent, of 4,000 total miles under operational control.[10]

Difficulties in accounting are further aggravated by the displacement effect, as walling in one area simply pushes illicit trade and traffic elsewhere. In the US, this has meant that the initial walling, which was successful in Texas and California, pushed illicit trade into Arizona. Former CBP Commissioner Alan Bersin remarked: "Criminal organizations have adapted to the increased resources, turning the Tucson sector of Arizona into a trafficking corridor for illegal immigrants and drugs."[11] The fence has also relocated drug-smuggling to the northern border. This logic of displacement is reiterated in interviews that I conducted with local officers in the field. As one border county sheriff described the problem: "take a balloon, clasp it between your hands and start blowing into it, it's going to start bloating ... [eventually] it's going to burst."[12]

In addition to problems of accounting, there has been a real shift in political and strategic thought at the border, with walls increasingly considered ineffective. Fencing quickly becomes financially unsustainable when combined with technology, as with SBI*net* which has been mocked as a "billion dollar-plus attempt to erect a 'virtual fence' across the Southwest border."[13] But there are also legitimate concerns that walling has actually made matters worse, as any success in closing off routes into the US has made the services of violent gangs more imperative for crossings, prompting vast increases in violence at the border – both sides – as gangs compete for access routes. More specifically, there are two types of problems that have risen to the fore since the advent of walling, both of which would persist even if the wall were to be completed: tunnels, which go underneath the wall and UAVs which go over it. Looking first at tunnels, the rate of tunneling has expanded exponentially since the advent of walling. From 1990 to 2011, US law enforcement unearthed 149 cross-border tunnels, along the US–Mexico border, 139 of which were discovered after 2001.

The Nogales sector of Arizona has become the fulcrum of the problem. One former Deputy Chief of Border Patrol remarked to me colorfully: "I have witnessed the discovery of over one hundred tunnels ... One of these days the entire city of Nogales, Arizona is going to drop about 50 feet because it is so catacombed with tunnels."[14] Tunnels also present especially dangerous problems for law enforcement. A local Border Patrol agent explains the dangers intrinsic to "crawling" the tunnels as follows:

It [is] very dangerous work [because] you never know who will be down in those tunnels with you ... [Agents] have smelled cigarette smoke in there, they have heard voices. Can you picture yourself about 45 feet under the ground, headed toward Mexico? ... You are underground, 90 feet from the opening and you find somebody in that tunnel with you.[15]

A second concern are ultralights or UAVs, which are low-flying aircraft that are able to transport drugs over the wall. Ultralights present a particular problem for lawmakers because they are small, inexpensive and quiet, evading sight and radar. They are flown across the southwest border year round, carrying hundreds of pounds of illegal drugs on each trip. They also provide drug cartels a form of inexpensive counter-surveillance. As one FBI agent puts it: "While we are watching them on the border with our sophisticated drones, they are also watching us."[16]

In addition, there are numerous other forms of breach popularized in recent years. Some go through the fence. The Police Chief of Nogales explains that the fence has a gap of about six inches between the bollards, so they make "packages that go right between those bars."[17] Another problem is the use of ramps which go up one side of the fence and down the other: "The fence is not a silver-bullet. It does impede their ability to drive at will with their loads by the thousands of pounds in vehicles, as they used to do ... [but] ramps go over the tops of fences."[18]

All told, policymakers have since come to realize that this solution was a problem unto itself, that it was "unreasonable and unsustainable."[19]

2012 and Beyond – the New Consciousness

Outside of heightened political rhetoric – especially in the 2012 and 2016 Presidential campaigns – the euphoria over fencing that dominated the 2000s has largely faded. Recently, largely in response to the economic recession and the climate of fiscal austerity, appropriations for tactical infrastructure have fallen precipitously. This de-funding of border walling reached its apex with the well-publicized cancelation of SBI*net*, which was discontinued because of its inefficacy. In 2010, Secretary Napolitano downgraded the program to a rump of its former self, explaining that SBI*net* "has been plagued with troubles from day one."[20] Senator Joseph Lieberman (I-Conn.), chair of the Senate Homeland Security and Governmental Affairs Committee, stated that "From the start, SBI*net*'s one-size-fits-all approach was unrealistic."[21]

Indicative of this change in thinking, in 2012 Border Patrol put out a new strategy, "The 2012–2016 National Strategy" toward border security, which moves away from previous notions of guarding the line. One security analyst explains that Border Patrol's new strategy emphasizes "risk-based approaches," rather than resource-based ones: "risk-based strategies are not based on *apprehension*, which is the catching of people that attempt transgression, but instead toward catching people before they come in, which is a form of *deterrence*."[22] This necessitates the "widening of the border" and "segmenting risk at the border." This move is more than semantic – it involves a whole change in consciousness toward what a twenty-first century border represents. This includes cooperative agreements between federal, state and local law enforcement agencies. It also includes an evolution in relations with Mexico and Canada. As a Border Patrol official explains:

[We want to move from a strategy of] coordination and collaboration to one where we have operational fusion with our partners. We want to be in an environment where we not only are planning together, but are executing jointly – not only within CBP, [but] with our international partners, whether they be the government of Mexico or the government of Canada.[23]

This shift in thinking is massive and has only recently been consecrated as policy – including agreements with Canada and Mexico, discussed in Chapter 3. Whereas in the past, walling was a centerpiece in border security, the new strategy cultivates an integrated border enforcement zone. The section to follow examines three parallel trends at the border, what I term the zones of *Surveillance*, *Heterogeneity* and *Vigilance*.

Trends in Bordering *at the Perimeter*: Widening the Net

Zone of Surveillance: Infrastructure, Technology and the Inland "Net"

There is an increased awareness that for borders to be effective, they cannot merely be "tall," they must also be "wide" and "layered," especially through the renewed commitment to use and deploy technology at the border. But what does this entail? At its most basic, this means widening the actual borderline – i.e. extending the border's "horizontal footprint" inland. There are several means of using technology and tactical infrastructure to widen the border. For example, some technology is being dedicated toward thickening the physical line through ground sensors. There are several types of sensors currently being deployed to the US border – seismic, magnetic, infrared – which are mostly placed within about half a mile from the border, but in some cases can even be extended as far as fifty to a hundred miles off the border. Unattended underground sensors enable the Border Patrol to react to any "sensor hit" at the border with the immediate deployment of patrol officers. In this way, sensors act as a "trip-wire."[24]

Presently, technology companies are fast at work cultivating new sensor systems. One technology developer explains that the "idea is to create a seismic zone along the border."[25] Their technology boasts it can detect people crossing a border at a range of 600 feet. Another company offers perimeter fencing with "buried cable detection systems," which complement fencing by providing an invisible "detection field" to protect a perimeter covertly with "software-controlled zoning."[26] Other sensors can be spread throughout the border area – like landmines – creating a zone of detection at intervals beneath the earth. In addition to same-side sensors, some systems create invisible fields of detection, emanating in both directions from the fence itself, to detect possible transgression in advance of the border.[27] These technologies contribute to the widening of border spaces, offering a different type of functionality than walling. As these technologies are covert, they are aimed at detection, not deterrence. Far from the purchase of the fence, which seeks visibility and demarcation, this technology is interested instead in invisibility and attempts to expand the border, rather than define it.

An alternate way to thicken the line, is through cameras and radars. The idea here is to extend the detection and pre-detection range of the border. As a local Police Chief on the US–Mexico border explained to me: "It's a net, basically. You are creating a new visual net and then having a response to that net."[28] This began with SBI*net*'s "Integrated Fixed Towers" system, which included cameras, night vision and radar that enabled "the Border Patrol to spot illegal immigrants at distances up to 7.5 miles away."[29] New camera systems serve as "the eyes of the border patrol agents," controlled remotely from a command center.[30] These new cameras correct for some of the earlier shortcomings of border cameras because they conceal where the cameras are pointing. These can be positioned to look inward from the border, mimicking the sensors, as well as across the other side of the line. These cameras work alongside radar systems that can track many miles out from the border, creating a pre-border buffer zone. These long-view detection systems work alongside covert reconnaissance cameras – such as "remote decoys" and "artificial rocks," which distract border-transgressors from the actual cameras and can be speckled throughout the border area to create a covert camera zone.[31]

In addition to fixed sites, cameras and radars operate via ultralight aircraft, unmanned aerial vehicles (UAVs) and Aerostats (radar balloons). UAVs are fairly common at borders, but interest in them has redoubled of late, as UAVs have capacity for extremely long-range surveillance power, including Electro-Optical (EO) sensors that "can identify an object the size of a milk carton from an altitude of 60,000 feet."[32] A DHS technology expert explains that the goal is to have a "wide-area" and "tiered air surveillance system" that coordinates the many different types of air surveillance units:

Much of the border is deserted, but we need to patrol it. We need a net out there. We are not going to build any fences, but at low cost we can provide eyes almost around the clock ... SBI*net* never made sense to me; airborne systems are the way of the future.[33]

Relatedly, cameras are increasingly being fixed to mobile units, such as portable long-range infrared sensors and truck-mounted mobile video surveillance systems, thereby perpetuating the net at the agent level. An industry leader explains: "We want to provide 'situation awareness', so [patrol officers] can see what is out there, miles around them, so they know where the danger is, so they know where there friends are and they know where to go and where not to go."[34]

Taking this inland "net" a step further are checkpoints – less a technology than an institutional site – which essentially recreate the border inland. These checkpoints, or "choke-points," allow the state to monitor and control traditional smuggling corridors – akin to the defense-in-depth strategy[35] deployed in ancient Rome. Chief of Border Patrol Michael Fisher explains that checkpoints are part of a layered approach that "extends our zone of security outward, ensuring that our physical border is not the first or last line of defense, but one of many;" they enable a "hardening at and between borders."[36] Locally, checkpoints are referred to as a "backstop" enabling agents a "second bite of the apple;" as importantly, they are unique legal spaces, as you "need no probable cause to stop a person."[37] Further, there are designs for roving checkpoints and temporary outposts to be speckled throughout the area.

In addition to aiding in detection and apprehension, checkpoints are "contact points" where border patrol has direct access to individuals and thus facilitate the capture of *biometrics* (usually fingerprints or irises). This subject is treated at great length in Chapters 5–7. This is a central mission of Border Patrol, which is now to "identify, not just catch." This is part of the broader move since 9/11 to create expansive identity profiles that link identities to international terror databanks. In fact, remote biometric capture first started in the military, with units in Iraq and Afghanistan capturing fingerprints and relaying that data via satellite to the US to see if the person linked to a terrorist watch database. These same uses now apply to Border Patrol.

For this reason, checkpoints have been controversial. After all, the Fourth Amendment protects "against unreasonable searches and seizures." To understand the climate, here is an exposition, about a contested checkpoint beside Arivaca, AZ:

Warrantless searches, property destruction and other alleged rights violations by Border Patrol have escalated … Tensions are running so high that local residents are operating their own surveillance operation to watch the watchmen.[38]

Normative concerns about life in the security zone are treated at the end of the chapter.

Zone of Heterogeneity: Federal, State, Local

Border areas in the US can increasingly be seen as discrete regions, due to the integration of different actors and agencies. Two aspects of this trend are noteworthy: intra-federal cooperation (including with information-sharing and joint operations), and the merging and cooperation of federal, state and local forces in the border regions into joint security initiatives. This broad integration strategy is referred to as a "whole of government" approach to border security.

Beginning with intra-federal integration, there is a general understanding in the federal government that effective risk-prevention at the border begins with information sharing. This may seem self-evident. However, historically there has been little to no information shared among agencies – a fact made manifest nationally by the inability of first responders to communicate on 9/11. This move toward intra- and inter-agency sharing at the border is formalized in the 2012–2016 Border Patrol agenda, which pledges to "continue to integrate our intelligence and enforcement capabilities [and] … to gather relevant intelligence and share it with our partners to enhance their ability to execute their portion of this effort."[39] The primary means by which this sharing is executed is through the integration of Border Patrol with intelligence entities and fusion centers – frequently on-site at the border, culling information throughout federal ranks.

But most importantly, interest in intra-agency cooperation has led to the decentralization of DHS. This shift in model is significant: whereas in the past the idea was to have a central knowledge bank, which circulated information to the perimeter, the plan now is to empower CBP officials who fan out throughout the border community. As one senior official explains: "at headquarters we have really flattened our organization … We have taken some high-level positions from headquarters and moved them out into the field."[40] Of course, getting real information sharing off the ground is not easy and there have been "turf wars." Nonetheless, significant inter-agency integration is underway. As a former head of CBP explains: "We have seen a level of sharing of information, certainly within the federal community, law enforcement and intelligence community, like we have never seen before."[41]

The second move has been toward the coordination of local and federal forces. This revolution in thinking is also derived from 9/11 and the linking of illegal immigration and terrorism – thereby collapsing much of the distinction between local and federal responsibilities and domestic and national security. The Homeland Security Act of 2002 and the Intelligence Reform and Terrorism Prevention Act of 2004, specifically mandated that DHS share information with local and state partners regarding terrorism and homeland security. In recent years, this transformation in thinking has really gained steam. In 2009, Julie Myers Wood, former head of ICE, encouraged the federal government to empower state and local officials to make decisions over immigration at the border, because the federal government had "not enough money and too few beds," to handle border issues on their own.[42] In 2010, DHS Secretary Napolitano stated that her main goal for the year was to encourage federal–state and federal–local sharing as regards border-related terrorism concerns: "Our goal is to give that front line of law enforcement the tools they need to confront and to disrupt terrorist threats."[43]

This change in thinking reached its peak with the 2012–2016 Border Patrol National Strategy. Michael Fisher explains the need for not just information-sharing but the full integration of the different forces at the border: "we are now doing things like integrated planning and integrated operation, which is different than just collaborating and coordinating with our partners ... What we're talking about [now is] pooling all capabilities, independent of the color of your uniform."[44] From the federal perspective this type of sharing is imperative. After all, in most border communities, the individuals most able to understand threats and observe suspicious activities are local officials, not federal ones.

Interest obtains on the local side as well. For example, the Sheriff of Hennepin County, MN explains that the integration of federal and local forces is essential because "more and more the technology and information that we all rely on are shared resources."[45] The Police Chief of Nogales, AZ attests that there has been a marked increase in coordination with federal officers in recent years:

We have [police officers who] get funded by the Federal government to assist Border Patrol, on border issues – immigration, smuggling, etc ... And we have people that go to Border Patrol briefings and we set our missions based on Border Patrol staffing. We now have a lot of Border Patrol channels that hadn't existed ever before on our radios, so we have communications abilities by getting encrypted codes that we were able to get because of this closer model working relationship that we have ... It's gotten so much better than it had been. There had been a lot of "no that's mine, no that yours, stay out of here." Its gotten to being more cooperative, with more communication.[46]

All told, there is a clear sense from both local and federal officers that the classic model of singular, federal control at the border cannot continue.

Zone of Vigilance: The Citizenry

In addition to intra- and inter-agency cooperation, there has also been an increase in civilian–state cooperation. There has of course always been some sort of state–civilian relationship at the perimeter – most notably amongst ranchers whose land abuts the border. However, Border Patrol is now explicitly cultivating a vigilant border community, especially as regards terrorism. This is embodied by the strategic move away from involving local border communities simply through "public relations" to what is termed "community engagement."[47] This is because practitioners are increasingly aware that the local community is the single most reliable source of information:

We used to think information came from government sources, shared down to the agent. Now we turn this upside: the agent has more information than anyone in Washington DC. But more than this: the local community actually has more information than the border patrol agents ... So you have gone from a top down [logic] – "information starts in DC and goes out to the agents at the border" – to this idea where border patrol agents have to interact with the community, engage with the community and win over the community. The community has to understand that those Border Patrol agents are here for a reason and [thus] want to share information with the agents.[48]

Border Patrol has recently put forth a number of programs to this effect. For example, Operation Detour and Drug Demand Reduction Outreach are schooling programs that educate students about border area dangers and coach them out of partaking in trans-border crime. These programs are preventative in nature, but also train students to react in ways that assist Border Patrol if they do learn about or get entangled with crime. In addition to educational programs, Border Patrol engages in what they call "community and stakeholder outreach."[49] Part of this program is to alert local borderland communities that there is a Border Patrol liaison who forges relations with local community leaders toward providing information and assistance to Border Patrol and enables stealthy assistance in return.

This "community engagement" also exists on the level of technological advancement – with new capabilities being developed so that individuals can enact their own self-governance. The most widely known of these campaigns is DHS's famous slogan "If You See Something, Say Something." But this logic of using citizen awareness for the purposes of homeland security is now enabled by technological applications – mostly funded by government grants. One example of this is the company Town Compass LLC, which made a Most Wanted Terrorist database available for download as a smartphone app. This software allows vigilant citizens to directly contact the FBI with information – i.e. as "first responders." On this point, one industry leader explains: "Notification systems are now becoming two-way, enabling people in the community [to] communicate from the field by whatever means available."[50] In fact, DHS itself has developed a First Responder Support Tools (FiRST) app for smartphones.

There is a veritable echo chamber within CBP about how vigilant border communities are the most effective line of defense. But this does not mean it is going to be easy or without cost. Potential ramifications are considered below.

Reconsidering the Peripheral State

The border is a complex space, with many actors and structures of control. What does this mean for governance? More to the point: how can we understand how authority is structured in such an environment? And what harms might inhere in this arrangement? This section hones in on the question of the place of the state in the borderlands. It first revisits the question of legitimate governance, then the problem of sovereignty.

The state is never simply a "thing" but rather a set of things – in this case, there is a heterogeneity of authority in the borderlands. Putatively, US border areas are controlled by Border Patrol, which is part of law enforcement – i.e., the police. But as is manifest above, there is much more than this. For example, the state is increasingly dependent on citizens for law enforcement. This is not harmless, as there is a thin line between *vigilance* and *vigilantism* – a line crossed famously by the "Minutemen" of Arizona, who militarized the role of self-policing. In this way, the border is decidedly *un*-modern. In the modern state, only state violence is tolerated; civilian violence is forbidden. As per Weber's formulation, the state does not simply control violence, it *monopolizes* it.

Another critical matter looms: the insertion of the US military into what are putatively domestic affairs. The militarization of the border after 9/11 was discussed briefly above. There have been two large outlays of National Guard troops to the border since 9/11: Operation Jump Start (2006–2008) and Operation Phalanx (2010–2011). There has also been a proliferation of US Air and Marine bases along the border – which had previously existed at the US–Mexico border, but which have now expanded to the US–Canada border. The merging of military and law enforcement functions is perhaps not that great a concern if it is exceptional, circumstantial and circumscribed. However, as the threat landscape shifts toward the merging of transnational crime (previously the domain of law enforcement) and terrorism (the domain of national security), the line between *security* and *defense* blurs – just like the distinctions between *foreign* and *domestic* in the intelligence community.

The question then is: what are the ramifications of this blurring? Should the military merely play an auxiliary role in the borderlands? Is its function surveillance or deterrence? Bert Tussing, of the US Army War College explains what is at stake:

This country is held together in many ways by an ethos that says we want our soldiers to be soldiers, not policemen. We want our military to be our servants, not our overseers ... In November 2001, a month and a half after the attacks, there were still National Guardsmen in some airports. [Did you think]: "what are these guys doing here? And why are they carrying those guns? Do they really need that stuff?" Don't feel bad about that ... We love our military, most of the time. But we know where we want our military to be, all of the time. So is this going to be an acceptable thing for the American people?[51]

Tussing brings up an important theoretical point about the projection of state power and the protection of its citizenry: we have an intuition that national security and law enforcement must be kept separate. But why is this true? One concern is that the presence of the military perpetuates the threat cycle, with threats to national security and law enforcement caught in an ever-expansive loop. Thus there is a blurring of security and law functions at the border, thereby enabling the two-headed hydra of the *military acting like police* and the *police acting like military*.

This feeds back into the discussion of vigilantism, or individual *discretion*, which can work in contravention of the law. Indeed, it is a hallmark of the modern state that everyday politics does not have face-to-face violence, but rather the depersonalization of political power, common to bureaucracy or administration. The personalization of authority is a serious concern. We need look no further than the classic voices of the canon for strong statements about how the only thing protecting us from tyranny is the law, as when Locke writes: "*Where-ever Law ends, Tyranny begins* ... Exceeding the Bounds of Authority is no more a Right in a great, than a petty Officer; no more justifiable in a King, than a Constable."[52]

It also raises specific points about the rise of the police as agents of statecraft – here they are not only law enforcement, but in the gray area of the border, something that resembles law creators – purveyors at once of choice and violence. Concerns over this were raised by Hannah Arendt regarding the question of stateless peoples, which created a shift in balance such that police discretion began to take weight over state laws:

The nation-state, incapable of providing a law for those who had lost the protection of a national government, transferred the whole matter to the police. This was the first time the police in Western Europe had received authority to act on its own, to rule directly over people; in one sphere of public life it was no longer an instrument to carry out and enforce the law, but had become a ruling authority independent of government.[53]

What transpired was violence, lawlessness and "illegal acts" by the police in the name of the state. Derrida also comments on the police – and specifically the border police – taking the law into their own hands:

> One has to be mindful of the profound problem of the role and the status of the police, of, in the first instance, border police, but also of a police without borders, without determinable limit, who from then become all-pervasive and elusive, as Benjamin noted in *Critique of Violence* just after the First World War. The police became omnipresent and spectral in the so-called civilized states once they undertake to *make the law*, instead of simply contenting themselves with applying it and seeing it observed.[54]

The question then arises: if authority is heterogeneous, how does sovereignty function in the periphery? What happens when there is an act of violence at the border, where law enforcement decides to take authority into its own hands, to act violently against perceived perpetration? This, in some sense is the ultimate sovereign act – looking here at sovereignty-*qua*-decisionism – as in this case it is the police that *decides on the exception*. Here it is important to revisit Schmitt:

> It is precisely the exception that makes relevant the subject of sovereignty, that is, the whole question of sovereignty. The precise details of an emergency cannot be anticipated, nor can one spell out what may take place in such a case … The precondition as well as the content of jurisdictional competence in such a case must necessarily be unlimited."[55]

In Schmitt's formulation the sovereign has two functions: to decide on the exception and to *decide what the exception is*. This is precisely the kind of authority that takes place at the border. There is a constant evaluation of what is or is not exceptional with every act of border transgression. There is no unitary state oversight; instead, there are numerous offices in which authority is overlapping. It is a sphere of constant judgment, of matters essential to the state, made by actors independent of the state itself. What actually happens in the state of exception? For Schmitt, the exception is a realm of unlimited authority "which means the suspension of the entire existing order. In such a situation it is clear that the state remains, whereas law recedes."[56]

It is no stretch to locate these concerns at the border. The border is the site where the exception arrives constantly at the doorstep of the state, where local officials react to a case that could not have been anticipated. The inevitability of this state erodes the normative basis of sovereignty – precisely because of the cultivation of a perpetual state of exception. The normative challenge is rendered clearest by Agamben, for whom the state of exception is the state of war turned inward, entailing the subversion of constitutional protections:

The paradigm is, on the one hand (in the state of siege) the extension of the military authority's wartime powers into the civil sphere and on the other hand a suspension of the constitution (or of those constitutional norms that protect individual liberties), in time the two models end up merging into a single juridical phenomenon that we call the state of exception.[57]

Agamben likens the state of exception to the pre-Montesquieuan state in which there is no separation between the executive, legislative and judiciary. Therefore the sovereign assumes full powers and abrogates legal constraints.

The challenges posed by the blurring of interwoven state, military and police forces are here made clear. As are the problem of individual border guards taking authority (of law enforcement) into their own hands, the different overlapping and unfolding layers of authority at the border and also the vigilantism of popular rule. Agamben continues:

When [*auctoritas* and *potestas*] coincide in a single person, when the state of exception, in which they are bound and blurred together, becomes the rule, then the juridicopolitical system transforms itself into a killing machine … The normative aspect of law can thus be obliterated and contradicted with impunity by a governmental violence that – while ignoring international law externally and producing a permanent state of exception internally – nevertheless still claims to be applying the law.[58]

The point here is not to suggest that the American border regime has anything in common with the type of "killing machine" that Agamben describes. But the threat of different layers of rule aligning in the hands of a single official is prevalent at the border. This should flag concern.

Point of Peripherality: Security and the Borderlands Subject

If we were to ask the question *What kind of space is the border region?*, we would answer: it is first and foremost a space of *security*. This has always been somewhat true, but this point is brought into particular clarity now, with the webs of personnel, infrastructure and surveillance that expand inland from the border, fundamentally altering the shape and character of the communities therein. One is here reminded of how Foucault described the panopticon, the "oldest dream of the oldest sovereign."[59] Indeed, the landscape thus described, of surveillance, visibility and control, in many ways recreates the panopticon in the open air of the borderlands. It is a space in which the state not only watches its subjects, but shapes them. In his essay, "The Eye of Power," Foucault explains: "[The system of surveillance has] no need for arms, physical violence, material constraints. Just a gaze. An inspecting gaze, a gaze which each individual under its weight will end by interiorizing to the point that he is his own overseer, each individual thus exercising this surveillance over, and against, himself."[60]

The peripheral subject is *conditioned* by surveillance. But is this sufficient to understand the harms of security on the peripheral subject? I argue that it is not, because there is something *specific* about the borderlands dweller. In particular, as much as security is aimed at their protection, it is also aimed at their control. Peripheral peoples are not *trusted* and so they are disciplined, not merely for fear of attacks from without, but also secession within. The people on the border have a double role: they are most *at risk* from outside threats, while at the same time *at risk of being a threat*. They are both the *subject* and *object* of security.

Center/Periphery: A Dialectic of Domination and Resistance

The borderlands are a panoptic space; they are also a peripheral space, thereby bringing into focus the complex relations between the *center* and *periphery* within a polity. With or without security installation, the border is a site of central presence and national iconography – replete with flags, uniforms, songs and other traditional representations, a performance of national identity which in the US has become ever more dramatic after 9/11. What is the point of this ostentatious declaration of state power and identity? These policies may be designed to make clear to the border-crosser the awesome power of the state. Or to convince citizens polity-wide that the state is being "tough on immigration." According to Wendy Brown this symbolic strength at the border is an attempt to regain sovereign power it has lost in the face of border porosity.[61] Surely these rationales are part of the story. But to focus only on state policies vis-à-vis the "outside" is to miss out on the function this projection of power has internally. The flags are also part of this effort to affirm the loyalty of the border community, the state's most *distant* self.

Turning our gaze toward the projection of central power on the periphery also illuminates a problem with the sovereignty-as-jurisdiction perspective. In our fixation on Westphalian sovereignty, the distinction of center-periphery has largely been lost. Indeed, the original challenge of statehood was to achieve homogenization within, not merely (and simplistically) to negate the world without. Indeed, the border is itself the center displaced at the periphery – an instrument of control used as much to subjugate the periphery as it is to defend it. In the US case, this re-claiming of the periphery by the center is embodied by some of the moves within CBP described above, such as the decentralization of CBP, the relocation of federal authority at the periphery and the appropriation of local law enforcement into asymmetrical power relations with federal agents – via integration and coordination. Still, this requires some unpacking. What do we mean when we suggest that states dominate their peripheries? I suggest this is best understood as a *local* colonial project.

This problem has deep roots. In ancient Rome, the frontier lands were comprised of dubiously loyal subjects, including some that were partially nomadic as a means of avoiding taxation. Consequently, the Roman state took great pains to cultivate some loyalties in these distant reaches of the interior. Indeed, one of the principle functions of early walling systems was "to divide the barbarians beyond from the barbarians within, who were in the process of becoming Roman."[62] In the Chinese empire too, boundaries were not simply designed to keep people out, but also to monitor the empire itself and keep imperial subjects from escaping:

It is assumed that an imperial border policy is concerned solely with keeping out the barbarians ... [But] an imperial boundary that is described as defensive, being supposedly designed to keep out unwanted barbarians, has in fact a double function: it serves not only to keep the outsiders from getting in but to prevent the insiders from getting out.[63]

The same can be said for early modern states. In the medieval period, the delineation of the border was more a spectacle than a delineation. Sahlins portrays the voyage of the king and his emissaries from the center to the periphery to anoint territory as part of a kingdom. Thus the border was a site of ceremony and festival, which intimated the far reaches of state power, but in fact had no further trappings as such. This grand voyage of the emissary was critical, as through the festival came identification with the center. With the king came wealth, culture and a view of progress that would have been impossible from the periphery.[64]

The colonization of the periphery became even more dominant with the rise of nationalism and centralized forms of administration. This point is made powerfully by Sheldon Wolin, who discusses how boundaries have the effect of cultivating likeness – the essential project of nationalism – achieved through political education and the *taming* of the polity, what he calls *domestication*.[65] This is true of any nationalization campaign. Marx made this point when he argued that taxation was a tool to garner homogeneity across the territory: "Taxes are the source of life for the bureaucracy ... [which] permits of uniform action from a supreme center on all points of this uniform mass."[66] With the rise of the bourgeois state, suddenly the enemy of the peasant was not the Cossack, but the bureaucrat.

In an entirely different geopolitical context, James C. Scott's work on upland Asia produces a similar story. Rather than perform fealty to the center, the local communities in frontier provinces could spurn the state, knowing that without difficulty they could move to a place beyond the outer-most post. As a consequence, reigning in the periphery has been an obsession of modern nation-states, enacted by "establishing armed border posts, moving loyal populations to the frontier and relocating or driving away 'disloyal' populations, clearing frontier lands for sedentary agriculture, building roads to the borders and registering hitherto fugitive peoples."[67] In this way, the state's attempt to nationalize the periphery is more than just a security measure designed to breed loyalty – it is an attempt to create in its own image the very place farthest from its likeness.

The point is simply that what we see in general in peripheral areas is something like what we might call *colonization*, except in this case it doesn't refer to the act of taking over distant lands for the plunder of the metropole. Instead, it describes the process by which the center generates loyalty out of its periphery. The link to the border is clear: we see it in the education of local citizens (*vigilance*), the co-optation of local authorities (*heterogeneity*) and of course the watchful eye of the central state (*surveillance*). This is a particular form of "nation-building" that targets the periphery, familiar from debates over multiculturalism. For example, Will Kymlicka's defense of minority groups from the majoritarian "nation-building" exercises by dint of which they have been marginalized.[68] His concern regards minorities. But this can be extended to peripheral peoples writ large.

This point about the center's subjugation of the periphery also forms the core of our debates over the *moment of founding* or what Connolly calls the "paradox of origins"[69] – i.e. that the inceptions of democracies are never themselves democratic, because the people are not present (Rousseau) or they are mired in violence (Arendt). The enduring legitimacy of democratic states is thus predicated on the forgetting of the transgressions of their founding. But if any space embodies the violence of founding it is the border, even if that violence or imposition was in the name of democracy itself. Borders thus retain the history of violence, like scars. This fact is lost when we speak of democracy's edges in pure abstraction, as limits; but borders are physical spaces at which that unfreedom is *maintained*, as those originary exclusions are re-created daily. The border remains unfree, even once the democratic experiment has begun and it must maintain itself as this space in order for democracy to persist.

The fact that founding is a process steeped in its own violence, in particular exacted by the center on the periphery, is brought out forcefully by Derrida:

All nation-states are born and found themselves in violence. I believe that truth to be irrecusable. Without even exhibiting atrocious spectacles on this subject, it suffices to underline a law of structure: the moment of foundation, the instituting moment, is anterior to the law or legitimacy which it founds. It is thus *outside the law* and violent by that fact ... Before the modern forms of what is called "colonialism," all States [have] their origin in an aggression of the *colonial* type. This foundational violence is not only forgotten. The foundation is made in *order* to hide it; by its essence it tends to organize amnesia.[70]

This colonization is precisely what we are doing in our peripheries. We can now see the positioning of the center at the periphery is not an accident; instead it is a historical outcome. We might now ask: Against whom was the violence of founding at the border conducted? Border ceremonies are as much designed to remind locals of who they *are*, as it is to tell outsiders who they *aren't*. The border fences *in*, as much as it fences *out*.

The Distant *Self & The Price of Security*

So who is this peripheral person – the one against whom centrist colonization efforts are at least in part designed? The concept of the *distant self* helps break down a central problem in thinking about borders, which is that on one side of the line is a *self*, taken to be homogenous, and on the other side of the line is an *other*, taken to be equally homogeneous. This classic rendering can be depicted as follows:

Figure 2.1

Country A – (BORDER) – Country B

However, at the border, national identities are not fundamentally distinct and homogeneous (like oil and water). They are to each the "other" but they are not foreign; rather they are familiar and (usually) equally indigenous. In a deep sense, they are *neighbors*. In the language of us/them, *they* are as much of the periphery as *we* are. Thus, identity at the border is intimately intertwined with *proximity* – with two peripheral peoples proximate to each other. A better diagram might be:

Figure 2.2

Center A – Periphery A – (BORDER) – Periphery B – Center B

No assumption should be made over whether nominal (Center A– Periphery A) loyalty is stronger than proximity (Periphery A–Periphery B); both pulls are present.

What the diagram in Figure 2.2 illustrates is not merely that state identification is heterogeneous but also that it has a *spatial dynamic*, subject to the vagaries of distance. It is not, as frequently assumed, evenly distributed across a territory like air or the coloration on a map. Indeed, we continue to view states cartographically, as circles of territory with a dot to represent the capital. But this pervasive image conceals the point that *functionally*, not all parts of a territory identify with the state equally. This discussion of peripherality clearly supports the unevenness of sovereignty thesis (discussed in Chapter 1). At their peripheries, states frequently have the properties of nations.

But Figure 2.2, while able to convey the complex relations of states and peoples in the borderlands, nonetheless excludes the border itself, which has an identity independent of both the center and the periphery. Indeed, in many ways, the border is the center implanted in the periphery – actually, two centers implanted at the site of their mutual peripherality. The border thus represents a center that is alien to its surrounds:

Figure 2.3

Center A – Periphery A – (Center A / Center B) – Periphery B – Center B

With this characterization, we can now return to the question: What is the harm of new security protocols? By what tools can we understand the ways in which peripheral peoples might be subjects of injustice? On some level it is the sheer act of living in a zone of *surveillance, heterogeneity* and *vigilance*. It would come as no surprise if people came to feel suspect, abused, unequal. (The problem of security vis-à-vis liberty is treated at length in Chapter 5.) But the problem as it is approached here is something we might classify, following Nancy Fraser, as an injustice of recognition. This harm usually encompasses a set of concerns, ranging from lack of representation, to cultural forms of domination and disrespect.[71] The point here is that institutions that misrecognize people are unjust because they prevent them from being equal participants in society, or that peoples have unequal access to this good. Such concerns are usually focused on minorities. But what about geographic pockets that suffer unequal treatment? Might it be said that peripheral people live in a constant state of non-equality for the sake of security? The claim here is that security policies do not just suspend liberty for the sake of security (treated later), but also that it suspends equality for the same reason.

Following Judith Butler, we might say that the harm of border colonization is that border dwellers are unequally grievable. And because this population is itself *interior*, it engenders a paradox as people need state protection from the very force by which they are subjugated. In this case, the target population (border dwellers) are not excluded from the power equation, but bounded and dominated by it. It is by their own law and own security, that they are dominated. This generates a particular form of precariousness, as:

the lives in question are not cast outside the polis in a state of radical exposure, but bound and constrained by power relations in a situation of forcible exposure. It is not the withdrawal of absence of law that produces precariousness, but the very effects of illegitimate legal coercion itself or the exercise of state power freed from the constraints of all law.[72]

What does it mean if not all subjects are equal and in particular large swathes of the population are put under forms of control that might be questionably legitimate? Such populations might feel that rather than have the state make them secure (i.e. solve the problem of security) they may instead feel insecure (and in fact that security is itself their problem). They are structurally insecure (by dint of being at the border). This is the *external* problem of security. But they are also insecure by dint of the colonizing center. This is the *internal* problem of security.

In terms of security, it would seem clear that we can say that border dwellers face categorically different conditions than other peoples throughout the territory of the state. The frontier is conditioned by constant insecurity. By what logic can a justifying explanation be given to these people – stuck between an insecurity that feels permanent (and thus the state cannot solve) and a state-imposed security designed for their protection, but manifests to them as more like colonization? What justification can be given, except to suggest that in the broader view it is better for the state, *generally*? Is this sufficient, given the permanent nature of security installations at the periphery? A model for solvency through citizenship is discussed in Chapter 3.

Conclusion

Looking ahead, we might ask some empirical questions. What happens to citizens as the lands around them become securitized – does their national allegiance strengthen? Why? And what about minorities? Do they take this as an affront or do they double down their commitments to the state? It seems there is a complicated interplay between numerous factors in borderlands – degree of national identification, degree of state strength and degree of physical development. What is the relationship between them? Another set of questions regards spatiality. Why does the capital benefit from being in the center? What would it lose as it incrementally inches toward the periphery? There may be a multifaceted relationship here, such that a state might want the periphery distant (i.e. enough to protect the capital) but not too distant (such that it wanders off and joins the enemy's ranks). Where is this point of perfect balance? When does the periphery become so distant that its removed-ness from the center diminishes loyalty entirely?

This chapter was interested principally in the question of the borderlands, looking at the new ways in which states – using the example of the US – are using security practices on their own peripheral lands. This point is expanded upon in the following chapter, in which new forms of *cross-border* security protocols are examined, following robust new forms of co-bordering present at the US borders with Canada and Mexico. This chapter will expand upon some of the issues discussed here, focusing on new challenges of sovereignty. It closes by sketching a model of citizenship to address some of the new normative challenges detailed on these pages.

Notes

1 DRS Technologies Advertisement. *Homeland Security Today*, March 2012.
2 Cited in Kirkham, Jeffrey Scott. "Police and the Southwest Border." Remarks by Kirkham, Nogales Police Chief. Border Security Expo, Phoenix, AZ, March 6, 2012.
3 Ahern, Jayson. Conference Chairman – Opening Remarks. Paper read at Border Security Expo, March 6, at Phoenix, AZ, 2012.
4 Gilbert, "Cooperative Efforts between Mexico, Canada and the U.S. in Law Enforcement and Prosecution."
5 Jay Kalath, CEO, Allied Mission Group LLC. Personal interview, Washington, DC, May 16, 2012.
6 Ibid.
7 The terms "fence" and "wall" are here used interchangeably to refer to forms of tactical infrastructure. The most popular is bollard fencing, which is comprised of vertical posts of metal or concrete, embedded into the ground at small enough intervals so as to be impassible. These are the strongest, but the most expensive. Bollard fencing has largely replaced the previous type of fence most common on the border, which was landing-mat fencing, made from surplus from the Vietnam War.
8 Rosenblum, Marc R. "Border Security: Immigration Enforcement Between Ports of Entry." In *Congressional Research Service Report for Congress 7–5700*, 2012, at ii.
9 Fisher, Michael. "Keynote Address," by Fisher, Chief, US Border Patrol. Border Security Expo, Phoenix, AZ, March 7, 2012.
10 Kimery, Anthony. "First in-Depth Inside Look at Border Patrol's New National Strategy, Issues and Implementation." *Homeland Security Today*, May 7, 2012; Kimery, Anthony. "Northern Border Intel-Sharing Deficient, Fed Audit, Officials Say." *Homeland Security Today*, March 8, 2011.
11 Quoted in McCarter, Mickey. "CBP Chief Lists Seven Principles for Agency's Success: Bersin Says Facilitating Trade as Important as Preventing Terror." *Homeland Security Today*, October 15, 2010.

12 Interview, Phoenix, AZ. March 6, 2012.
13 Silverberg, David. "Ten Years after 9/11." *Homeland Security Today*, September 8, 2011.
14 Colburn, Ronald. "Border Enforcement by Land-Air-Sea (Detection and Deterrence)." Remarks by Colburn, Principal, Command Consulting Group and Former Deputy Chief, US Border Patrol, DHS. Border Security Expo, Phoenix, AZ, March 7, 2012.
15 Lawson, Leslie. Update from Border Patrol Sector Chiefs – Panel Discussion with Leslie Lawson, Chief Patrol Agent, Tucson Sector/Nogales Station. Paper read at Border Management Conference & Technology Expo, October 16, 2012, at Judson F William Convention Center, El Paso, Texas.
16 Valdemar, Richard. "Patrolling the Border: Special Issues in the South." Remarks by Valdemar, Gang Task Force, FBI. Counter Terror Expo Conference, Washington DC, May 16, 2012.
17 Kirkham, "Police and the Southwest Border."
18 Colburn, "Border Enforcement by Land-Air-Sea (Detection and Deterrence)."
19 Basham, Ralph. 2013. Bi-Lateral Cooperation: Joint Operational Efforts, US–Canada – Panel Discussion by Ralph Basham, former head of Customs and Border Protection. Paper read at Border Security Expo, March 12, at Phoenix, AZ.
20 McCarter, Mickey. "DHS Programs under Review Get No Funding: Cargo Screening? SBI*net*? General Aviation? Under Review." *Homeland Security Today*, February 25, 2010.
21 McCarter, Mickey. "Disagreements over Virtual Fence Decision." *Homeland Security Today*, 2011.
22 Shiffman, Gary M. "Patrolling the Border: The New National Strategy." Remarks by Shiffman, former CBP Chief of Staff, Managing Director, Chertoff Group. Counter Terror Expo Conference, Washington DC, May 16, 2012.
23 Chavez, Felix. "2012–2016 Border Patrol Strategic Plan." Remarks by Chavez, Deputy Chief, Operations Division, Office of Border Patrol. Border Management Conference & Technology Expo, El Paso, Texas, October 16, 2012.
24 Padilla, Sonia. "Investing in Proven Technologies: Integrated Fixed Towers and Mobile Surveillance Systems." Remarks by Padilla, Executive Director, Office of Technology Innovation and Acquisition, US Customs and Border Protection. Border Management Conference & Technology Expo, El Paso, Texas, October 17, 2012.
25 King, Mike. "Filling a Need: How IDENTISEIS Was Born." Remarks by King, Vice President, Border Technology, Inc. Border Management Conference & Technology Expo, El Paso, Texas, October 17, 2012.
26 "Integrated Perimeter Security Solutions." Southwest Microwave Advertisement, 2012.
27 "Senstar: The Trusted Choice for Perimeter Security Technology & Products." Senstar Advertisement, 2011.
28 Jeffrey Scott Kirkham, Nogales Police Chief. Personal interview, Nogales, AZ, March 20, 2012.

29 Goodwin, Jacob. "With SBI*net* Behind It, CBP Develops a New Procurement Strategy." *Government Security News*, February 2012, at 26.
30 Padilla, "Investing in Proven Technologies."
31 "Rti350 Wireless Remote Trigger & Illuminator." RECONYX Advertisement, 2012.
32 Hardin, Peter. "Eyes in the Skies." *Richmond Times-Dispatch*, October 30, 2003, at 1.
33 Interview, Washington, DC, May 17, 2012.
34 Mora, Manny. "Keynote Speech," by Mora, Senior Vice President, Strategic Business Development & Integration, General Dynamics C4 Systems. Border Management Conference & Technology Expo, El Paso, Texas, 2012.
35 Bonner, Robert C. "Perspectives on Border Security: Past, Present, Future." Remarks by Robert C. Bonner, former Commissioner, CBP; Former Administrator, DEA; and Former US District Judge for California's Central District. Border Security Expo, Phoenix, AZ, March 13, 2013.
36 Fisher, Michael. "Testimony of Michael J. Fisher, Chief, U.S. Border Patrol, U.S. Customs and Border Protection, Department of Homeland Security." 1–10: House Committee on Homeland Security, Subcommittee on Border and Maritime Security, 2012, at 2; Fisher, Michael. "Securing Ports of Entry." Remarks at the Border Security Expo, Phoenix, AZ, March 7, 2012.
37 Interviews, El Paso, TX, October 16, 2012.
38 Nowrasteh, Alex and Patrick G. Eddington. "How Effective Is Border Security?" *Cato Institute Online*, March 4, 2016.
39 Cited in Kimery, "Northern Border Intel-Sharing Deficient."
40 Chavez, "2012–2016 Border Patrol Strategic Plan."
41 Bonner, Robert C. "Terrorism and Transnational Criminal Organizations: Growing Confluence." Remarks by Bonner, former Commissioner, CBP; Former Administrator, DEA; and Former US District Judge for California's Central District. Border Security Expo, Phoenix, AZ, March 13, 2013.
42 Quoted in McCarter, Mickey. "287(G) Vital to Immigration Reform: Ex-Chief of ICE Calls for More Flexibility to Enforce Law." *Homeland Security Today*, November 12, 2009.
43 Quoted on McCarter, Mickey. "Napolitano Outlines DHS Priorities for 2010: At Top: Aviation, Borders, Information Sharing, Immigration Reform." *Homeland Security Today*, January 27, 2010.
44 Fisher, "Securing Ports of Entry."
45 Stanek, Richard. "Tackling Gang Violence before it Hits the U.S." Remarks by Stanek, Sheriff, Hennepin County, MN. Border Management Conference & Technology Expo, El Paso, Texas, October 17, 2012.
46 Kirkham, personal interview.
47 Fisher, "Securing Ports of Entry."
48 Shiffman, "Patrolling the Border."
49 2012–2016 Border Patrol National Strategy. 2012. US Border Patrol, at 20–1.
50 Quoted in Leggiere, Philip. "Beyond the One-Way Alert." *Homeland Security Today*, March 2012, at 11.
51 Tussing, Bert. "The Changing Role of the Military in Border Security Operations." Remarks by Tussing, Director, Homeland Defense and Security,

US Army War College. Border Management Conference & Technology Expo, El Paso, Texas, October 16, 2012.
52 Locke, *Two Treatises of Government*, at 400–1.
53 Arendt, Hannah. *The Origins of Totalitarianism*. New York: Harcourt, 1976 [1951], at 288.
54 Derrida, Jacques. *On Cosmopolitanism and Forgiveness*. Translated by Mark Dooley and Michael Hughes. New York: Routledge, 2001, at 14.
55 Schmitt, Carl. *Political Theology: Four Chapters on the Concept of Sovereignty*. Translated by G. Schwab. Chicago: University of Chicago Press, 2005, at 6–7.
56 Ibid., at 12.
57 Agamben, Giorgio. 2005. *State of Exception*. Translated by K. Attell. Chicago: University of Chicago Press, at 5.
58 Ibid., at 86–7.
59 Foucault, *Security, Territory, Population*, at 66.
60 Foucault, Michel. "The Eye of Power," in *Power/Knowledge*, at 155.
61 Brown, *Walled States, Waning Sovereignty*, at 25.
62 Luttwak, *The Grand Strategy of the Roman Empire*, at 78.
63 Lattimore, *Inner Asian Frontiers of China*, at 239–40.
64 Sahlins, *Boundaries*, 27.
65 For example, he writes: "Boundaries work to foster the impression of a circumscribed space in which likeness dwells, the likeness of natives, of an autochthonous people or of a nationality or of citizens with equal rights. Likeness is prized because it appears as the prime ingredient of unity." Wolin, "Fugitive Democracy," in *Democracy and Difference*, at 32–3.
66 Marx, Karl. "The Eighteenth Brumaire of Louis Bonaparte," in *The Marx–Engels Reader*. Edited by Robert C. Tucker. New York: W. W. Norton & Company, 1978, at 612.
67 Scott, *The Art of Not Being Governed*, at 19.
68 Kymlicka, Will. *Contemporary Political Philosophy: An Introduction*. Oxford: Oxford University Press, 2002, at 351.
69 Connolly, *Identity/Difference*.
70 Derrida, "On Forgiveness," in *On Cosmopolitanism and Forgiveness*, at 57.
71 For example, Fraser writes: "to view recognition as a matter of justice is to treat it as an issue of *social status* ... What makes misrecognition morally wrong, in this view, is that it denies some individuals and groups the possibility of participating on a par with others in social interaction." Fraser, Nancy, in Fraser, Nancy and Axel Honneth. *Redistribution or Recognition? A Political–Philosophical Exchange*. New York: Verso, 2003, at 29–31.
72 Butler, *Frames of War*, at 29.

3   One Border, Two Sovereigns?

Every day [cooperation] is going on ... Is this collaboration perfect?
No. But it is a far cry better than it was when I started in San Diego,
when the only thing you would exchange were middle fingers.
                                    – Border Patrol Agent, Tucson Sector, AZ, 2012[1]

We intend to build on existing bilateral law enforcement programs to
develop the next generation of integrated cross-border law enforcement operations that leverage cross-designated officers and resources
to jointly identify, assess, and interdict ... serious offenders and violent
criminals on both sides of the border.
                                    – US President Barack Obama, 2011[2]

In his "Two Essays on Liberty," Isaiah Berlin remarked that the central
question of politics is that of obedience and coercion: " 'Why should I (or
anyone else) obey anyone else?' ... 'If I disobey, may I be coerced?' 'By
whom, and to what degree, and in the name of what, and for the sake
of what?' "[3] These are fascinating questions but, for most of us, dormant
ones. We might protest the policies our state enacts, but we do not doubt
under which state we are subjects. What is remarkable about the trend
discussed here – co-bordering, or the dual management of border areas –
is that for large swaths of the population, this might begin to change.
    The United States understands its borders not merely to be increas-
ingly wide and zonal, but also *jointly-administered*. This is because, insofar
as border security is concerned, success requires a joint effort between
states – i.e. throughout the government "there is a robust sense in which
one 'cannot go it alone'."[4] Politically this shift is embodied by two groundbreaking agreements, the Beyond the Border Agreement (2011) between
the US and Canada, and the Twenty-First Century Border Initiative
(2010), between the US and Mexico. Additionally, the US Border Patrol
strategic plan (2012–2016) engendered a radical shift in US bordering practice toward cross-border policies of risk-management and co-
location. In this rubric, borders are jointly managed – a clear challenge
to notions of sovereignty derived from the Westphalian ordering of states.

The institutionalization of cross-border management exists with both Canada and Mexico. Deputy Chief of Border Patrol, Felix Chavez makes this broad point here:

We want to be in an environment where we not only are planning together, but are executing jointly [with] our international partners, whether they be the Government of Mexico or the Government of Canada ... We are going to do this by supporting an integrated intelligence platform that promotes information-sharing throughout the domestic and foreign law enforcement community.[5]

The process began in US–Canada maritime waters, with the Shiprider program – i.e. the placement of US border patrol officers on Canadian ships in Canadian waters, and Canadian border patrol officers on US ships in US waters. Although less formalized than on the northern border, this bilateralism is also taking place on the US–Mexico border.

These changes embody a holistic shift in thinking toward bilateral control over US borders – drawing on the logic of *widening*, discussed in Chapter 2, but in a way that is two-sided. The strategy attempts to rethink the security of border spaces *in tandem*, with the assumption that neighboring states are partners in a joint effort at eliminating a common threat (illegal migration, smuggling, terrorism), rather than antagonistic states linked only by a thin zone of truce. In the pages that follow, these policy advances will be discussed at length via in-depth looks at the different borders of the US, beginning with Canada, then Mexico, and finally the Caribbean-maritime region, "America's third border." This cooperation comes in two basic forms. The first is simple information- and intelligence-sharing, and operational cooperation. The second pertains to actually placing forces across the border, in what is known as co-location – i.e. forces from each side are to be located together (on each side of the line).

Given this empirical material, this chapter argues that what is emerging is a form of heterodox sovereignty – in this case, with joint controls over a shared perimeter. More specifically, the focus of this chapter is on *territoriality*, or the idea that states are territorially defined, bounded political units, comprised of three attributes – territory, autonomy and independence. By contrast, the more radical move suggested by my research engenders a territorial form of horizontality in which there is horizontal overlap *without any corollary vertical extent*. This notion of what we might call *divisible horizontality* is greatly destabilizing to the logic of the territorially ordained Westphalian system, in which external sovereignty cannot be disaggregated. In this new rubric, borders are no longer simply marks of *division* between states but rather spaces of *joint maintenance* (such that borders are still *defining*, but not necessarily *unitary*). As such, they come to resemble more closely economic and cultural boundaries; they also reflect the new geopolitical realities of globalized mobility. Whereas in previous geopolitical eras, states used to be concerned with each other, today they are primarily concerned with the flow of people – frequently a problem that neighboring states share.

Thereafter, the chapter offers some conceptual innovations. Regarding sovereignty, it offers further evidence for thinking not in binary terms, but *spectral* ones, with states more or less able to control their territories, such that there are *degrees of sovereignty*, understood as *spatial*, rather than territorial. A kind of rule that is *spectral* and *spatial*, starts to resemble *imperium*. The basic difference between sovereignty and *imperium* is that the latter is not territorially circumscribed. This chapter also asks us to think of adjoining states as *neighbors* – like Siamese twins, structurally conjoined. As such, neighbors present for each other problems of negative externality. The point is compounded by the fact that the local populations – the *distant self* and the *proximate other* – themselves are often artificially divided by the border. Just as peripheral areas of modern states were often subjects of colonization campaigns from the center (acts of inclusion), borderlands were often areas of division by centers in consort, or by other distant metropoles (acts of separation). In such cases, (re-)unification can perhaps rectify past ills.

Given the potential for harm intrinsic to co-bordering, the chapter concludes with a speculative proposal for limited cross-border citizenship for border dwellers, who are increasingly subject to two sovereigns (and thus, uncertain sovereignty). This model claims that the perimeter zone – comprised of the proximate regions of two neighboring states – might be able to offer a form of distinct citizenship that would enable participation in the decision-making process as regards border policies (and especially in decisions that directly affect local communities). As such, the responsibilities that border communities already bear (as they are disproportionately affected by border policy) would now match increases in representation and voice.

Cross-Border Cooperation I – the US and Canada

The story of cross-border US–Canada cooperation, like much of this narrative, begins with 9/11. Prior to that event there had been minimal cooperation between the US and Canada – indeed, both countries had for years boasted having the longest open border in the world. September 11 changed that; its immediate aftermath produced a frenzied demand to shut down the border. But this proved untenable due to its enormous cost to trade. Given these conflicting imperatives – security on the one hand, and trade on the other – both sides realized that cooperation was essential. A Canadian Senator explains the shift in thinking:

> [After 9/11] the United States understandably had a laser-like focus on secur-ing its borders, and we were fearful about what would happen to [our trade]. At that time, we sold 87% of everything we made and created in this country into the U.S. market. The US response was, quite rightly, that security trumps trade. But the Canadian government of the day took that as an affront to our sover-eignty, and actually rejected the offer of a perimeter security arrangement ... So we began to see the incredible lines of trucks and cars at the border; the paper burden for businesses grew ... [We came to understand] if we want an efficient flow of trade, if we want people at our shared border, able to cross our shared border, then we have to be part of this perimeter security approach.[6]

Thus, in December 2001, DHS director Tom Ridge and Canadian Minister of Foreign Affairs John Manley agreed to the "Smart Border Declaration." This agreement first used the idea of a US–Canada bor-der zone – as in a "zone of confidence against terrorist activities" – and promised to harmonize US and Canadian border policies and integrate their practices based on four "pillars": the secure flow of people, the secure flow of goods, a secure cross-border critical infrastructure, and coordination and information-sharing. Following on the heels of this landmark agreement, in April 2004 the Canadian government issued a national security policy statement entitled "Securing an Open Society" in which the US and Canada were declared to be "Partners" in their shared border security: the 2001 Smart Border Agreement would be a model for not just a trilateral region (including Mexico) but globally. This partnership is part of the bedrock on which the current collab-oration is founded. In addition, the agreement included a number of initiatives dedicated to secure, speedy trade such as opening new Free and Secure Trade (FAST) lanes at ports of entry.

These agreements immediately following 9/11 were largely diplomatic – making public shows of cooperation and overtures toward friendship, but without creating real policy changes. However, they did put into motion a few pilot programs of interest, planting seeds for future cooper-ation. The first of these is the binational Integrated Border Enforcement Teams (IBET), which opened the door for intelligence sharing, and even shared access to databases of biometric information. A spinoff of IBET is the Border Enforcement of Security Team (BEST), which focuses more on interdiction, and is now present at both the Canadian and Mexican borders. It is a joint task force, run by Homeland Security Investigations, a branch within ICE, and comprised of members of numerous federal agencies, in addition to local and international partners. The central purchase of IBET and BEST is the sharing of resources and personnel; in addition, they provide a template for numerous other cross-border engagements, detailed below.

Shiprider: The Pilot

The first breakthrough at the US–Canada border was the "Shiprider" program, put forth in 2005 as a pilot and designed to address maritime security. This program enabled armed officers from the United States Coast Guard and the Royal Canadian Mounted Police to patrol their maritime border areas together – as part of a single joint mission in shared waters – with the jurisdictional flexibility to pursue border transgressors on either side of the territorial divide. Furthermore, the Shiprider program "allowed each government to confer upon the other country's participating law enforcement officers the authority of peace officers in order to facilitate the enforcement of their respective laws across the international border."[7] The program began as an outgrowth of the IBET team in the Detroit/Windsor region, but in 2007 it expanded to all sectors of the US–Canada maritime border, including the coastal waters between Washington state and British Columbia.

The logic behind Shiprider is simple, but goes against conventional wisdom. An official in the Royal Canadian Mounted Police explained the system to me as follows:

The border is going to be there. We are going to be sovereign ... but by eliminating the border as a barrier to law enforcement, it allows us to follow the criminality across the border, instead of having an incident where the border is there, and we have to stop. [With] the Shiprider concept, the border is gone. If [criminality] starts in the US and comes into Canada, then all of a sudden there becomes a Canadian officer in charge ... Vice-versa, you cross that frontier, and US laws kick in. The key is to have all of our people specially trained and designated. [They] all have to meet the standard, to know all of the right sovereignty issues, all of the laws have to be respected.[8]

In addition to riding on shared vessels, law enforcement officials are trained in each other's laws at a special academy in South Carolina. This ensures that the laws of both countries are protected, even though foreign officers are crossing sovereign soil.

The Shiprider concept was immediately attractive – heralded as a way to "solve" the problem of the border. However, it was not an easy policy to bring into existence – even at the pilot level – due to legal issues present in both countries. What was being proposed had legitimately never been proposed before, and so both countries had to "look the other way" in order to get it on its feet. A Superintendent of the RCMP explains:

[For Shiprider to work] there had to be a certain amount of administrative forbearance on the part of both countries because it was recognized that our laws didn't permit this to happen, but both countries agreed to a diplomatic note – an MOU – to just look the other way on that count, and conduct a pilot to determine if this is the most effective model on the border, and it has been a success.[9]

This gives a window into how complicated it was for this policy to get underway – after all, it required a lot of trust between parties. The data being shared is extremely sensitive, and the types of joint operation were pathbreaking. As one industry leader in the US explained to me, the only way it got off the ground is with "a handshake that we will go through the formalities later."[10] Both the "handshake," and the Memorandum of Understanding get at the same point: the changes afoot are extremely difficult to negotiate because they go against our most powerful state institutions (and intuitions).

Difficulties aside, this program is deemed widely successful. In May 2009 the pilot program was negotiated into the more formal Canada–US Framework Agreement on Integrated Cross-Border Maritime Law Enforcement Operations (ICMLEO-Shiprider). The agreement was further formalized in July 2010, through the finalization of the Joint Border Threat and Risk Assessment, made public in March 2011. Shiprider has now been regularized across the northern border, with a new pilot project underway for integrated cargo security. Going a step further, the Beyond the Border Agreement envisions bringing it to land, "with fully co-located and cross-designated officers from both countries working together on investigations, [with] a uniform presence on a border-patrol like model, as well as intelligence all co-located into one office."[11] This is the future of integrated law enforcement. Pilots for a land-based shiprider are already underway.

The Beyond the Border Agreement

Shiprider was an enormous leap forward in re-thinking toward border security. Building on this success, President Obama and Canadian Prime Minister Stephen Harper signed a joint declaration, the "Beyond the Border" agreement, on February 4, 2011, to broaden security cooperation along larger swaths of the perimeter (i.e. not merely international waterways). This represents a more holistic attempt at integrated law enforcement along the shared US–Canada border, bringing together numerous projects that had been in pilot-stage and formalizing them into law. This discussion will focus on two central attributes: the integration of law enforcement missions through interoperable technology and joint communications centers; and, the joint management and protection of critical infrastructure along the border. Beginning with integrated law enforcement and interoperable communications, Canada and the US agreed to create an inventory of existing domain awareness (or monitoring) capabilities at the border, with an eye toward radio interoperability. This inventory was completed on October 31, 2012.

DHS refers to this general push toward binational interoperability as its Next Generation (NextGen) strategy. Interoperability here refers to the ability for two sides to share information (voice or data) on a particular technological platform (such as, for example, radio). For this policy to take effect, there cannot just be co-located forces on the ground, but also centralized databases where information can be shared and processed including radio interoperability. Right now the two inventories are on the same map, but there is a ways to go before they become effectively integrated. Nonetheless, this is the goal: "Within three years, Canada and the U.S. will implement a binational radio interoperability system to permit law enforcement agencies to coordinate effective binational investigations and timely responses to border incidents."[12]

Radio interoperability sounds like a very banal subject, but is in fact extremely groundbreaking – and infrequently exists between agencies within the same country, nevertheless across the border. Indeed, direct contact between country officials is in many cases forbidden by law. Thus, where there is a need for communication between officials on the two sides – especially in the case of first responders, when time is of the essence – it frequently occurred in contravention of the law. The problem presently is that when first responders cross the border, they have to say "'Here is one of my radios, give me one of yours'. That is how they communicate. They cannot just flick a switch and share the same channel."[13] This is the type of issue that interoperability would solve. A first step in this direction was made in 2015, whereby an amendment to a 1952 treaty now enables frequency sharing between the two countries.

The US and Canada are also aiming toward interoperable sensor and radar systems, co-positioned to "map" a joint border. The Manager of the RCMP Engineering Technology Program, explains this process as follows:

One of the things that we have done is divide the whole border up into zones. This follows an American model, as they are a little bit ahead of us in terms of geospatial understanding. But on top of that [we have a] hot map, where bright red will be a high concentration of sensors in that zone. And then, when you look at the map, you can say "Hey, on the Canadian side it is transparent," meaning there are no sensors … Eventually, we are going to tie this to risk assessment, [so we can] map smuggling roots.[14]

At present a sensor-sharing pilot is on its way, with the US and Canada agreeing to share sensor data across the border. Ultimately this will allow "security agencies to talk to one another having a common operating picture of what is [happening] on the ground."[15] Whereas in the past technology was an impediment to the shared management of the border, it is increasingly an asset.

The Beyond the Border agreement also paves the way for shared critical infrastructure along the border. The logic here is simple, it is frequently true of border areas that the closest emergency response units to any crisis are situated on the opposite side of the border. This means that effective responses to local governance situations require interoperable communications between different jurisdictions. Going a step further, according to DHS the plan is actually to "co-locate and integrate our assets and personnel with those in Canada, and offering reciprocal opportunities to our colleagues, consistent with applicable laws and authorities … and among all partners on both sides of the border."[16] This type of cooperation originally got underway in the Maine-New Brunswick area, where DHS and Public Safety Canada signed an MOU in April 2009 to start a pilot project in which Canadian federal and provincial administrations would use the DHS Automated Critical Asset Management System (ACAMS), a web-based portal that aids local governments design critical infrastructure protection programs.

In July 2010, the Canada–US Action Plan for Critical Infrastructure pledged a cross-border, binational strategy for critical infrastructure protection in which DHS and the US Department of State work cooperatively with Canadian counterparts through the Emergency Management Consultative Group (EMCG), "to improve the resiliency of communities that straddle the border and ensure they have clear and coordinated approaches to emergency management and response."[17] They also launched a Regional Resilience Assessment Program (RRAP) to determine the resilience and interdependence of local critical infrastructure on each side of the border. The point here is that in the case of disasters, there would be a cross-border, zonal form of sharing.

A second aspect of this idea of joint critical infrastructure is the cultivation of joint communities that are vigilant in each other's protection. This type of commitment is very similar to the type of policy the US engages on its own side of the border, bringing the borderland citizens into the service of the state, except here this has been re-conceived as a cross-border endeavor. Moreover, taking this a step further, this plan includes not merely state-community cooperation on each side, but there are actually community–community cooperative exercises across the border. Some of this community preparedness has already occurred. For example, in June 2012, federal and state representatives of Washington State and British Columbia, participated in the Evergreen Quake catastrophic earthquake exercise. This collaborative effort drew from previous experience of joint cross-border security exercises held during the 2010 Winter Olympics in Vancouver. These new collaborative cross-border exercises are now planned for the coming year in the Eastern States and Provinces along with a National Level Exercise.

Looking Ahead

These pilot endeavors are currently underway, making slow but steady progress toward co-location and cross-designation. It is worth highlighting two of these programs – Shiprider, and IBET/BEST – in terms of their future projections, both of which have "Next Generation" models in the works. Looking first at Shiprider, Canada and the US plan to regularize the program, via dual ratifications in their respective states. The first two official Shipriders are to be deployed in the Pacific Region and Detroit-Windsor; two additional Shiprider teams are to be established in 2015–2016, by which time they will be equipped with a binational radio interoperability system. Thereafter, the plan is to create integrated teams on land. Test pilots are underway, but the locations remain undisclosed.

As part of their Next Generation vision, IBET and BEST intend to expand and develop in such a way as to include full co-location, with a cross-designated law enforcement capability.[18] IBET has grown considerably in recent years, to the point where at present it has over 250 trained US and Canadian law enforcement officers, versed in the laws of both countries, such that they are prepared for lawful engagement on either side of the border. BEST too has been considerably revamped, such that there are now thirty BESTs with over 800 members and 100 participating agencies. Since its creation, BEST has seized over ninety-five million dollars, 6,500 weapons, over 800,000 pounds of narcotics, and made over 7,800 criminal arrests. The RCMP Chief Superintendent puts the future of Shiprider, IBET & BEST into relief:

> We started off with coordination and cooperation and we are moving now towards integration … The Next Generation is to take a bit or the best of [the existing Shiprider, IBET and BEST platforms] and build a future police force that will strengthen security along the border, maximize resources we have and

achieve efficiency ... Instead of duplicating the technology, we really need to start moving towards integrated platforms.[19]

These points of progress are examples of the ways in which US–Canadian relations are evolving at the border. There is a lot of forward-thinking here. When asked about the future of the US–Canadian border, one border trade expert replied that he foresees borderline "economic zones in which both countries laws are in effect," calling for Border Enforcement Facilitation Teams empowered to perform duties within the "plaza to plaza" areas of land borders.[20] Another imagines a point in the near future where there will be cross-borderland municipal forces – like police, or fire units. One RCMP official could even imagine a circumstance in which there is some form of joint badge on uniforms, denoting binational border guard units.[21]

This concept of a fully integrated border police force is still far afield; nonetheless, the fact that it is central to contemporary political discourse is illuminating.

Cross-Border Cooperation II – the US and Mexico (and The Caribbean)

In the American reckoning, if Canada is the gentle giant to the north, Mexico is an inferno to the south. The question thus remains: what can these changes in Canada tell us about Mexico? Obviously, the US–Canada border is a far easier border to test out such hybrid-jurisdiction pilots; but change is underway on the southwest border as well. Despite numerous differences between the two borders, the problems that warrant co-location are the same – namely the need to interdict across jurisdictions. While a formal agreement is still a far ways off, recent years have seen several breakthroughs akin to Beyond the Border, discussed above. Chief among these is the Twenty-First Century Border Management Declaration with Mexico, signed in 2010, which prompted Secretary Napolitano to praise then CBP Commissioner Alan Bersin for "fostering an unprecedented level of cooperation with Mexico."[22] This venture, alongside others throughout the region, is discussed below.

Mexico, Merida and the Twenty-First Century

In the US relationship with Mexico, there has historically been limited cooperation on border security – as is true of nearly every asymmetrical relationship between migration source countries (Mexico) and recipient countries (the US). Of course, there has been cross-border cooperation in the past, such as in the *Bracero* Program (1942–1964). But this has occurred over issues of labor and immigration, and notably *not* included border security. This remained true during the debates over the North American Free Trade Agreement (NAFTA), which began in 1986 and were finalized on January 1, 1994. The first US–Mexico agreement that placed any real emphasis on border security was a May 1997 joint declaration between President Clinton and President Zedillo. Nonetheless, substantive progress only really got underway after 9/11. Beginning in March 2002, President Bush and President Fox signed a twenty-two-point Border Partnership Action Plan, in which they agreed to share data sufficient to facilitate fast-lanes and frequent traveler programs – a matter discussed in Chapter 6, with respect to the ports. The US and Mexican presidents also signed the Partnership for Prosperity agreement, which became the trilateral (with Canada) Security and Prosperity Partnership for North America (2005), to further encourage secure trade within the NAFTA region. These agreements treated border security explicitly, but focused on preparing border trade for a post-9/11 world.

The first major breakthrough in US–Mexico relations toward cooperation over border security was the Merida agreement, announced in October 2007, which centered on the US providing funding and training to the Mexican government to counter drug trafficking. In 2008, Congress pledged 1.8 billion dollars toward the problem, dedicated toward training and staffing Mexican forces. On June 5, 2009, this basic cross-border strategy expanded with the US Office of National Drug Control Policy (ONDCP)'s Southwest Border Counternarcotics Strategy, under which CBP, ICE, Coast Guard and FBI agreed to share information as a means of cooperating to stop Mexico-bound weapons smuggling and currency, for which effort they would also share information and coordinate with the government of Mexico. Also in 2009, DHS announced a new set of border initiatives, including an expansion of "Operation Firewall" and "Project Gunrunner," two campaigns to reduce gun and money smuggling, and which focused heavily on joint-cooperation between US and Mexican officials.

The Merida initiative is widely considered a success, and all told, from 2008–2010 the US contributed $1.3 billion to Mexico. In May 2010, Obama announced plans to expand the Merida Initiative to explicitly focus on border infrastructure and signed the Twenty-First Century Border Management Declaration with President Calderon. This vastly increased the character and scope of US–Mexico cooperation – and enabled real cooperation over border security, and not just as regards immigration and drugs. As one DHS official explains, the US–Mexico strategy is on the same path as US–Canada:

[The Twenty-First Century Border Management Declaration] shifted the paradigm [from] guarding and policing the border [to] coordination with Mexico to facilitate legitimate trade and travel and address common security concerns. This was unthinkable 5–10 years ago. When I was the attaché down in Mexico City, the "sovereignty flag" was always thrown up by the Mexican officials. It was us always encroaching on their sovereignty. Today you very rarely hear that. It is "how can we work and make our border more secure."[23]

The point here is that it is a mistake to think of the two US borders as fundamentally different. Instead, the US strategy is to treat the northern border as a testing ground for projects that, if successful, will be introduced in the south.

As with Canada, US–Mexico collaboration has produced a number of joint projects, mostly about drugs. For example, in 2011, CBP, DEA and DoD put together a Border Intelligence Fusion Section in the El Paso Intelligence Center, for the point of developing a common intelligence picture for all of the US federal, local and tribal partners. Another such initiative along the Southwest border is the Alliance to Combat Transnational Threats (ACTT) in Arizona, which teams federal and local forces with the Government of Mexico to interdict criminal organizations. What is important here is the increasingly collaborative nature of these efforts. Speaking in 2011, Border Patrol Chief, Michael Fisher explains that the US is working with "Mexico to develop an interoperable, cross-border communications network that will improve our ability to coordinate law enforcement and public safety issues."[24]

In 2012, the Merida initiative graduated the first Mexican ICE class out of its academy – designed to work alongside its American counterparts. An important outgrowth of this training strategy has been the formation of Mexican border units, which had existed in the past but which were disbanded in the 1960s. The Mexican attitude had been that the border was a US problem, as the main flow was south-to-north. Thus, until recently, Mexico only had what was called "Grupo Beta" which is a federal unit that makes some effort at policing; by contrast on the southern border with Guatemala, Mexico does have a border patrol. However, as of 2012 the Mexican authorities have started a unit called the "Border Police" – part of the Federal District Police (SSP). This fits into the broader US awareness that "you can't successfully manage the border just from one side."[25] Indeed, cooperative perimeter policing was one of the central goals of the revamped Merida Initiative. A former Chief of Border Patrol explains:

[Merida enabled] information-sharing that has never occurred before between the United States government and the Mexican government ... Its going to take a partnership with the Mexicans on the south side to secure the border like it needs to be secured … We are beginning to see Mexican law enforcement between the ports of entry, which was something we used to fear. If you go back in the 80s and 90s or early 2000s [you] didn't want them out there, because you didn't know what was going on. Now [you] shake hands across the fence and jointly work and have joint communication. [It is essential] that we work closely together. As I mentioned, we can't do it alone.[26]

This attitude, of seeing Mexico as a neighbor, and the border as a joint problem, is a remarkable change. This is true to the point where the idea of militarizing the border is now being rejected precisely because it will sour this neighborly attitude and compromise the US' ability to cooperate with Mexican law enforcement at the border. Moreover, these are not just platitudes from Washington and Mexico City. On a local level, change is already palpable, with the two sides already cooperating. Each sector of border patrol has its own liaison unit, with coordinated schedules and protocol meetings with Mexican officials. There are also already coordinated tactical operations. Indeed, this type of cooperation is quite common. One agent describes coordinated law enforcement during tunnel-raids – a process that follows the same logic as Shiprider:

What we are doing in Nogales are binational sweeps of the joint tunnels we have … Our agents, unarmed, go into Mexico with Mexican partners to go into the tunnels and sweep. The Mexicans then hand off the weapons to their partners, come across with us and we protect them … CBP is [also planning] *Espejo Ops* – mirrored Ops – where they will be [on their side], and we will be [on our side] … In specific instances [we] have actually put [Mexican officers] on our [helicopter] and flown into Mexico, looking for a suspect.[27]

Cooperation is increasingly occurring regarding information as well. For example, there are now intelligence officers assigned in the US, from the Federal Police in Mexico [SSP], and vice-versa. Their explicit purpose is information sharing. This is also true as regards centralized data. For example, the US and Mexico increasingly collaborate on their UAV program, sharing feeds and collaborating on usage – such that the US grants Mexican authorities permission to use American UAVs for their purposes.

What is perhaps most encouraging is the high level of optimism that stronger forms of institutional cooperation are forthcoming. For example, when asked whether the US–Mexico border would come to approximate the US–Canada border – and specifically whether Shiprider would work in the south – one border patrol agent replied: "We haven't gotten to that point yet. At some point [we will] … but we haven't actually had people as a rider over there … It is something to look forward to in the future."[28] When asked if what is happening in

Canada was conceivable on the Mexican border, another agent replied that the goal "would be a dual-sovereign zone, almost like a Eurozone. We were talking about it being a Canada-Mexico-NAFTA zone, like Schengen."[29]

This vision of the US–Mexico border is nothing short of radical; but there are still obvious concerns about sovereignty. Who would adjudicate between sovereigns in a joint sovereign regime? What information is to be shared? The same agent explains:

Sovereignty issues are a concern. [Mexico and Canada are wary] of the United States being the 800 pound gorilla ... [Mexican authorities] still have sovereignty squawks when certain things happen. But [now] welcome our air support, welcome our assistance [this is new] ... [There are many] cutting-edge questions – what can I share? ... There is a lot of fear on both sides. Do we trust the Americans not to come in and try to tell us how to run our country? And on our side, do we trust [giving] information to the Mexicans, because they are all corrupt. But we are going to have to work through this.[30]

As with the US–Canada border, there will ultimately need to be legislation, but the point is that political will is increasingly there. Full colocation on the US–Mexican border is not imminent. However, thinking about the border is progressing at a breakneck speed – the implications of which are considerable.

Projecting Outward – The Caribbean and Latin America

The practices of the US Border Patrol also extend throughout the region – i.e., America's "third border," which includes the Caribbean, Central America and the northernmost countries of South America. This area has been a central focus of DHS, which has sought on the one hand to extend US influence over regional bordering practices, and on the other to actually train regional states to work together at their own borders – i.e. exporting the very model discussed above. This focus is understandable, as regional borders are interconnected by definition. Just as US border security is dependent on Mexico, it is also dependent on Mexico's southern border with Guatemala. One border security expert refers to our broader regional strategy as a "hurdles process;" the goal is to help develop border security throughout the region, to make it ever more difficult to even get to the US.[31] A DHS official explains that the goal is to take our bordering capabilities and "move them outward," building similar institutions in Central America.[32]

As transnational criminal and terrorist networks become linked, various disparate state porosities meld into a single problem. Gustavo Mohar, a former national security official in the Government of Mexico presents this point from Mexico's perspective:

> Mexico is facing a very difficult challenge at its Southern border, [due to] a systemic and severe crisis of stability in Central America ... The border is the place where expressions of crime become public. But the origins of these problems are far away from the border, in the southern part of Mexico they come from Columbia and Peru ... Transnational crime has no respect for any border.[33]

As such, the US has become invested in deploying assets toward regional management. DHS has contributed to boosting law enforcement regimes in numerous Latin American countries, such as Colombia and Peru; the Coast Guard has also been linked to international law enforcement agreements throughout the region, including the Caribbean Basin Security Initiative, and the Central American Regional Security Initiative, which is designed to bring Merida-type assistance for law enforcement initiatives to countries including Belize, Costa Rica, El Salvador, Guatemala, Honduras, Nicaragua and Panama. DHS's Joint Interagency Task Force-South, facilitates transnational cooperative counter-narcotic and counterterrorism efforts throughout the region, including using unmanned aircraft systems and long-range patrol aircraft. In this arrangement, the US coordinates border security with eleven different regional countries. Plans are also underway for collaborative maritime security missions with Puerto Rico. For example, Luis Fortuño, the Governor of Puerto Rico, has called for a joint US–Caribbean Border Initiative, with "the same level of commitment that has been provided to combat the drug trade along the Southwest and northern borders."[34]

The important point here is not just that the US is interested in pushing crime away from its border – a natural extension of defense-in-depth – but that DHS is seeking to replicate US border control in other borders throughout the region. This goes so far as to include the training of new cadres of border patrol in joint schools. For example, Border Patrol set up a regional border academy in Panama, which graduated its first class in September 2012. Panama is at the center of the export of US bordering practice. Indeed, the Government of Panama is even re-making its governance structure along the lines of US Customs and Border Protection. Columbian National Police also participate in the regional border academy and are presently included in BEST units.

The US's pan-American dream is of course self-regarding: training Latin American border patrols saves US dollars at its own borderline and expands US influence. But there are also bilateral agreements between Central American states, independent of US participation, centered around the Central American Security Initiative, where regional ministers meet in tandem on a quarterly basis to discuss security issues – a matter expanded upon in Chapter 4. In both cases, these co-bordering initiatives are radically shaping the nature of border security throughout the region.

Sovereignty, Security and Territoriality – Reconceptualizing Neighbors

Sovereignty and Territoriality

States have borders. This is part of their definition: a state is a territorially- bounded political unit, a "bordered power container,"[35] in which "mutually recognized borders delimit spheres of jurisdiction."[36] The border is "the precise line at which jurisdictions meet, usually demarcated and controlled by customs, police and military personnel."[37] It is a *defining* space; in particular, it is definitive of sovereignty. The border – in particular, the *perimeter* – delimits the territory over which sovereignty has dominion. It also provides the basis for the classic distinction between interiority (internal authority, or autonomy) and exteriority (external authority, or independence). These attributes – territory, autonomy and independence – together comprise the central tenets of what we call sovereignty-qua-*territoriality*.[38] Internally, or within a sovereign jurisdiction, the rule of the sovereign is absolute vis-à-vis competing powers. Externally, a sovereign jurisdiction is impermeable, such that other sovereigns recognize the principle of non-interference in each other's affairs. This definition of sovereignty, and especially its external component defines the international state system, formed on the basis of the mutual sovereign recognition of juridically equivalent units. In any internal/external division, the border plays a defining role.

It shall be immediately clear that co-bordering – i.e. regimes of dual-sovereign management at the border – is deeply destabilizing to this classic conception of sovereignty. In particular, it creates a sovereignty that is heterogeneous, with joint or overlapping domains over a single territory. These challenges to sovereignty are in some sense familiar.[39] But for the most part, the unity of sovereignty and territory has persisted even in the face of border porosity. As Christopher K. Ansell explains, "the *organizing principle* of territoriality remains intact."[40] Arguments about de-territorialized sovereignty in the EU are equally unsatisfying,[41] as the EU "might be better described as a 'rebundling' of territorialities than an 'un-bundling'."[42]

The point is that while territoriality is perhaps the most embattled tenet of sovereignty, it has nonetheless largely remained intact through globalization. After all, even supranational organizations (like the EU) and international organizations (like the UN) are composed of member states that retain territorial authority. But co-bordering shows how sovereignty can be *horizontally* overlapping, not merely *vertically* overlapping, as we see in most examples of global institutions. To be clear, "horizontal sovereignty" is not a new concept. We are familiar, for example, with the "'horizontal' or 'nonterritorial' dispersal of sovereign powers over branches of government, agencies."[43] Yet, this usage of "horizontal authority" is by definition "nonterritorial" – it simply describes powers that spread across government branches. By contrast, the more radical move suggested by my research neither entails the spread of power within a state (horizontal) or a higher authority that transcends the state (vertical), but rather a territorial form of horizontality in which there is horizontal overlap *without any corollary vertical extent.* This notion of what we might call *divisible horizontality* is greatly destabilizing to the territorially ordained Westphalian system, in which external sovereignty cannot be disaggregated.

This question about territoriality and whether it is changing warrants further clarification. Here *territoriality* is understood as the ultimate, indivisible sovereign rule over a particular territory. It must be one-to-one in nature; it cannot be two-to-one or n-to-one. *Territoriality* is at its root a negative conception: it modifies where sovereigns cannot intervene, rather than indicate any particular set of competences internally. On face, co-bordering appears to directly challenge this notion: creating overlapping jurisdictions in which two sovereigns can exercise authority over the same stretch of territory. To determine whether this is meaningful, it is important to disaggregate sovereignty according to its *de jure* and *de facto* components. On a *de jure* level, this critique remains fairly weak. After all, while there may be overlapping controls, in fact the two states remain identifiably discrete. In the case of USA–Canada, in the borderlands there are American and Canadian law enforcement officials each with bilateral capacities. However, at no point do the states become mutually unrecognizable. In short, on US soil, Canadian and American law enforcement officials *enforce American law* – they don't mutually enforce Canadian–American law. Thus, there is still a clear link between law and territory; what appears to have blurred regards enforcement.

To this point, the Beyond the Border agreement explicitly discusses the monopolistic nature of sovereignty – i.e. that each state maintains sovereign control of its own territory. For example, the wording of the bill in its Canadian form "recognizes that integrated cross-border operations must respect the sovereignty of each state and [be] conducted in accordance with the rule of law."[44] Several provisions have been written into the various agreements to ensure the preservation of sovereignty. Co-location is to be restricted to officers with joint training in both countries' laws to ensure that all local laws and policies are respected. Further, even though officers may be co-located on foreign soil, they must be under the guidance of officers from that home country.

Skepticism that the types of changes chronicled here will ever amount to a full challenge to *de jure* sovereignty is warranted; however, this conclusion is not foregone. The developments identified on these pages are in their nascence – many of them even at the pilot level, driven by Memoranda of Understanding (MOUs) – but include within them the potential to expand into more comprehensive programs. As these institutions take hold and establish a legal basis in national legislatures, they could come to engender a system of legal pluralism, in which more than one legal regime presides over a given territory.[45] At its weakest, such pluralism could mean vertically overlapping legal systems, as is now common in transnational or cosmopolitan law, in which there are potential legal conflicts between types of law. But what is being discussed here is of a different sort: here pluralism refers to overlapping authorities *within* the same type of law (in this case, two equally sovereign states). These trends are inchoate, but there is a lot of momentum toward more robust forms of integrated border management. Indeed, as part of the Beyond the Border Agreement, Canada and the US are discussing *aligning their laws* in the border areas.[46]

On a *de facto* level, the challenge to sovereignty is considerably stronger – and potentially radical. After all, co-location is already under way: in select sites along the border, a citizen of X can be held to a law enforced both by the officials of X and of Y. While the laws have not changed, decisions are increasingly made in tandem, and infrastructure is being used in tandem. All information being used and generated is under this system shared – a remarkable point in its own right, as such *information cannot be un-learned*. Matters of border security, central to state sovereignty by any measure, are now governed by joint decision making and a great deal of trust. This issue – the *politics of trust* – is treated at length in Chapter 6. Here it is sufficient to frame the point, as trust is greatly antithetical to sovereignty as we generally understand it.

As evidence that sovereignty is being ceded in a very real way, one need look no further than the statements made at the time. For example, Trevor Bhupsingh, of Public Safety Canada remarked:

> The whole idea of having foreign law enforcement officers – and having the ability to enforce laws in the host country – has raised difficult questions, and sovereignty concerns, in both our countries. That said, the two governments and officials on both sides have been working really hard to establish some basic principles and rules of the game.[47]

Further, there was considerable resistance voiced against these policies, especially by Canadians concerned about the sheer amount of information given to the US:

> In retrospect, [we] should never have treated intelligence sharing between our two countries as anything but problematic ... We have now come to another realization – that in fashioning an informational border security policy, we put the proverbial cart ahead of the horse. Intelligence taps were opened to maximum flow before we had a tool for assessing common threats which could help us define how best to share intelligence.[48]

Concern that there is now *too much* information sharing between the two states is, of course, a nasty underside to ceding this facet of sovereign authority.

Certainly, the lack of *de jure* challenges to sovereignty, diminish these *de facto* shifts. But concerns of this sort are overblown, and arise from a penchant in political theory to overstate the legal aspects of sovereignty and understate the political ones: i.e. to emphasize questions of *authority* (and jurisdiction) over *control*. But matters of control are as integral to sovereignty – if a state cannot control its borders, it cannot be considered sovereign over them. For example, Habermas defines sovereignty with specific reference not merely to jurisdiction, but capacity: "A state is sovereign only if it can both maintain law and order internally and protect its borders against external threats."[49] More recently, scholars have variously remarked that "sovereignty refers not merely to the right to regulate various aspects of life within a territory, but also ... *the capacity to exclude other political agents from control of the territory*," and that "a state is sovereign if it exercises *effective control* over its territorial boundaries and population through a governing apparatus able to maintain law and order."[50] Just as ought implies can, authority implies capacity.

Indeed, the main thrust of writings on globalization detailed how the sovereign state was losing *control*, due to mobilities it could not contain. Malcolm Anderson wrote:

The policies and practices of governments are constrained by the degree of *de facto* control which they have over the state frontier ... The incapacity of governments in the contemporary world to control much of the traffic of persons, goods and information across their frontiers is changing the nature of states.[51]

This book takes this argument further because the loss of control described here is itself state-sanctioned – the state *ceding sovereignty for security*. Far from the globalization-era critique that sovereignty is waning; it is here instead revealed to be transforming. Further, we have good reason to believe that the type of joint peripheral management described on these pages may well come to generate a new legal environment. In short: co-bordering schemes of control may come to delimit *authority* as well.

Imperium

How might we go about understanding sovereignty without territory? We need a new conceptual vocabulary. Drawing on *de facto* sovereignty, we might first think of sovereignty not as binary – a state either is or isn't sovereign over a jurisdiction – but rather as *spectral*, with states more or less able to control their territories. In this way there would be *degrees of sovereignty*. Allen Buchanan makes this point:

[A common] assumption equates "state" with "sovereign political unit," and then makes the mistake of thinking that sovereignty is an all-or-nothing affair ... This is a mistake because there are no such political entities. Sovereignty is a matter of degree ... A political unit can have much control over some matters but lesser control over others.[52]

Another way to render sovereignty is *spatial*, such that the sovereign has power over as much space as it has capacity to control. Going a step further, if we take this notion of sovereignty that is *spectral* and *spatial*, we start to see a resemblance between the kind of authority we expect in sovereign states, and that of empire – *imperium* – first introduced in Chapter 1.

The basic difference between sovereignty and *imperium* is that the former is territorially bounded and the latter is not. The reason we would not ordinarily describe Rome as sovereign is because its frontiers were zonal, and thus there could be no clear logic of interiority/exteriority. In either case, the boundary lies at the center of this discussion. This bears out in scholarly treatments. By one account, the scope of "military action" that might fit under the umbrella of *imperium* was broad enough to include any kind of administration of territories outside the metropole:

When we come to examine [*imperium*] in a *militiae* context, it is immediately apparent that there is a whole gamut of meanings from the most abstract (that is "power" with little or no territorial implication) to the most concrete ("empire" in the sense of a sharply delimited area) ... When Cicero, his contemporaries, and predecessors used imperium to describe a national or political structure, they had in mind something less well-defined. A similar usage might be found in the English word "power."[53]

Another account is as follows: "The *imperium populi Romani* was the power Romans exercised over other peoples, viewed in its widest sense ... If the limits to the *imperium* of a Roman magistrate on the boundaries of Roman power were not strictly defined, this implies that the boundaries of the *imperium Romanum* itself were uncertain."[54]

The notion of *imperium* is important, because, as states extend their authority in important ways across the border, they start to resemble empires – with all of the benefits and concerns that accompany this conception. This is taken up below, and again in Chapter 4.

Two Concepts – Neighbors, and the Proximate Other

So far this re-conceptualization of binational borders has focused on the question of sovereignty. But a recurring theme in this book pertains to *neighbors* – i.e. states that share a border at their mutual peripheries. This is a separate category of interstate relations. *Neighbors* share a different set of relations than mere allies, as they are structurally united, even if there are no formal relations at their shared periphery. Unfortunately, because of our *thin* conception of borders as sites of *division* rather than *shared peripherality*, this insight has been concealed. However, neighboring states have for centuries found cross-border solutions to cross-border problems. For example, in the eighteenth century, cooperation between the French and Spanish kings was a common means of catching smugglers:

As early as 1722, when the two states had not yet resolved their territorial disputes in the [Pyrenees], the Paris and Madrid courts each agreed to return all "thieves, assassins, and deserters" who took refuge in the opposing kingdom ... But it was their concern to repress smuggling that, above all, led the two governments to cooperate ... The 1768 convention explicitly allowed authorities of each crown to transgress the limits of France and Spain: "The troops and guards of the two crowns may move freely beyond their reciprocal boundaries to stop the smugglers, provided that they mutually return the citizens arrested on the lands of one or the other power" … [The] 1774 agreement specified that customs employees and soldiers of each state could "unite" and "mutually assist" each other on both territories while pursuing smugglers.[55]

But even if we establish the idea of the neighbor as *existing*, we might still ask whether they have a special role in each other's affairs? What is fascinating about neighbors is that they, on some level, explode the very friend/enemy category. This is because these states share peripheral spaces, and in this sense they share some rudimentary form of *selfhood*. That selfhood might be loving or loathing, but the structural connectedness is not in dispute. For example, it is against neighbors that all forms of expansion are zero-sum. Thus, neighbors – vis-à-vis territory – are in a relationship of normative coexistence that other states are not, as in Locke's discussion of land usurpation, which is just only insofar as it does not impede anyone else's.[56] In the case of the mutual exhaustion of the earth, it is against the neighbor (initially, and necessarily) that harms of usurpation arise. It is for this reason we might question the role that neighbors may have in terms of humanitarian intervention. Bernard Williams, for example, argues that neighbors have to be considered as a separate category of possible interveners, because they are by nature invested in the outcome.[57]

The notion of the neighbor also matters in international law, especially as pertains to the notion of refugees – and *non-refoulement*, through which states have special obligations to the citizens of neighbors by dint of their proximity. For example, the UN 1951 Convention Relative to the Status of Refugees, "implies that geographical proximity to a host state is relevant to delineating the latter's obligations to entrants."[58] The same is true in contested areas, such as "debatable lands" that maintain a "border identity" and "a rough-and-ready system of law,"[59] and in conflict zones. Butler's remarks about Israel and Palestine throws into relief the structural entanglement of neighboring polities:

Israel (what is called "Israel" – its borders constantly expand and it is difficult to localize at any given moment) and "Palestine" (its borders contract all the time) [are] joined inextricably, without contract, without reciprocal agreement, and yet ineluctably. So the question emerges: what obligations are to be derived from this dependency, contiguity and unwilled proximity that now defines each population, which exposes each to the fear of destruction …?[60]

This sets up the normative point. Because borders necessarily have two sides, border policies on one side necessarily have an effect on the people and land on the other side. As such, neighbors present for each other

problems of collateral damage – something we recognize is a moral problem in the case of war, but rarely think about in terms of ordinary states.
Before closing this discussion of the neighbor, it is helpful to hone
in on the particular populations of the (neighboring) borderlands, what
I term the *distant self* and the *proximate other*. In many cases these two
populations are artificially divided by the border. Just as peripheral areas
of modern states were often subjects of colonization campaigns from the
center (acts of inclusion) – treated in Chapter 2 – for much of the world
borderlands were areas of division by centers in consort, or by other
distant metropoles (acts of separation).[61] But because of the arbitrary
nature of these divisions, peripheral peoples frequently had as much in
common with each other than with the central state. The periphery was
frequently a site of cohabitation, even among disparate ethnic communities, which were to each the "other" but (usually) equally indigenous.
    Why does this matter? Because insofar as unification might be a norma-
tive good – undoing the harm of previous acts of division – co-bordering
might be a means of this attainment. This is taken up in Chapter 4.

Borderlands Citizenship – A Sketch

This discussion has brought to the fore several concerns intrinsic to new
forms of border security. In what follows, I outline a proposal for limited
cross-border citizenship for border dwellers, who are increasingly subject
to two sovereigns (and thus, uncertain sovereignty). The principle harm
this model may alleviate pertains to misrepresentation (and misrecognition). This is a solution to a *timeless* problem – borders by their nature
have negative externalities – but also a *timely* problem, as this citizenship
would help counteract some of the new harms of co-bordering.

Perimeter Zone Citizenship

This model proposes that the perimeter zone – comprised of the proximate regions of two neighboring states – should offer a form of distinct
citizenship. This would entail some role in the decision-making process
as regards border policies (and especially in decisions that directly affect
local communities), as well as reciprocal obligations for participation.
It would also require cross-border institutions within the border zones
of the two communities. Citizens in this zone would retain their own
national membership but be afforded special rights and responsibilities
unique to the perimeter zone itself.
    At its very basic, borderland citizenship would entail the demarcation of
explicit territories of adjoining states. For example, in the United States,

there is a US county (Douglas) that abuts a Mexican county (Sonora) in the deserts of Arizona. This model would appropriate some version of these jurisdictional parameters, such that citizens within these districts would have special rights and permissions. To some degree, this already exists. In Sonora, there are special permissions to apply for an easy-entry pass into the US (via SENTRI), which are not available to citizens of inland provinces (for example, Sinaloa). This model would expand upon this principle to both designate special privileges on a national level in each state, and at the same time enable joint-level rights and institutions *between* states, such as voting on decisions of border management. Thus, this special citizen status would have both a national and a binational component.

Of course, the more rights and responsibilities that come along with borderland citizenship, the more likely it will prove meaningful. At the very least, cross-border institutions of citizenship and governance can enable the voice of borderland citizens in shaping policies pertinent to them – such as about economic and ecological issues that are joint (a variation of the all-affected principle). Some limitations are to be expected. For example, while it might enable borderland citizens to cross freely between states and vote on shared issues, it might not enable the same privileges of residency. In this case, rather than "remove" the line, it creates a *graduated* line, as while the *membership* line would now be moved inland, the *residency* line would stay in place. In doing so, this model would cultivate a zone *legally* that already exists economically and culturally. As such, the responsibilities that border communities already bear (as they are disproportionately affected by border policy) would now match increases in representation and voice.

This model advances a recent trend in discussions on citizenship that emphasizes the idea of *residency*, but differentiates itself in critical ways. Contemporary writing on citizenship vis-à-vis *residency* is primarily interested in the question of when immigrants earn the so-called "right to stay." As Joseph Carens explains, "at some point a threshold is crossed, and they acquire a moral claim to have their actual social membership legally recognized."[62] This also motivates Ayelet Shachar's argument about *jus nexi* – i.e. "earned citizenship" that derives its moral strength from the idea of "rootedness" in a community.[63] Her model is based on the notion that an individual deserves citizenship based on the relationship they have with the society in which they live. Rainer Baubock makes a similar claim with his "stakeholder" citizenship.[64]

The model of citizenship presented here shares sympathies with this literature. However, the difference is that borderland-derivative citizenship would be predicated not on *time of stay* but rather mere residency as such – individuals in border communities are *already there*. They do not "earn" citizenship by an act of becoming local; these people are already local. Their claim to citizenship is borne instead of a change in jurisdictional awareness. Borders are now beginning to be understood for what they are, cross-national communities. This form of citizenship is less *proactive* than *retroactive*; it is a corrective of past injustices written into the Westpahalian state system.

In this way, even though this citizenship is local, it is global as well. By locating the democratic process at multiple sites, with overlapping jurisdictions as a means of preserving the voice of local communities within a global institutional frame, it fulfills many of the goals of cosmopolitanism – discussed in Chapter 4.[65]

Citizenship as Solvency – Smoothing out the Border

With this rough frame in mind, perimeter zone citizenship has two particular benefits. The first is *representation*. Peripheral peoples are frequently the least represented, even *in their own polities*, including regarding policies specific to the border. In the US, there is a very real problem in that the securitization of the border is largely prompted by votes from citizens thousands of miles from the border, frequently against the wishes of the border dwellers themselves.[66] Is it fair for a demos to vote for policies that disproportionately affect a small subset of the population, even against the will of that group? We frequently think of this question in terms of minority rights, we rarely do so in terms of territorial ones.

Additionally, perimeter zone citizenship would assist residents on the "opposite side of the line," who are directly affected by the border policies emanating from both centers, not just their own. They may have *minimal* voice in their own polity, but they have *no* voice in the opposite one, even though those policies implicate them directly. This is clearly an error of what Nancy Fraser terms "justice as representation." She asks: "Do the boundaries of the political community wrongly exclude some who are actually entitled to *representation?*"[67] Perimeters, in this rubric, can be re-fashioned not as democratic wastelands, but as independent sites for democratic norm formation, with different groups taking authorship of their interests.

The benefit to peoples on the other side of the line follows the rough logic of *affectedness*, namely the principle that those people who are affected by a policy should have a say in its formulation. This is a much-embattled concept, as it nearly impossible to establish who is or isn't affected – in some sense, in a globalized world, don't policies affect everyone? But it remains a guide, especially as regards borders, where issues directly and *necessarily* affect people on either side of the line, establishing a far more restrictive notion of affectedness. To make this point, David Held cites examples ranging from "transboundary pollution such as acid rain or river pollutants" to the "siting and operation of nuclear power plants, for instance that at Chernobyl."[68] The border is an institution that clearly has externalities on either side. Thus, in so far as this presents an injustice of representation, some form of cross-border citizenship can be a corrective.

At the core of this problem is a central question in political theory, namely: *how do you legitimate coercion*? This is a general problem for democracies, but it is most extreme on the border, where populations on the other side of the line are coerced but no effort is made toward cultivating justifications for that coercion. Arash Abizadeh makes a compelling case that from the vantage of democratic theory, a justification is owed to all people subject to coercion – including both citizens on the other side of the line, as well as immigrants that arrive at the door, because border control "subjects both members *and nonmembers* to the state's coercive exercise of power."[69] How wide we take this claim to be is subject for the debate. However, *at least* we owe a justification to people that live in borderlands.

Another aspect of representation pertains to matters of community – namely, that creating small borderland units enables a kind of community cultivation that might be lost in a larger polity. This argument has deep roots, beginning with Aristotle's community of speech, but reaching its full form in republican and communitarian traditions of thought. Generally, if borderlands are comprised of people with shared concerns over border issues, having a proximate forum for participation is a good thing. A related purchase of cross-border citizenship pertains to deliberative democracy – a normative ideal based on the idea of public reasonableness, which prioritizes the public deliberation of free and equal citizens as a mechanism for legitimating political decision-making. A central proponent of deliberative models of citizenship is Habermas, who believes that it is only through deliberative models of democratic will-formation that space can be made for the better arguments to come into play, sufficient to secure a fair bargaining process between participants – a model he calls the *"decentered society."*[70]

A second benefit pertains to *minority rights*, and *multiculturalism*. If multiculturalism is good, then cross-border intermixing is good, especially as borders frequently artificially separate peoples that might seek re-unification. A cross-border citizenship model could quite easily be a space of multicultural preservation and interaction. This is true both because the border *generates* obligations on both sides and because people feel obligations to people on the other side – often more even than people in the center. Indeed, in the borderlands the local communities are *equally indigeneous*, as are forms of intercultural hybridity. The fact that this is even an issue gets at a classic problem of rooting liberal principles in bounded political communities. For example, Kymlicka provocatively asks: "Why should someone in Maine feel more solidarity with a resident of Texas, 4,000 miles away, than with a resident of New Brunswick, 5 miles across the border with Canada?"[71] This is a question we may also flip: knowing as we do that a person in Maine *also* has loyalties to the person in New Brunswick, what should we do about it? Perhaps cross-border communities can consolidate local-level affinities.

But more than this, cross-border zones offer a way to protect local minority communities, and foster multiculturalism, without tying citizenship to those ethnicities – here citizenship is a purely geographic construct. This is a different type of institution than those suggested by proponents of so-called group-differentiated citizenship – like Kymlicka, who defends multicultural rights when they supplement individual rights. In this case, these are not ethnic communities, but rather structural ones. As such, cross-border citizenship can amplify voice and assist an ordinarily marginalized population, *peripheral peoples*, frequently overlooked in our hurry to discuss the plight of immigrants. This type of citizenship is integrative – only *across* bounded communities, rather than *within* them.

A final benefit warrants mention here. Borderlands dwellers are frequently people that have suffered particular and discrete injustices as a result of the border. Thus we might also inquire into whether cross-border citizenship might offer some solvency for *reparative justice*. Insofar as the border meted out injustices in the past, one way in which reparation can be meted out, short of restitution (or the returning of territory once taken away) is to provide the means for representation and participation. This is a form of "as-if" restitution, and perhaps a better one, as this form of reparation doesn't create any new generation of harmed individuals (those from whom reparations have been taken).

This said, one issue emerges that warrants address – *secession*. Certainly, borderland citizenship could lead toward demands for self-determination. But this should not be assumed – a region may be at the same time loyal to its center, as well as to its compatriots across the border. Further, there is no reason to assume that regional and nationalistic identities align at the border any more than that they deviate – i.e. that cross-border affiliations, such as between the Basque people in Spain and France, are any more likely or common than uniform nationalisms. To the contrary, better voice in border decisions – and better institutions – might strengthen loyalty to the center, not weaken it. One of the central causes of separatism has been the exclusion of separatist groups, rather than methods of integration.[72] Cross-border citizenship is not the same as autonomy; it is the merging of larger units, not the siphoning away of smaller ones. As such, this model of citizenship need not create any *necessary* form of centripetal pull away from the state.

In fact, cross-border citizenship could actually help soften problems of self-determination, or the belief that states and nations should be co-extensive, by *perhaps* constraining nationalism's decent into extremism borne of the mutual exclusivity of binary nation-state antagonisms. As borders become thick, collaborative spaces, the roots of contestation – the fixed interior/exterior division – may more or less fall away. Having institutionally linked perimeter zone communities, with binational structures of governance and shared rights and responsibilities can help maintain the benefits of national identification, while eliminating some of the harms, especially as pertains territorial revanchism.

Indeed, we might go a step further and suggest that forging unity in regions *over and above* questions of nation/state overlap might actually help solve the problem of contested lands. For example, regarding the problem of "debatable lands," David Miller looks into how we can ground the legitimate claims to this kind of territory. There are two commonplace solutions: plebiscites (let the people decide where they want to live) or partitions (let them pick one territory or the other). But he argues that plebiscites cannot work without disenfranchising minorities, and partition simply perpetuates the problem (re-draws the line). His solution looks a lot like the joint management of border regions:

[A solution to the debatable lands problem] must involve at least two and possibly three levels of government. Within the territory what is needed is a power-sharing form of government with significant powers in the field of economic and social policy, especially, so that development within the region is controlled by the people living there ... Meanwhile, at a higher level, the larger states must agree to divide powers over the territory between them. That is to say, they must either exercise them jointly, by forming a combined authority to supervise policing or military defence, or they must exercise them side-by-side, with two national flags flying over public buildings, two national television stations broadcasting throughout the region, and so forth. In this way both states maintain not only some measure of control but also an important symbolic presence in the disputed territory.[73]

There is considerable convergence between his position and the one that I articulate here. But the argument can be taken considerably further than Miller envisions, as cross-border citizenship need not be only a solution for contested borders, but rather for *normal borders too*.

Toward a New Kind of Citizenship

Thus far, cross-border citizenship has been expressed as a palliative to systemic issues deriving from the border. But some of the questions it raises are larger. How do we even begin to think about binational communities of citizens? Or more deeply: how do we start to treat the other as one of our own? Following Butler, if we believe that the normative task that faces us is to diminish the unequal grievability of people, then perhaps creating joint spaces is the best way to do this. But beyond this, perhaps this type of citizenship is doing something new. It is geared, not toward establishing a set of rights for members – i.e. a citizenship of interiority, but rather toward establishing new kinds of membership that break down distinctions of interiority/exteriority. In doing so, this new form of citizenship has normative purchase: it softens points of distinction and invigorates the interstitial spaces between peoples. The question then is: What is the means by which this may do so? The answer is that it is through a form of *localization* – or the *turning local* of a community that was once geopolitical, by enabling and unifying practices of peoples on both sides of borders. Here I follow what Tully calls the "diverse" citizenship tradition, which has a local variant he calls *civic* (as opposed to *civil*) and a global variant, which he calls *glocal* (as opposed to *cosmopolitan*). The key here for this discussion is the concept of the glocal, or the "global networking of local practices of civic citizenship."[74] Cross-border citizenship could be called glocal insofar as it pertains to the existing activities and behaviors of borderlands citizens.

By breaking down forms of sovereign exclusion, one can open up the possibility of local action and engagement. In this way, it is the enabling of a civic realm, as much as institutionalizing a civil one. To this point, Tully prioritizes the relationship between citizens, or

the relationships citizens form whenever and wherever they "act together" *as* citizens in various activities. The relationships are civic and democratic partnerships among equals negotiating and acting together ... This is the realm of civic freedom as *isegoria*, citizens speaking to each other in equal relationships about their common concerns, rather than *parrhesia*, speaking to their governors in unequal relationships.[75]

In this way, cross-border citizenship can be seen as a kind of civil–civic hybrid, allowing civil forms of engagement to catch up to civic ones.

Conclusion

At the US borders with Canada and Mexico, there has been a shift in consciousness about what the twenty-first century border should look like, driven by the realization that in today's world, governments cannot administer their borders alone. Instead, borders must be bilaterally managed and administered – preferably with forces co-located and cross-designated on either side of the line. This reflects the new geopolitical realities of globalized mobility. Whereas in previous geopolitical eras, states were primarily concerned with each other, now they are mostly concerned with flows (of people and goods) – which is frequently a problem that neighboring states share. Today, borders are not designed for states to oppose one another or oppose migratory flows, but rather are places where states join forces in the *shared* fight against transnational migratory flows.

The research presented in Chapters 2 and 3 reveals that, in the United States, border perimeters are getting *wider* and are increasingly *dual-managed*. These specific observations, drawn from the American case, are extended in Chapter 4 toward a more international discussion. It then explores this point normatively, inquiring into whether this is on balance harmful or beneficial (and how we might go about shaping it).

Notes

1 Interview, El Paso, Texas, October 16, 2012.
2 "Declaration by President Obama and Prime Minister Harper of Canada – Beyond the Border." The White House, Office of the Press Secretary, 2011.
3 Berlin, Isaiah. "Two Concepts of Liberty." In *The Proper Study of Mankind: An Anthology of Essays*, edited by Henry Hardy and Roger Hausheer. New York: Farrar, Straus and Giroux, 2000, at 193.
4 Shiffman, "Patrolling the Border."
5 Chavez, "2012–2016 Border Patrol Strategic Plan."
6 Wallin, Pamela. "Plenary Address," by Wallin, Chair, Senate Committee on National Security. Canadian Association of Defence and Security Industries (CADSI) SecureTech Conference, Ottawa, Canada, October 30, 2012.
7 Kostiuk, Christine. "Bill C-60: Keeping Canadians Safe (Protecting Borders) Act." Parliamentary Information and Research Service Legislative Summary LS-670E, 2010, at 2.
8 Zarins, Andris. "Canada–US Beyond the Border Initiative: Efficient Border Crossing for People – Innovate to Address Threats Early." Remarks by Inspector Zarins, Officer in Charge, Integrated Border Enforcement Team Operations, RCMP. Canadian Association of Defence and Security Industries (CADSI) SecureTech Conference, Ottawa, Canada, October 30, 2012.
9 Coons, Warren. "Cooperative Efforts between Mexico, Canada and the U.S. in Law Enforcement and Prosecution." Remarks by Coons, Superintendent of

the Royal Canadian Mounted Police. Border Security Expo, Phoenix, AZ, March 6, 2012.

10 Jay Kalath, CEO, Allied Mission Group LLC. Personal interview, Washington, DC, May 16, 2012.

11 Coons, "Cooperative Efforts between Mexico, Canada and the U.S. in Law Enforcement and Prosecution."

12 Zarins, "Canada–US Beyond the Border Initiative."

13 Eric Torunski, Executive Director, Canadian Interoperability Technology Interest Group (CITIG). Personal interview, Ottawa, Canada, October 31, 2012.

14 Hawkins, George. "Technology Serving Integrated Cross-Border Law Enforcement Operations." Remarks by Hawkins, Manager, RCMP Engineering Technology Program. Canadian Association of Defence and Security Industries (CADSI) SecureTech Conference, Ottawa, Canada, October 30, 2012.

15 Meunier, Pierre. "Canada–US Beyond the Border Initiative: Efficient Border Crossing for People – Innovate to Address Threats Early." Remarks by Meunier, Head, Borders & Critical Infrastructure, DRDC Centre Security Science. Canadian Association of Defence and Security Industries (CADSI) SecureTech Conference, Ottawa, Canada, October 30, 2012.

16 Department of Homeland Security (DHS). 2012. "Northern Border Strategy," at 15–16.

17 Ibid., at 6.

18 Coons, "Cooperative Efforts between Mexico, Canada and the U.S. in Law Enforcement and Prosecution."

19 Oliver, Joe. "Technology Serving Integrated Cross-Border Law Enforcement Operations." Remarks by Chief Superintendent Oliver, Director General Border Integrity, RCMP. Canadian Association of Defence and Security Industries (CADSI) SecureTech Conference, Ottawa, Canada, October 30, 2012.

20 Phillips, Jim. Canada–US Beyond the Border Initiative: Expedited Cargo Clearance – Panel Discussion by Jim Phillips, President Canadian American Border Trade Alliance. Paper read at Canadian Association of Defence and Security Industries (CADSI) SecureTech Conference, October 31, 2012, at Ottawa Convention Centre, Ottawa, Canada.

21 He explains with guarded optimism: "You would have your own uniform, but there would have to be some kind of designation, whether it would be a shoulder-flash like the United Nations has, but you would have to clearly designate to both countries that you are a police officer." Interview, Phoenix, AZ, March 12, 2013.

22 Quoted in McCarter, Mickey. "Bersin Steps Down as CBP Chief."

23 Alvarez, Luis. Emerging Threats and DHS's Western Hemisphere Strategy to Combat Transnational Crime – Speech by Luis Alvarez, Deputy Assistant Secretary for International Affairs, Department of Homeland Security. Paper read at Border Management Conference & Technology Expo, October 17, 2012, at Judson F William Convention Center, El Paso, Texas.

24 Quoted on Kimery, "Northern Border Intel-Sharing Deficient."

25 Reyes, Silvestre. Focusing Attention and Resources on the US–Mexico Border – Speech by Congressman Silvestre Reyes, 16th District of Texas, US House of Representatives. Paper read at Border Management Conference & Technology Expo, October 16, 2012, at Judson F William Convention Center, El Paso, Texas.

26 Gilbert, "Cooperative Efforts between Mexico, Canada and the U.S. in Law Enforcement and Prosecution."

27 Interview, El Paso, Texas, October 16, 2012.

28 Interview, El Paso, Texas, October 16, 2012.

29 Interview, El Paso, Texas, October 16, 2012.

30 Ibid.

31 Ahern, Jayson. "Perspectives on Border Security: Past, Present, Future." Remarks by Ahern, former Acting Commissioner, US Customs & Border Protection. Border Security Expo, Phoenix, AZ, March 13, 2013.

32 Alvarez, "Emerging Threats and DHS's Western Hemisphere Strategy to Combat Transnational Crime."

33 Mohar, Gustavo. "The Globalization of Crime: International Initiatives – Lessons Learned, Success Stories." Remarks by Mohar, Former Secretary General, Center for Investigation & National Security (CISEN), Government of Mexico. Border Security Expo, Phoenix, AZ, March 13, 2013.

34 Quoted in McCarter, Mickey. "Governor of Puerto Rico Calls for US Caribbean Border Initiative to Combat Drug Cartels." *Homeland Security Today*, June 22, 2012.

35 Giddens, *The Nation-State and Violence*, at 120.

36 Spruyt, *The Sovereign State and Its Competitors*, at 35.

37 Anderson, *Frontiers*, at 9.

38 For a definition of *territory*, see Buchanan, Allen. "The Making and Unmaking of Boundaries: What Liberalism Has to Say." In *States, Nations and Borders: The Ethics of Making Boundaries*, edited by Allen Buchanan and Margaret Moore, 231–61. Cambridge: Cambridge University Press, 2003, at 232–3. For a definition of internal/external sovereignty, see Cavallero, Eric. "Global Federative Democracy." *Metaphilosophy* 40, no. 1 (January 2009): 43–64, at 43–4.

39 Ruggie, John Gerard. "Territoriality and Beyond: Problematizing Modernity in International Relations." *International Organization* 47, no. 1 (1993): 139–74; Krasner, Stephen D. "Problematic Sovereignty." In *Problematic Sovereignty: Contested Rules and Political Possibilities*, edited by Stephen D. Krasner, 1–23. New York: Columbia University Press, 2001.

40 Ansell, Christopher K. "Territoriality, Authority and Democracy." In *Restructuring Territoriality: Europe and the United States Compared*, edited by Christopher K. Ansell and Giuseppe Di Palma, 225–45. Cambridge, UK: Cambridge University Press, 2004, at 225.

41 While there is indeed supra-national sovereign control, the basic units of that sovereign order are still territorially defined member states. As Di Palma explains: "Even a strong regional regime is not a regime that thereby marginalizes states … even as it builds its institutions, a regional regime may continue to rely on the authenticity conferred by member states as these

share jurisdictions with and within the regime … the logic of territoriality, while significantly repositioned, is not easily discarded." Di Palma, Giuseppe. "Postscript: What Inefficient History and Malleable Practices Say About Nation-States and Supranational Democracy When Territoriality Is No Longer Exclusive," in *Restructuring Territoriality*, at 259.

42 Ansell, Christopher K. "Restructuring Authority and Territoriality," in *Restructuring Territoriality*, at 5.
43 Cavallero, "Global Federative Democracy," at 45.
44 Kostiuk, "Bill C-60."
45 See e.g. Walker, Neil. "Beyond Boundary Disputes and Basic Grids: Mapping the Global Disorder of Normative Orders." *International Journal of Constitutional Law* 6 (July/October 2008): 378–96.
46 Coons, "Cooperative Efforts between Mexico, Canada and the U.S. in Law Enforcement and Prosecution."
47 Bhupsingh, Trevor. "Technology Serving Integrated Cross-Border Law Enforcement Operations." Remarks by Bhupsingh, Director General, Law Enforcement and Border Strategies, Public Safety Canada. Canadian Association of Defence and Security Industries (CADSI) SecureTech Conference, Ottawa, Canada, October 30, 2012.
48 See Wesley Wark's column in Callahan, Mary Ellen and Wesley Wark. "Privacy and Information Sharing: The Search for an Intelligent Border." In *One Issue Two Voices*, 1–23: Woodrow Wilson International Center for Scholars, 2010, at 16–17.
49 Habermas, Jurgen. *The Inclusion of the Other: Studies in Political Theory*. Edited by C. Cronin and P. D. Greif. Cambridge: MIT Press, 1998, at 108.
50 Buchanan, Allen and Margaret Moore. "Introduction: The Making and Unmaking of Boundaries," in *States, Nations and Borders*, at 28, italics mine.
51 Anderson, *Frontiers*, at 2.
52 Buchanan, "The Making and Unmaking of Boundaries," at 236.
53 Richardson, J. S. "Imperium Romanum: Empire and the Language of Power." *The Journal of Roman Studies* 81 (1991): 1–9, at 5–7.
54 Lintott, Andrew. "What Was the 'Imperium Romanum'?" *Greece & Rome* 28, no. 1 (1981): 53–67, at 53–4; 64.
55 Sahlins, *Boundaries*, at 89–91.
56 Locke, *Two Treatises of Government*, at 291–2.
57 Williams, *In the Beginning Was the Deed*, at 148–9.
58 Fabre, Cecile. *Justice in a Changing World*. Cambridge, UK: Polity Press, 2007, at 114.
59 Miller, David. "Debatable Lands." *International Theory* 6, no. 1 (March 2014): 104–21, at 104–5.
60 Butler, *Frames of War*, at xxvi.
61 For example, in *Imagined Communities*, Benedict Anderson details how imperial states instilled territorial parameters and limitations into popular consciousness by drawing borders on maps (especially between 1760 and 1900). Once the borders were drawn then all other factors – "lines of longitude and latitude, place names, signs for rivers, seas, and mountains, neighbours" – disappeared. Anderson, *Imagined Communities*, at 175.

62 Carens, Joseph. *Immigrants and the Right to Stay.* Cambridge, MA: The MIT Press, 2010, at 18.

63 Shachar, Ayelet. *The Birthright Lottery: Citizenship and Global Inequality.* Cambridge, MA: Harvard University Press, 2009.

64 Baubock, Rainer. "Global Justice, Freedom of Movement and Democratic Citizenship." *Arch. Europ. Sociol.* 1: 1–31, 2009, at 21–2.

65 Pogge, Thomas. "Cosmopolitanism and Sovereignty." *Ethics* 103 (October 1992): 48–75; Held, David. *Democracy and the Global Order.* Palo Alto: Stanford University Press, 1995; Kuper, Andrew. 2004. *Democracy Beyond Borders: Justice and Representation in Global Institutions.* Oxford: Oxford University Press.

66 For an empirical account see Payan, Tony and Amanda Vasquez. "The Cost of Homeland Security." In *Borderlands: Comparing Border Security in North America and Europe*, edited by Emmanuel Brunet-Jailly, 231–58. Ottawa: University of Ottawa Press, 2007, at 245.

67 Fraser, *Scales of Justice*, at 17–18.

68 Held, David. *Models of Democracy.* Cambridge, UK: Polity, 2006, at 303.

69 Abizadeh, Arash. "Democratic Theory and Border Coercion: No Right to Unilaterally Control Your Own Borders." *Political Theory* 36 (1): 37–65, 2008, at 44–5.

70 Habermas, Jurgen. "Three Normative Models of Democracy," in *Democracy and Difference*, at 27.

71 Kymlicka, *Contemporary Political Philosophy*, at 254–5.

72 For a review of the empirical literature, see ibid., at 352.

73 Miller, "Debatable Lands," at 114–15.

74 Tully, *On Global Citizenship*, at 7.

75 Ibid., 61–2.

4 Co-Bordering, Cosmopolitanism and the Specter of Empire

> Who said that all states are bad, but the worst state of all is no state at all?
>
> – Giovanni Poggi[1]

The state is a spatial construct, an embodied political form. But what should the body look like? Foucault engages this discussion using the writings of Alexandre Le Maitre, for whom the relationship between the capital and the territory:

> must be a geometrical relationship in the sense that a good country is one that, in short, must have the form of a circle, and the capital must be right at the center of the circle ... Le Maitre dreams of connecting the political effectiveness of sovereignty to a spatial distribution. A good sovereign, be it a collective or individual sovereign, is someone well placed within a territory, and a territory that is well policed in terms of its obedience to the sovereign is a territory that has a good spatial layout.[2]

This is exactly how we see states – as circles of territory with a dot in the center to represent the capital. This is the state in its distilled form: a center and its border. The last chapters have challenged the myriad assumptions intrinsic to this depiction. But Foucault's question is provocative. What is the perfect state form – should such a thing exist? And for whom is this ideal? A central aim of this book is to reopen the question of the *politics of unit*. If we are ever to discover Aristotle's best regime, we must also consider its territorial encasing. With this in mind, this chapter asks whether or not co-bordering can approximate some form of territorial ideal.

The chapter begins by establishing that the cross-border collaborations detailed in previous chapters are part of a global story, nested at various levels in sites across the world. To make this point empirically, evidence is provided from cases around the world, with a detailed focus on Europe and South Africa – two disparate settings that illustrate this broader point. As in the US case, there is a clear understanding that problems threatening states – terrorism, illegal trade, immigration – threaten *all states alike.* This globalization of threats increasingly requires states to operate together. Indeed, once considered the essential bulwarks of states, borders are now seen as impediments to security. Counter-state forces cross borders fluidly, but states are forced – by the same international agreements that once consolidated state supremacy – to abide by the rules of sovereignty. Here, multilateralism conspires to weaken transnationalism, rather than strengthen it.

With these points in mind, this chapter asks what this means normatively. Co-bordering presents a dilemma. On the one hand, it appears to present avenues toward fulfilling the global project of cosmopolitanism – especially in the form of multilateral sharing and regional integration. But on the other hand, it seems to perpetuate asymmetrical power relations between neighboring states. This chapter adjudicates between these views, placing co-bordering on the familiar spectrum between cosmopolitanism and empire. I argue that, left to its own course, this evolution in bordering practice foretells great harm, akin to a form of neo-imperialism, due to *hierarchical relations of power.* Instead, co-bordering is a normative model to which we aspire – i.e. conditions of *heterarchy.* With the right institutions, however, the corrosive effects of power can perhaps be held in check. With this in mind, I outline another citizenship model that might neutralize such harms.

It is worth saying a few words on the two sides of this debate. Certainly, the concept of jointly managed borders has normative promise. Indeed, this form of bi- and multilateral institutionalism opens the door for radically re-thinking the international state system, especially along the lines of the global project of cosmopolitanism. Co-bordering can clearly be in the service of this type of arrangement at the local-level – via a form of federalism, or the repooling of sovereignty between states – providing building blocks to a regional schema and a framework for how states can form political institutions in tandem. In this rubric, co-bordering would provide the glue, adhering member states, which would be compatible with a supranational constitutional structure. At an advanced level, co-bordering could pave the way for a legal-synching between neighboring polities – a form of legal pluralism through which the seeds can be planted for an enduring form of *heterarchy* – i.e. the formal and informal equivalence of units. To this point, co-bordering appears essential to developing the *federative ideal* – the Kantian dream of an expansive and peaceful federation of states – frequently at the core of even statist visions of the global sphere.

This said, there are also myriad potential harms to co-bordering. For the discussion of harms, it is helpful to start by outlining some reasons why the present system of bordering might be considered worth preserving – i.e. what co-bordering might undermine. The principle concern is that powerful states would use co-bordering as a means of legitimating predatory actions against weaker states. After all, borders as institutions can help protect weak states from strong ones. Once the black box of mono-sovereign borders is opened, this protection falls away. Thus, the blurring of territorial fixity might actually free powerful states to embrace imperial modes of domination. This is because borders are necessarily *restrictive*, but frontiers are by nature *expansive*. This would enable forms of imperialism between *neighbors* that we normally associate with the more distant abroad – i.e. a form of *proximate colonialism*, or *occupation*.

Because of these concerns, the chapter sketches another citizenship model that draws from the cross-border citizenship discussed in Chapter 3 while opening up the question of migrants and Third Country Nationals (TCNs). This could be an area in which there are preferential rights afforded to migrants, who are offered the possibility of working and cultivating lives in these borderlands zones – essentially, areas in which they would be given a larger range of permissions that would exist in a separate polity. Such a model of membership might also entail political rights – such as, not merely voting in local elections but holding office. This would have the benefit of furnishing an institutional basis whereby certain human rights can be protected. This chapter provides a preliminary sketch of what such a scheme might offer.

A Global Question?

The USA, Technology Transfer and Regional Modeling

The US has played an active role in perpetuating its own border management policies abroad. In particular, it is at the cutting edge of technological development, funneling unprecedented quantities of money into border technologies, developed by US companies, many of which have international affiliates. A small handful of companies drives the bordering industry worldwide, and thus the exact products that are driving the markets in the US are proliferating globally. Put simply: "the homeland security enterprise is a global one."[3]

American contractors are increasingly multinational. One perimeter technology firm boasts "53,000 systems in more than 80 countries;" another is present "in over 100 countries."[4] Another boasts clients across Asia, Europe and the Middle East, and is now responsible for developing border security systems in Saudi Arabia and the United Arab Emirates, its largest international customers.[5] The US is also increasingly subsidizing foreign technology developers, mostly European. Given the emphasis on standardization and interoperability, companies with global reach are becoming progressively more successful. For example, the list of the top twenty-five leading contractors for DHS, now has more international companies than ever.[6] The highest-ranked companies in terms of grants obtained from DHS are European Aeronautic Defense and Space Company (EADS) (The Netherlands; sixth), Safran (France; seventh), Securitas AB (Sweden; eighteenth) and Siemens AG (Germany; nineteenth). Additionally, in a separate study of emerging contractors – the so-called "rising ten," or younger technology developers – a number of European firms emerged.

In addition to funding international technology developers and US companies that peddle their wares globally, the US is also at the center of this global movement politically, propagating its system of border management internationally. This is most immediately evident *regionally*, with DHS exporting its brand of border security throughout the Western hemisphere. This has already been discussed with regards to Canadian and Mexican policies that "mirror" US programs. But this extends beyond neighboring states. For example, DHS has created a border academy in Panama, trained by US Border Patrol. Indeed, Panama is fully re-modeling its border administration structure along the model of CBP. José Raul Mulino, Vice-Minister of Public Safety and Security, Government of Panama, advocates collective border security in the region, including the "integration of central American forces."[7]

The US–Panama agreement is a test case for exporting bordering education abroad. DHS wants to expand this model throughout the region:

Our future plan [is] expanding the DHS concept into other areas of the world ... The idea would be to kick something off in Central America, and use that as an example, and move on to other regions of the world ... We have done a great job with Panama ... [Now] we are using the relationship with our Panamanian counterparts to pave the road for the other countries in our area.[8]

In the words of one DHS official, the focus in the region has changed: "Before it used to be migrants coming across the border, and making sure they move in a humanitarian way. Now the shift is moving toward securing the border."[9]

It comes as no surprise that the US is intimately engaged in the politics of the region. However, this project is also increasingly *global*. As outlined in the introduction, the new threat environment is understood to involve the merging of terrorist threats (like al-Qaeda) with organized crime (like the drug cartels) into a multiheaded hydra. These are global concerns, not regional ones. This means that attempts at regulated border control has to adapt into a multi-national affair, which need not stop at the regional extremity. Consequently, the US has taken to promoting global information-sharing and express collaboration amongst law enforcement officials. The US goal is not to replace international organizations in cross-border interdictions, but rather to strengthen global policing commitments. Further, the US sees international policing efforts as part of a broader aim of using internationalism as a means of exporting US methods.

The US model of cultivating bilateral agreements that can be woven into a multilateral framework is an alternative model to the classic framework of international organizations. But, the strategy has broad global appeal, including from the UN, for whom bilateral cross-border collaboration is a necessary predicate for global governance. The UN Office for Drugs and Organized Crime (UNODC) attests:

> Since crime has gone global, purely national responses are inadequate: they displace the problem from one country to another ... States have to look beyond borders to protect their sovereignty ... If police stop at borders while criminals cross them freely, sovereignty is already breached – actually, it is surrendered to those who break the law. Therefore, trans-border intelligence-sharing and law enforcement cooperation are essential.[10]

This point about state-level cross-border cooperation is further brought forth by Ban Ki-moon, the former UN Secretary-General: "with transnational threats, states have no choice but to work together. We are all affected ... we have a shared responsibility to act."[11] The problem here is, to date, global law enforcement mechanisms have been ineffective. What the UN actually calls for is a schema of bi- and multi-national policing efforts. This point is critical: there is an alternative global order emerging which is discrete from international organizations, but is instead based on bilateral, state–state agreements that are spreading across the globe.

And of course, there is also a tremendous amount of direct US involvement in the border security measures of other states. Recent examples include the US funding a "Border Security Mobile Surveillance Sensor Security System" in Egypt and the installation of border surveillance system in Tunisia,[12] as well as the highest levels of military cooperation with India.[13]

Europe

The European Union (EU) is a parent figure to this project, due to the erasing of the internal borders of Europe after the Schengen Accord.[14]

Direct comparisons with the US are not easy, as while there is a commonly accepted external frontier to the EU, member states control their own peripheries. Nonetheless, the EU shows a parallel trajectory to some of the developments in the US. As with the United States, the terror attacks of 9/11 prompted the expansion of the border security institutions put in place in the 1990s, so-called "Frontier Europe," built in response to the growing challenge of immigration.[15] A key aspect of the post-9/11 window of border enhancement hinged on risk-management and data-sharing protocols, rather than tactical infrastructure. In short, Europe has undergone its own realization that "walls don't work." New border technologies mirror some of the same developments we see in the US, including remote control (perimeter controls at a distance from the perimeter itself), pre-detection technologies, and perimeter-zone sweeps. This point is familiar: such technology aims to make the border the last line of defense, rather than the first.

Additionally, the immediate post-9/11 window led to a rethinking of European policy toward *collective* border security. In October 2001, several member states conducted a feasibility study about creating a single, unified "European Border Police." These and other debates produced an organizational framework for discussing border issues – the Strategic Committee on Immigration, Frontiers and Asylum (SCIFA), as well as heads of national border police (or SCIFA+). These institutional moves were important first steps toward collaborative border security, although they fell far short in practice. One European Commission official complained:

[SCIFA] wasn't particularly useful co-operation, but it was something that everybody felt was needed, to take this next step after the 9/11 attacks etc. and what was happening in the US. But the US built a mastodon [DHS], we simply just disintegrated ourselves.[16]

Change was slow, but these events galvanized interest in border security, leading to the development of Frontex in 2005. Although member states retained ultimate authority over their own borders. This has led to first steps toward the centralized coordination of border control – referred to in this context as "integrated border management" or joint border operations. Although still inchoate, this type of integrated management is designed to include joint border patrols, inter-agency cooperation, and data-sharing across member states and institutions.[17]

Frontex is in the process of truly becoming a coordinated agency. In fact, the European Commission is establishing a European Border and Coast Guard, governed by risk analysis and "increased screening, registration and debriefing activities."[18] They also discuss needing to expand their operations to include access to SIS, VIS, Eurodac, Europol and Interpol databases – in short data collaboration. Here is a general remark from Frontex about layered approaches at the border:

Increasingly, while movements across the external air borders are managed through a layered approach, where the border is divided into four tiers, the physical border is increasingly becoming a secondary layer for risk assessment, meaning that checking and screening start well before passengers cross bordercontrol posts at airports. Border management will increasingly be riskbased, to ensure that interventions are focused on highrisk movements of people, while lowrisk movements are facilitated smoothly.[19]

Beyond this consolidation, what is of interest here is that Frontex realizes that the central predicate of its own success is whether member states receive help from a neighbor (as opposed to going it alone). For example, in its 2016 report, Frontex explained that the cooperation between Spain and Morocco was the key determinant in controlling the land route between the two countries – indeed, it has been so effective, that it has largely displaced migrants to other crossings, such as Libya.[20] The same was true on the Western African route, where there is a very small number of migrant, which Frontex attributed to "the Memorandum of Understanding between Spain, Senegal and Mauritania, that includes joint surveillance activities and effective return of those detected crossing the border illegally."[21] Once again, the coordinated appeal was the successful one. This same pattern was mirrored in the Arctic Route, which connects Norway and Finland with Russia and only saw its number decrease when "the Russian Federation resumed its practice of preventing the exit of travellers without a travel document that would allow them to enter the EU."[22]

Moreover, the EU is collaborating directly with neighboring governments, and indeed using those states' soil for their own operations. For example, the EU response to the migration crises in Greece was a military solution to take place in Libya, on Libyan soil – i.e. to use Libya as a buffer state, a country of "last transit of irregular migrants and asylum seekers."[23] The EU has also over the last few years continually offered carrots to Turkey in order to deal with immigrants on their soil, rather than let them get to the EU border.[24]

Any way you cut it, the same kind of thinking that drives US endeavors at its borders is also structuring and shaping EU policy toward its external frontiers – European states increasingly realize that they "can't go it alone."

South Africa

South Africa is also reconsidering its border strategy. As with the US, there is a general sense amongst South African border officials and practitioners that present forms of border management are unsustainable. One aspect of this is the understanding that security forces at the border are no longer primarily oriented against other militaries, but rather flows of goods and peoples. As one colonel in the South African National Defense Force (SANDF) explained to me in an interview: "Having many battle tanks is not going to prevent billions [of dollars] of contraband coming into the country. Fighter aircraft is not going to prevent that."[25]

There is also an understanding that while the impulse in border security is toward walling, this is nonetheless not an effective solution. For example, mirroring the precise language used in the US, one defense strategist explains the problems of border walling by saying: "You are not going to solve the problem with a big bang approach."[26] Another SANDF colonel explains this fact, with specific reference to US attempts at building a wall on its border with Mexico:

Pre-1994, before the new government took over, we looked to the outside and said "keep it out." But this cannot work if you participate in an open economy, which we all do ... You will always have migration ... And there is no system in the world that is going to stop it. The classic example of this is the "Berlin Wall" approach. Not even the Berlin Wall worked ... The US recently tried this on its border with Mexico, although it wasn't a wall made of bricks, it was a fence. But did it work? No ... There is no system that is going to keep people out. No Berlin Wall, no deep trench with water and crocodiles. Irrespective of how many people you shoot, you are not going to keep them out.[27]

For him, the exclusionary strategy failed in the US, just as it had in South Africa, before the end of Apartheid.

The sum of this changing awareness of the border environment has led South Africa to come to its own version of the *can't go it alone* conclusion – i.e. there has to be some form of cross-border cooperation to manage borders effectively:

You can't just look after yourself. We are part of the continent and we are part of the region ... That implies that we cannot [separate] our border safeguarding from our regional responsibilities ... There should be an effective, integrated border management approach ... [The goal is] a joint inter-departmental, inter-agency, and multi-national approach [that will work as a] collective, because we cannot provide anything [alone].[28]

Put another way: "[Today] border safeguarding operations are distinguished by *alliance and coordination*, rather than *control*."[29]

This *can't go it alone* attitude has two components. Internally, South Africa is dedicated to turning the border into a zone, in which to catch potential transgressors. This means first and foremost what they call – using the same language prevalent in the US – a "whole of government approach," or "Operations-in-Depth," meaning the integration of South African forces along the border, with increased interoperability and information-sharing. The same overtures are made toward information sharing, with data management and sharing across all players, because "the SANDF cannot do it alone. In fact, no single department can do it alone."[30] Externally, this plan includes *cross-border* communication, with "joint integrated, inter-agency, and multi-national operations at tactical and operational levels."[31] On every level, commitment to the idea of a joint bordering scheme is strong. By one account: "a joint border would be ideal … We need to involve our counterpart on the other side."[32]

South Africa has already begun to cooperate with its neighbors. Here is an account of how this type of strategic thinking can move forward:

[We need] to have a system which includes collaboration between states … We have developed systems over a couple of years already, whereby the South African Defense Force will collaborate with Botswana Police, or Botswana Defense Force across the border, to make border control operations more effective, to access information … One of the elements of operations-in-depth, is to have an external-internal liaison because the problem does not begin at the border, and it does not end at the border. And if we recognize this, we have won 50% of the battle.[33]

Much of this change in thinking about borders security derived from successful experience during the Soccer World Cup in 2010, when South Africa and its neighbors conducted joint missions. There are also agreements for bi- and tri-lateral policing of coastal waters between South Africa, Mozambique and Tanzania for collective security against piracy – based on MOUs, just as in the Shiprider program in the US.

Evidence from Around the World

September 11 inspired a rethinking of bordering practice worldwide. As evidence of this, it is perhaps best to start with one of the least likely sites of cross-border cooperation between neighboring states, on the Israeli–Egyptian border in the Sinai. Despite obvious technological and military advantages, Israeli forces increasingly realize that changing threats require coordination with the Egyptian forces on the other side of the line – coordinating borderline defense against shared concerns over mobility, in this case by radical Islamists. Roei Elkabetz, an official in the Israel Defense Forces, explains: "The nature of war is changing, we all know it. [There are no more] big wars ... no tanks, no airforce. [Now] they use robots and UAVs to challenge us." Today, Israel uses much of the same technology that the US uses at the border – twenty-four-hour radar, etc. But the important point is this: once they have knowledge of a threat approaching the border, they coordinate with Egyptian forces. Elkabetz continues:

> Cooperation with the Egyptians at the tactical level is very good. We are speaking on a daily basis, in real time ... [This cooperation] has been happening for the last few years. Before there was no need ... there were only some immigrants ... [But] it has become crucial in the last two years. So we are speaking with their generals, we have meetings ... We decided that if the global jihad, or the salafiyya is a mutual enemy, then lets coordinate. We know now that the same enemies are against Egypt and against Israel.[34]

Of course, the story of Israeli and Egyptian cooperation is a fickle one. But the sheer fact of joint border coordination is a powerful example of this rising shift in awareness.

A similar system is in place in the West Bank – a vastly different geopolitical terrain which does not divide sovereign states, but rather a sovereign state (Israel) from a contested territory (the Palestinian Authority). Nonetheless, even though the Israeli wall – or "Security Fence" – has received the bulk of critical attention, it constitutes only a small part of Israeli security policy. Israel's aim in the West Bank is first and foremost to create a buffer zone between itself and the Palestinian population of the West Bank. The fence is designed to be the last line of defense – the endpoint of a comprehensive network of roads, settlements and checkpoints, designed to create an Israeli security zone that prevents Palestinians from ever even getting to the fence, nevertheless crossing it. In this way, checkpoints are a sort of filling-out strategy in the West Bank, which is part of what makes the wall function as it does. As one analyst for the UN Office for the Coordination of Humanitarian Affairs (OCHA) explains, the security fence and internal checkpoints act as part of a "coordinated system."[35] Not surprisingly, this argument is echoed by Palestinian observers: "it is a system of control ... the checkpoint system cooperates with the segregation wall."[36]

One of the global regions in which changes to border perimeter security is most prevalent is in the East African Community – largely modeled on the EU – comprised of Tanzania, Kenya, Uganda, Rwanda, Burundi and South Sudan. This collective has made significant steps toward the joint management of its common borders, driven by transnational criminal threats. An official at the Kenya Revenue Authority explains the origin of thinking about shared borders in the EAC:

In 1998 there were simultaneous bomb blasts in Nairobi and Dar es Salaam by terrorists. This was an eye-opener, as we got to know just how porous our borders were. All of the materials used in the construction of those bombs had passed through our borders. And because the [Kenyan and Tanzanian] agencies were not connected, they were able to penetrate and comfortably bomb the two capital cities … Now we have general meetings at the border stations, and coordinated verifications are taking place … We have started practicing this, bringing all of the regional agencies [together] – all of the customs, immigrations, departments and other agencies … Now, for example, all of the goods that are being exported from Kenya to Uganda [are processed] on the Ugandan side, where we sit together and do the clearance [together].[37]

Real changes in border administration are very recent, as with the 2012 Collaborative Border Management agreement. Today, the EAC is planning to move toward a more comprehensive joint border management scheme, pilots of which are already underway:

Right now we are doing joint patrols, both at the local and the regional level … [For example] the Kenyan Revenue Authority and the Uganda Revenue Authority are jointly patrolling the borders. [Around] Lake Victoria all of the countries [coordinate with] patrol boats and motorcycles … All of this is about integration. Eventually we shall involve other parties as well into these patrols.[38]

As another Kenyan official explained to me in an interview, at the perimeter the different law enforcement agencies "come together as a team;" under this new regime of joint border management, authority is situated in a joint "defense council."[39] Should disputes arise, they are to be negotiated in a shared EAC Court, although the legal powers of this court are still being finalized.

Other examples abound, especially in contested areas. For example, in North Africa, Tunisia and Egypt are pushing for regional border security arrangements, as a result of the now nearly five-year-old insurgency led by al-Qaida-related and Islamic State-related groups. Abdel-Fattah el-Sissi, President of Egypt is leading calls for a "regional military task force" to deal with shared forms of transnational threats, emanating from the instability of Libya.[40] When asked what Turkey's new border wall with Syria would look like, Turkish Finance Minister Mehmet Simsek explained that they would prioritize "systems that would locate and track terrorists and their border crossings" and would include "mine detection systems, anti-IED equipment, surveillance aircraft, cameras, sensors and drones."[41] Another example of unlikely cross-border cooperation is that between India and China. Right now their officials are in the process of rolling out a bilateral Border Defense Cooperation Agreement (BDCA), first signed in October 2013, on their mutually contested border. Their goal was to establish "a formal mechanism to improve security along their 4,056-kilometer border ... [and increase] cooperation on a military-to-military basis."[42]

Co-Bordering – Weighing Normative Concerns

The global trend toward co-bordering helps reshape the debate over the effect of globalization on the international state system. Sovereignty is transforming in response to globalized flows, with states collaborating against shared threats. We are in a position, with the closing of the era of globalization and the rise of securitization, to rethink global institutions. The question now is: what does this mean normatively?

Potential Benefits

The concept of jointly managed borders certainly has normative promise. Indeed, this form of bi- and multilateral institutionalism opens the door for radically re-thinking the international state-system. For many scholars, borders represent a problem in politics because they are *morally arbitrary, anti-democratic*, and perpetuate *global inequality*. For proponents of these views, borders should be superseded. To understand how co-bordering might offer some form of solvency, it is helpful to revisit these points.

The bounded polity – the nation-state – poses a challenge to liberal democracy, as carving the limits of state membership necessarily creates a category of exclusion. Those left outside of state lines enjoy none of the privileges of those inside; worse still, the borders separating without from within are themselves frequently arbitrary. This is referred to as the "boundary problem," or the problem of "constituting the demos."[43] As Whelan explains, democracy "cannot be brought to bear on the logically prior matter of the constitution of the group, the existence of which it presupposes."[44] In this discussion, the boundary is an abstract concept.[45] With regard to territorial borders, Pierre Manent explains: "the difficulty of democracy is that, in relation to the principle, the body is arbitrary."[46] Thus, democracy in the nation-state container is an incomplete ethical project. If democracy is defined as a state of consent, then those that are excluded should have chosen to opt out. But those excluded made no such choice. Indeed, frequently those on the outside risk their lives to enter states to which others, often just a few miles away, were entitled by no particular investiture of their own – merely by the "accident" of their birth. Indeed, in many ways the Westphalian border is the model institution against equality, as national concerns trump universal ones.

To solve the problem of arbitrary borders, theorists have either tried to "democratize transnational institutions" or "transnationalize democracy." There are two commonly articulated viewpoints: that the world needs bounded political units, such as nation-states, which should all be equally democratic (in this way, states are like pieces to a comprehensive democratic puzzle); or that there should be some sort of global administration through which the rights of all are equally protected (doing away with state lines entirely, or building upon them a super-structure of governance). On the one hand, work within the nation-state system; on the other hand, scrap it in favor of a higher law. For example, Jean Cohen distinguishes between *sovereigntists* (those who want to work within the Westphalian frame) and *cosmopolitans* (those who wish to transcend the state-system via international institutions); in a similar vein, Nancy Fraser distinguishes between an *affirmative approach* to thinking about transnational governance (those who want to work within the state system) and the *transformative approach* (those who want to transcend it).[47]

These schools represent a spectrum, ranging from support for national borders to some form of world government. For an example of the former, Cohen argues that global institutions should work alongside state sovereignty, rather than trump it – what she calls dualism. Most common within this literature are hybrid solutions that envision some form of regional or transnational legal and political institutions that work alongside the existing state systems. Benhabib defends what she calls "republican federalism," or the "constitutionally structured reaggregation of the markers of sovereignty, in a set of interlocking institutions each responsible and accountable to the other,"[48] such that states preserve their sovereignty, but are delimited by international legal norms, thereby enabling the spread of democracy across borders – via what she terms "democratic iterations." Habermas champions international political institutions, especially at the regional level, building upon the model of the EU as a stepping stone toward a "constitutionalized world society ... a multi-level system that can make possible a global domestic politics," or even a "*supranational* world organization."[49] Going a step further, other scholars argue for some form of world government. For example, Eric Cavallero argues for what he calls global federative democracy, or a system of democratic decision-making at the global level in order to guarantee that all those affected by a policy can be participant to the decision, but at the same time, smaller units can make decisions on behalf of people disproportionately affected at the local level.[50]

What, if anything, can co-bordering contribute to these debates? If it is to move the debate at all, it will be in the middle level – via a form of federalism, or the repooling of sovereignty between states. In Benhabib's model, republican federalism is a situation in which multiple territories and legal units have overlapping jurisdictions – including at sub- and supra-national levels – with varying degrees of vertical authority (and accountability), usually linked by a republican constitution. Co-bordering can clearly be in the service of this type of arrangement at the local level, providing building blocks to a regional schema, presided over by a republican constitution. Specifically, co-bordering can provide a framework for understanding how states can form political institutions in tandem, and even create the terms for overlapping legal zones, while at the same time preserving basic aspects of sovereignty.

At an advanced level, co-bordering could pave the way for a legal synching between neighboring polities – a form of legal pluralism. As Neil Walker explains, legal pluralism "tends to emphasize the advantage of a 'bottom up' evolutionary landscape of diverse legal orders over a 'top down' programmed arrangement." The benefits of pluralism are appreciable:

in terms of the greater capacity of each order to check and counter the legitimacy deficits and to moderate the excesses of the others; in terms of pluralism's encouragement of tie-breaking compromise or dialogue; in terms of its propensity toward equal recognition of different and diverse constituencies and their corresponding legal regimes; and in terms of a general willingness to recognize and embrace the emergence of new such constituencies and regimes.[51]

Co-bordering is suggestive of all of these benefits, derived from the fact that local communities can create their laws in tandem.

It is through this local-level legal synching that the seeds can be planted for an enduring form of *heterarchy* – i.e., the formal and informal equivalence of units. A principle attribute of nearly any variant of cosmopolitan regimes is the horizontal dispersal of power (ideally amongst equals) rather than the vertical distribution of power, as in classic asymmetric relations. The European Union is putatively an example of such a structure, although there are holes in this logic – as detailed in Chapter 3. Indeed, even discussions of horizontal sovereignty do little but describe power that is distributed horizontally across organs, not sovereign systems without vertical ones as well.[52]

What is remarkable about co-bordering is precisely the potential for horizontal relations across units. This is essential, as nearly all forms of cosmopolitanism retain some form of the state unit, maintaining some form of border. For all their merit, these solutions retain the cell-unit of the state, and envision broader forms of international and transnational legal constraints operating alongside the state system. Borders in these systems are transcended by legal structure; they are rarely shared. By contrast, co-bordering enables a system by which borders can be shared – thus, there are still borders but they are not mono-sovereign. This is precisely what Benhabib calls for when she describes borders as "active sites of transnational conversations and interactions."[53]

Up to this point, co-bordering appears essential to developing the *federative ideal*. One particular model of federalism that co-bordering appears to strengthen is Jean Cohen's, which seeks to preserve unit-sovereignty, while eliminating classic forms of statehood – thereby supporting both federalism and global constitutionalism. For such a system to work, she advocates for an alternate form of polity, which is state-like, but not exactly a state (although it remains a constitutional body). In this rubric, federalism enables units small enough for individuals to view themselves as the authors of their own laws (*pace* Kant, Habermas), with a public sphere sufficiently proximate to enable popular expression, and safeguard fears of autocracy, common to larger polities. But the central normative purchase of Cohen's federalism – like most forms of global or regional federation discussed in contemporary theory – is that such a union is *heterarchical*:

A federation consists of two public powers (member states and federal), whose constitutional legal orders are involved in heterarchical rather than hierarchical interrelations, in which an ineradicable plurality of political existences coexist and which institutionalizes political structures providing for shared rule and self-rule, along with legal structures registering independence and interdependence.[54]

Co-bordering is a complimentary, localized piece of this narrative. It describes a site of interaction where states can accede to federal union over a particular quadrant of territory (their mutual peripheries), enabling a level of bi- and multilateral organization heretofore unimaginable at the mutual borderlines between states. It further supports a number of specific points toward the furtherance of this system. For example, co-bordering appears to create the terms by which greater representation, in smaller units can be afforded to more people, without sacrificing the polity-size required under conditions of globalization. As Cohen remarks, the constraints of contemporary politics requires that states get larger to be able to compete on the global stage; but democracy requires the preservation of small units in which democratic will formation can be best served. Federalism creates the terms where such a trade-off is rendered obsolete; co-bordering strengthens the structural basis of this edifice while potentially increasing the number of spaces in which democratic voice is enabled and representation is possible.

Co-bordering also has a practical benefit for such theories. Federal logic is attractive in the abstract but, as with the European Union, member states in such polities are always capable of exiting the order. This means that the structure never quite gets beyond the statist principle. What federalism requires in practice is a system in which members have a difficult time extricating from the union. This is precisely what co-bordering provides. It is through this system of entangled, joint peripheries that members become inextricably intertwined at their peripheries – i.e. glued together. These units are just as state-like as the ones Cohen and other proponents of federalism describe, but there is an added mechanism of structural commitment to the union.

This point about *mechanism* – the glue – is important. What international systems need is first and foremost the experience of collaboration – after all, it is through collaboration that future forms of collaboration can be born. In short, one of the possible normatively positive effects of this system is that it can actually make borders behave as bridges – thereby cultivating cross-border communities. This follows a constructivist attitude toward institutions, i.e. that through the process of collaboration, states change their nature.[55] Although Alexander Wendt and John Rawls are perhaps surprising bedfellows, this follows the latter's point in his *Law of Peoples*: for global institutions to have the same properties of attachment and responsibility that states do, there first have to be deep levels of cross-border social cooperation. Rawls is optimistic that bonds of interrelation grow over time, helping develop effective international institutions.[56]

This discussion of mechanism brings us to a classic question: how do we form such communal attachments, or more specifically, how do feelings of belonging get translated into meaningful political community? By creating the terms of institutional enagement and interaction, co-bordering plausibly assists in this process. Moreover, in so far as national attachments are things we sometimes fear, co-bordering presents the possibility of transforming national bonds into a productive geopolitical forces, especially in so far as it may allow us to build up from small level nationalisms toward a more global picture. This answers a popular call in democratic theory, for democratic institutions to "scale up" from the local to the global.[57] This is the kind of thing that co-bordering can enable because of the creation of local sites of citizen interaction – presaged in Chapter 3.

Taking a step back, if you think states are good, then you think borders are good. But if you think that states are morally suspect, then co-bordering presents a role to solvency. The other half of this equation is treated below.

Potential Harms

For the discussion of harms, it is helpful to start by outlining some rea-sons why the present system of bordering might be considered worth pre-serving – i.e. what co-bordering might undermine. A number of defenses obtain. A central one pertains to democratic freedom. For many, the state provides the basic terms for the flourishing of democracy and the rule of law. Certainly this was the motivating concern for early modern theorists of sovereignty, like Hobbes and Bodin. As Manent explains: "democracy, in order to become a reality, needs a *body*, a population marked out by borders and other characteristics, namely a *defined* realm."[58] It is within bounded states that citizens can be confident of the authority to which they are subject. This lies at the core of citizens' rights in the modern state. The republican account of citizenship explicitly places freedom within a bounded unit: "I am free as a *citizen* of a particular state, a state that promotes the common good of non-domination."[59]

Further to this point that states as bounded political units can be bas-tions of freedom comes Walzer's position on self-determination – that, given the conditions of global moral pluralism, bounded states provide spheres of justice in which popular sovereignty is possible. This position provides the core of Walzer's defense of why sovereign states have the right to police their own borders, or that "the recognition of sovereignty is the only way we have of establishing an arena within which freedom can be fought for and sometimes won," and that "the distinctiveness of cultures and groups depends upon closure and, without it, can not be conceived as a stable feature of human life."[60] For Walzer, there is a moral interest in preserving units in which people feel that they are in a community of like-minded people and participate in shared political institutions, which further supports the administrative benefits of bounded states. Liberal nationalists also defend the merits of an intimate, bounded community, but more for pluralism and the protection of minorities, whose prefer-ences can be lost within the current of broader democratic politics.[61] This latter point supports the claim that good fences make good neighbors.

Another argument pertains to the nature of authority, which to be meaningful must be clear and stable. Indeed, a central criticism against co-bordering would come from those who believe that there has to be singular state authority over territory. On this point, David Miller writes:

[State] functions cannot be carried out effectively unless the state has author-ity over a determinate territory ... The existence of such authority makes it possible for people at any given location to know which legal regime they are subject to, and which other policies apply to them ... Imagine two commu-nities intermingled on the same territory, each subject to a different political authority responsible for law enforcement etc … It would [be] very difficult for their members to cooperate with one another, or to solve all kinds of collective problems such as where to build roads, or how to control environmental pollution. Even simple person-to-person dealings … would be hard to conduct until it was agreed whose law should govern them.[62]

Miller critiques specifically the logic of the dual-controlled zone. He links it to the Middle Ages, when this type of organization led to chaos.

This said, defenses of conventional borders need not be defenses of states, but rather of norms of sovereignty and the stabilizing function of the international state system. Indeed, to whatever degree the Westphalian system of states can be considered stable is due largely to agreements on fixed, mono-sovereign borders. On this point, Lord Curzon famously noted that borders are a constraint to power, representing "a prevention of misunderstanding, a check to territorial cupidity, and an agency of peace."[63] In international legal thought, there are several reasons for why boundaries are effective at keeping powers in check, notably by providing clarity to the limits of jurisdiction, thereby securing "a basis for coexistence and cooperation through the precise allocation of the jurisdiction and authority over territory as between one political community and another."[64] Indeed, the state system was originally designed as a safeguard against the expansionary appetites of individual states.

Here is where borders come in: it is at least clear that borders as institutions can help protect weak states from strong ones. Once the black box of mono-sovereign borders is opened, this protection falls away. Thus, the blurring of territorial fixity might actually free strong states to embrace imperial modes of domination. This is because borders are necessarily *restrictive*, but frontiers are by nature *expansive*. This would enable forms of imperialism between *neighbors* that we normally associate with the more distant abroad – i.e. it is a form of *proximate colonialism*, or *occupation*. It is for this reason that Charles Maier makes an error in writing about empire when he writes: "Something there may be that doesn't love a wall, but it isn't imperial power."[65] In fact, walls are impediments to empires, and in this regard, looking at the contemporary US, the wall is *the least normatively concerning aspect of the border*.

Indeed, principally, borders protect small states. This feeds back into the subject of sovereignty, and the importance of distinguishing between *de facto* and *de jure* variants. As Andrew Hurrell explains, the problem of big and small states can be summarized as follows: for small states, their juridical sovereignty is more important than their empirical sovereignty; for big states, their empirical sovereignty is more important then their juridical sovereignty.[66] It comes as no surprise that small states were the main proponents of human rights, especially in the immediate postwar period. And of course, the big states all vetoed any international mechanisms of enforcement against their sovereignty.[67] The idea that sovereignty is a means by which small states can be protected from big ones comes out in a lot of writing in International Relations. As Wendt explains, small states lean on norms of sovereignty for collective security:

> What keeps the United States from conquering the Bahamas, or Nigeria from seizing Togo, or Australia from occupying Vanuatu? Clearly, power is not the issue ... This lack of interest can only be understood in terms of their recognition of weak states' sovereignty ... Ironically, it is the great powers, the states with the greatest national means, that may have the hardest time learning this lesson; small powers do not have the luxury of relying on national means and may therefore learn faster that collective recognition is a cornerstone of security.[68]

Otherwise put: sovereignty and security align for small states, but not for big ones. Going a step further, we can even say that it is *because* we live in a world where sovereignty exists as a norm of mutual recognition between states that makes them able to co-border. Without recognized sovereignty, states would never cede sovereignty in any way. But because states feel comfortable vis-à-vis other states, and comfortable in their sovereign status, they are able to co-border (against their new threat, globalized mobilities).

It is valuable to revisit the good aspects of states, and sovereignty, as this is precisely the system that might be destabilized by joint border administrations. What harms might such a destabilized system engender? The likely answer is some form of neo-imperialism, borne of *asymmetry*. There is a natural tension between states as bounded units and power. Weak states value borders most, as they offer a form of protection from the outside. As states become more powerful, boundaries become an impediment from which they may seek to break free. This law of the powerful has been around since ancient Athens and the Melian Dialogue: "The strong do what they will, the weak do when they must."[69] On this point, Stephen Krasner, for whom sovereignty is always just a mask for asymmetry, argues that strong states always find ways to "break the rules" or alter them to their favor.[70] We should not be sanguine – power asymmetry is the fact of the world. As Krasner warns: "Power is asymmetrical. There is no hierarchical authority. Logics of consequence have trumped Westphalian logics of appropriateness."[71] Thus we need to take as our normative starting point conditions of hierarchy, not heterarchy.

Asymmetry is a fact of international politics, but how do we connect co-bordering to neo-imperialism? For this, I return to Michael Doyle's definition of empire, introduced in Chapter 1, as "effective control, whether formal or informal, of a subordinated society by an imperial society."[72] Doyle chooses to define empire by using effective control (a *de facto* measure) rather than legal annexation (a *de jure* measure) because, ultimately, it is the latter that defines the type of dominating relationship we associate as imperial. It is this subject of imperial behavior that is of essence here; after all, co-bordering is putatively voluntary. Doyle further distinguishes between formal and informal control; this discussion engages the latter, as it pertains to the question of influence.[73] The concern with co-bordering is twofold: first that the stronger power coerces the weaker one to agree to joint border controls; second that even voluntary accords ultimately transform into means of hierarchical domination. Either route presents a version of co-bordering that looks like nation-state imperialism. It also shares an affinity with the Roman imperial strategy of cultivating neighboring states as clients – very similar to what we today would call buffers – which would form "an active barrier between the perimeters of the empire and the possibly still more dangerous barbarians deeper inland."[74] Such a system allowed Rome to be hegemonic without necessarily expanding territorially. Could co-border regions essentially become clients for big states?

The types of arrangement facilitated by co-bordering are unlikely to be overtly coercive. Initially, co-bordering agreements are likely to be two-sided and voluntary, and in the case of coercion, violence may be threatened but not performed. At least at the outset, the asymmetrically inferior side must agree to being commanded. Or, in the words of Roman jurists, *Etsi coactus tamen volui* ("I may have been compelled, but in the final analysis I committed my will").[75] The degree to which co-bordering becomes truly oppressive is mostly contingent on the extant power asymmetries between the contracting states. For example, returning to the co-location of forces between the US and Canada, once operations become intertwined, it becomes costly to extricate. Thus, should the US decide to exercise its might, Canada would be faced with two substandard options: extricate from co-location, which would be costly; or, submit to US influence. In the US–Mexico case the stakes are higher due to drug violence. What measures are in place to stop the zone of influence of the border from expanding according to US will? The previous pages established simply that decisions at the border were *joint*; this does not mean they are *equal*.

Another form this may take is through institutional abuse. Indeed, liberal institutionalism should not be assumed to be part of the solution – after all, international institutions are run in the interests of strong states too. Indeed, historically, liberal multilateralism has masked a type of imperialism. Remarkably, Hurrell expresses this point invoking similar language of "we cannot do it alone" trope, cited throughout this book:

For many states and other groups, the rhetoric of liberal multilateralism covered the reality of its top-down, prescriptive, and often coercive character. The substantive outcomes appeared to be stacked in favour of the most powerful ... The hard-line hegemonist "we can do it alone" is clearly wrong. But the liberal hegemonist version, "we can do it together" depends on who "we" are, on what "it" is, and what is meant by "together."[76]

And the same types of concerns are prevalent in regional associations, where strong states will frequently use the regional platform as a way of exercising their hegemony – as is evident in US policies in the Americas. Indeed, the idea that the US has used its power in such a way as to promote "joint decision-making" in its favor is an old trick on the international economic domain. Hurrell calls this the "paradox of regionalism" – i.e. "that a successful move beyond the state depends on the existence of reasonably well-functioning states."[77]

Cross-Border Citizenship – An Addendum

Because these trends are inchoate, any further analysis will be speculative. This said, it is plain to see that, if left on it its own, co-bordering might metastasize into a form of neo-imperial overreach, with borders transforming into sites of asymmetrical co-optation. This is because, to be normatively affirming, joint sovereignty schemes must embody *heterarchy*, but in fact are more likely to mask *hierarchy*. But if *heterarchy* is a model to which we aspire, we might then ask how we might go about attaining it. As first discussed in Chapter 3, democratic institutions can be designed to bring about normatively desirable change in the border regions. The suggestion there was to bring about a form of cross-border citizenship to protect and enable citizens of neighboring states. Certainly this suggestion remains applicable in light of the discussion above. But what about migrants? Surely there is potential for harm here too, given that a principal reason for cross-border collaboration is the maximization of state capacities to control border flows. For example, the US and Mexico are working together to more efficiently "deal with" illegal aliens and maximize their capacity to control migration.[78] Similar levels of state cooperation against migrants are common worldwide, as in the case of Greece and Turkey, mentioned above.[79]

One way to think through solvency is to augment the citizenship model first introduced in Chapter 3, to include an accomodation of *migrants*. This could mean designating an area in which there are preferential rights afforded to migrants, who are offered the possibility of working and cultivating lives in these borderlands zones – essentially, areas in which they would be given a larger scope of permissions than would exist in a home polity. In a *thin* rendering, the border zone could be a place afforded for the re-settlement of refugees and asylum seekers – migrants for whom states have special obligations in international law, through the convention of *non-refoulement*. These are people toward whom states already have legal obligations (from the UN 1951 Convention Relative to the Status of Refugees (article 33) and are (often) already located at borders. It would seem that co-bordering offers promise in enabling a zone of permissive repatriation. A *thick* rendering might also afford spaces where economic migrants can work. The point is that if border zones can become housing areas for immigrants, you in principle can ameliorate the harms against them (by giving them a space to live and work) without requiring that states have a fully open borders policy. Of course, this would only work if such zones didn't make states less likely to accommodate migrants in other portions of the state.

What facets of citizenship could be afforded to migrants in such a scheme? Clearly this would allow permission to enter into the border zone. But we might also want them to be allowed to participate in the cross-border institutions. Perhaps there would have to be a time-window, after a migrant moves and establishes work and residency, before they would be allowed full participation rights. An even stronger model would also pave the way toward a more full type of inclusion into a polity, as with membership. Broadly speaking, there are a number of different levels of integration, with different types of demands, ranging from the provision of mother-tongue language services to the cultivation of safeguarding institutions whereby immigrants can be sure to have their rights protected and live in communities of respect. The point here is simply to point out that a border zone safe haven could provide a site and mechanism to help ensure that integration procedures are fair and policies are inclusive.

The normative purchase of such a model is manifold. For example, it would seem to offer an institutional basis whereby certain human rights can be protected – essentially creating Human Rights Havens. Indeed, it might create sites – physical and legal locations – whereby state institutions might be checked by international forces and powers. Such a scheme would also aid in refugee relocation – the problem that there are people whom no state wishes to take in. Having collaborative zones in which repatriation can occur might mediate such a concern, as it could be the type of zone in which states can share the cost of the accommodation of TCNs. Best of all, co-bordering citizenship zones would in principle be places where migrants would come to feel empowered. On this point, Bonnie Honig writes of the importance of distinguishing "the status of the immigrant as an object of charity of hospitality ... from an alternative status, one that does better from the vantage point of democratic theory, that positions the immigrant as a full agent empowered to make (always contestable) claims or take rights on her own behalf."[80] Given the problem migration poses to contemporary societies, the idea of a healthy, empowered migrant population is something many of us would find inspiring.

Conclusion

What has become crystal clear is that the changing world security situation since September 11, 2001, has destabilized the principle of formal sovereign equality of states ... so which is it: the rise of cosmopolitan norms or the spread of empire?

– Seyla Benhabib[81]

The story depicted here – of a patchwork of bilateral state unions that sit somewhere in between independent states and a unitary global order – provides material to rethink the international system. For example, if border zones increasingly become polities, such that two states jointly control a territory – this would signal the emergence of the *condominium* as a political unit.[82] We might also see different forms of regional association, as for example in Kalypso Nicolaïdis' models for the EU – her *Euro-Limes, Euro-Spheres,* and *Euro-World* concepts – all of which derive from the vagueness of European borders.[83] The question now facing us is how to shape these new forms of cooperation.

This chapter showed the scope of the empirical reach of co-bordering, and raised broad normative questions about the ethical contours of this phenomenon. It argued that while there are strong potential benefits of such a system, they are unlikely to obtain without democratic institutions planted to help shape their course. Another form of citizenship might help engender such change. This topic concludes the discussion of the perimeter; however, similar issues on the global stage are re-introduced in Chapter 7 regarding changes at the ports of entry. Indeed, nearly all of these themes – global justice, sovereignty and citizenship – are revisited in Part II.

Notes

1 Poggi, *The State,* at 196.
2 Foucault, *Security, Territory, Population,* at 13–14.
3 Silverberg, David. "10 Years After 9/11," *Homeland Security Today,* September 8.

4 "Integrated Perimeter Security Solutions." Southwest Microwave, 2012; "Cochrane USA: Perimeter Security Barrier Specialist." Cochrane USA, Product Guide, Volume SP1, 2012.

5 FLIR Systems cited in Finnegan, Philip. "Analyst's Notebook: FLIR + ICX = New Opportunities." *Homeland Security Today* June 8, 2012.

6 Finnegan, Philip and Peter Barnes. "Homeland Security Today's Top 25 of 2011." *Homeland Security Today*, April 2012, 24–9, at 26.

7 Mulino, José Raul. "The Globalization of Crime: International Initiatives – Lessons Learned, Success Stories." Remarks by Mulino, Vice-Minister of Public Safety and Security, Government of Panama. Border Security Expo, Phoenix, AZ, March 13, 2013.

8 Alvarez, "Emerging Threats and DHS's Western Hemisphere Strategy to Combat Transnational Crime."

9 Ibid.

10 Costa, Antonio Mario. "The Globalization of Crime: A Transnational Organized Crime Threat Assessment." 1–303: United Nations Office on Drugs and Crime (UNODC) Report, 2010, at ii–iii.

11 Cited on Ibid., at 19.

12 Nikala, Oscar. "Tunisia to Install Surveillance Gear on New Libyan Border Wall." *DefenseNews*, February 19, 2016.

13 Ganapathy, Nirmala. "US, India Move Towards Sharing Logistics." *Strait Times*, April 13, 2016.

14 The EU is treated here as a single, supranational polity, rather than a set of neighboring states with open internal borders; as such, changes to the *internal* borders of Europe fall outside of this discussion.

15 By one account: "The terrorist attacks on 11 September 2001 led to the identification of a wide range of measures aiming to reinforce 'homeland' security, including the tightening up of external border controls." Leonard, Sarah. "The Creation of FRONTEX and the Politics of Institutionalisation in the EU External Borders Policy." *Journal of Contemporary European Research* 5 (3):371–88, 2009, at 376.

16 Quoted in Neal, Andrew W. "Securitization and Risk at the EU Border: The Origins of FRONTEX." *Journal of Common Market Studies* 47 (2): 333–56, 2009, at 342.

17 See e.g., Leonard, "The Creation of FRONTEX," at 373ff.

18 "Risk Analysis for 2016," Frontex, at 5.

19 Ibid., at 61.

20 For a detailed account, see ibid., at 21.

21 Ibid., at 21.

22 Ibid., at 6–7.

23 Triandafyllidou, Anna. "Governing Migrant Smuggling: A Criminality Approach Is Not Sufficient." *openDemocracy.net*, April 6, 2016.

24 Ibid.

25 Grundling, Anton. "Keynote Address: Border Safeguarding – a Whole of Government Approach." Remarks by Colonel Grundling, SSO Plan Joint Operations, South African National Defense Forces (SANDF). Border Management Southern Africa Conference, Pretoria, South Africa, January 22, 2013.

26 Goncalves, Duarte. System Engineer – Defence, Peace, Safety & Security, The Council for Scientific and Industrial Research (CSIR). Personal interview, Pretoria, South Africa, January 22, 2013.
27 Interview, Pretoria, South Africa, January 23, 2013.
28 Grundling, "Keynote Address."
29 Valentine, Cobus. "Remarks," by Valentine, Senior Domain Specialist C41, Saab Grintek Defence, South Africa. Border Management Southern Africa Conference, Pretoria, South Africa, January 22, 2013.
30 Goncalves, Duarte. "Border Safeguarding – a Whole of Government Approach." Remarks by Goncalves, System Engineer – Defence, Peace, Safety & Security, the Council for Scientific and Industrial Research (CSIR). Border Management Southern Africa Conference, Pretoria, South Africa, January 22, 2013.
31 Valentine, "Remarks."
32 Goncalves, personal interview.
33 Interview, Pretoria, South Africa, January 23, 2013.
34 Elkabetz, Roei. "Defending Israel's Borders." Remarks by Brigadier General Elkabetz, Chief of Staff, Southern Command, Israel Defense Forces. Border Management Conference & Technology Expo, El Paso, Texas, October 16, 2012.
35 Lein, Yehezkel. Analyst for the UN Office for the Coordination of Humanitarian Affairs (UN OCHA). Personal interview, East Jerusalem, July 14, 2009.
36 Suhail Khalilieh, Applied Research Institute of Jerusalem (ARIJ). Personal interview, Bil'in, West Bank, June 5, 2008.
37 Nganga, Kamau. "Case Study: The Kenyan Experience at Our Border Stations." Remarks by Kamau Nganga, Deputy Commissioner, Kenya Revenue Authority. Border Management Southern Africa, Pretoria, South Africa, January 22, 2013.
38 Ibid.
39 Interview, Pretoria, South Africa, January 22, 2013.
40 Nikala, "Tunisia to Install Surveillance Gear on New Libyan Border Wall."
41 Bekdil, Burak Ege. "Turkey to Shop for Border Security Equipment." *Defense News*, September 5, 2015.
42 Raghuvashani, Vivek. "Indian Defense Minister to Visit China, Discuss Boundary." *DefenseNews*, March 16, 2016.
43 Whelan, Frederick G. "Democratic Theory and the Boundary Problem." In *Liberal Democracy*, edited by J. R. Pennock and J. W. Chapman, 13–47. New York: New York University Press, 1983; Goodin, Robert E. "Enfranchising All Affected Interests and Its Alternatives." *Philosophy & Public Affairs* 25, no. 1, 2007.
44 Whelan, "Democratic Theory and the Boundary Problem," at 40.
45 Goodin goes so far as to critique the term "boundary" as too geographic sounding – further contributing to the general sense that borders should be dismissed as territorial spaces. See Goodin, "Enfranchising All Affected Interests and Its Alternatives," at 40ff.
46 Manent, Pierre. *A World Beyond Politics A Defense of the Nation-State*. Princeton: Princeton University Press, 2006, at 68.

47 Cohen, "Sovereign Equality vs. Imperial Right," at 485; Fraser, *Scales of Justice*, at 22.
48 Benhabib, *Dignity in Adversity*, at 112.
49 Habermas, Jurgen. *Between Naturalism and Religion*. Translated by C. Cronin. Cambridge: Polity, 2008, at 332–6. Along similar lines, global constitutionalists defend the spread of constitutional norms between disparate national courts, with verdicts made on one national stage being used in another. See e.g., Brunkhorst, Hauke. "Globalizing Democracy without a State: Weak Public, Strong Public, Global Constitutionalism." *Millenium: Journal of International Studies* 31, no. 3 (2002): 675–90.
50 Cavallero, "Global Federative Democracy," at 52–3; see also Kuper, *Democracy Beyond Borders*.
51 Walker, Neil. "Beyond Boundary Disputes and Basic Grids: Mapping the Global Disorder of Normative Orders." *International Journal of Constitutional Law* 6: 378–396, 2008, at 390–1.
52 See e.g., Cavallero, "Global Federative Democracy," at 45.
53 Benhabib, *Dignity in Adversity*, at 36.
54 Cohen, *Globalization and Sovereignty*, at 152–3.
55 For example, Wendt writes: "even if egoistic reasons were its starting point, the process of cooperating tends to redefine those reasons by reconstituting identities and interests in terms of new intersubjective understandings and commitments." Wendt, Alexander. "Anarchy Is What States Make of It: The Social Construction of Power Politics." *International Organization* 46, no. 2 (Spring 1992): 391–425, at 417–18.
56 Rawls, John. *The Law of Peoples*. Cambridge, MA: Harvard University Press, 1999, 112–13.
57 See e.g., Held, *Models of Democracy*, at 283–4.
58 Manent, *A World Beyond Politics*, at 68.
59 Laborde, Cecile. *Critical Republicanism*. Oxford: Oxford University Press, 2008, at 1–2.
60 Walzer, Michael. "The Moral Standing of States." *Philosophy and Public Affairs* 9 (1980): 209–29, at 214; Walzer, *Spheres of Justice*, at 39; see also Sandel, Michael. *Liberalism and the Limits of Justice*. Oxford: Oxford University Press, 1982.
61 Miller, David. *Citizenship and National Identity*. Cambridge: Polity Press, 2000; Kymlicka, Will. "Territorial Boundaries: A Liberal-Egalitarian Perspective." In *Boundaries and Justice. Diverse Ethical Perspectives*, edited by D. Miller and S. H. Hashmi, 249–76. Princeton: Princeton University Press, 2001; On minorities, see Kymlicka, Will. *Multicultural Citizenship: A Liberal Theory of Minority Rights*. Oxford, UK: Oxford University Press, 1995.
62 Miller, David. *National Responsibility and Global Justice*. Oxford: Oxford University Press, 2007, at 214–15.
63 Cited in Hurrell, Andrew. "International Law and the Making and Unmaking of Boundaries." In *States, Nations and Borders*, at 279.
64 Ibid, at 279.
65 Maier, *Among Empires*, at 101.
66 Hurrell, Andrew. *On Global Order: Power, Values and the Constitution of International Society*. Oxford: Oxford University Press, 2007, at 246.

67 Beitz, Charles R. *The Idea of Human Rights*. Oxford: Oxford University Press, at 24–5.
68 Wendt, Anarchy Is What States Make of It," at 414–15.
69 Cited in Doyle, *Empires*, at 28.
70 He writes: "The international system is characterized by power asymmetries. Stronger actors can, in some cases, conquer weaker ones … But rulers might also choose to reconfigure domestic authority structures in other states, accepting their juridical independence but compromising their de facto autonomy … Rulers have found that it is in their interest to break the rules." Krasner, Stephen D. *Sovereignty: Organized Hypocrisy*. Princeton: Princeton University Press, 1999, at 6–7.
71 Ibid., at 41.
72 Doyle, *Empires*, at 30.
73 He writes: "Imperial control is one form of the exercise of asymmetrical influence and power … Power is a subset of influence. It can be considered the ability of the powerful actor to achieve effects that the influenced actors would not choose to have occur." Ibid., at 34.
74 Luttwak, *The Grand Strategy of the Roman Empire*, at 36.
75 Poggi, *The State*, at 6.
76 Hurrell, *On Global Order*, at 283.
77 Ibid., at 259.
78 Johnson, Jeh. "Statement by Secretary Jeh C. Johnson on Southwest Border Security." news release, March 9, 2016, https://www.dhs.gov/news/2016/03/09/statement-secretary-jeh-c-johnson-southwest-border-security.
79 Gidda, Mirren. "As Routes to Europe Close, Refugees Are Starting to Consider One of the Oldest and Deadliest Crossings." *Newsweek*, April 12, 2016.
80 Honig, Bonnie. *Democracy and the Foreigner*. Princeton: Princeton University Press, 2001, at 61–2.
81 Benhabib, *Dignity in Adversity*, at 96–7.
82 I am grateful to Rainer Baubock for pointing this out to me, at APSA 2015.
83 Nicolaïdis, Kalypso. "Europe's Ends." In *The Meanings of Europe: Changes and Exchanges of a Contested Concept* edited by Claudia Wiesner and Mieke Schmidt-Gleim, 236–57. London: Routledge, 2014, at 250–4.

Part II

The Ports of Entry

5   The Tiniest Constable: Big Data, Security and the *Politics of Identification*

You know the TSA. We're the ones who make you take off your shoes before padding through a metal detector in your socks (hopefully without holes in them). We're the ones who make you throw out your water bottles. We're the ones who end up on the evening news when someone's grandma gets patted down or a child's toy gets confiscated as a security risk. If you're a frequent traveler, you probably hate us.

– Former director of the Transportation Security
Administration (TSA), Kip Hawley 2012.[1]

All cargo is not created equal ... No package will ever complain about being profiled.

– Mike Rogers, Subcommittee
on Transportation Security, 2011.[2]

No theorist has understood the problem of boundaries better than Michel Foucault, who in his lectures at the College de France, engages a thoughtful discussion on the spatial organization of late medieval towns. In the Middle Ages, towns were bounded spaces: they had walls. This physical manifestation of security enabled a clear division between those who were cozy and safe within the city, and those who were excluded – abandoned to the desolation of the surrounding woods. However, a great change occurred in the eighteenth century, when cities no longer walled themselves. In short order, the constraints on town life were lifted and denizens were free to move in and out as they pleased. In one sense this was freedom embodied; but in another sense it signified its end, as without walls local conditions frequently deteriorated into banditry and violence. Thus, the removal of the city walls actually led to a reduction of liberty – in this sense, the capacity to flourish without fear of bodily harm. Without boundaries, the familiar friend/enemy distinction blurred; suddenly anyone was potentially an enemy. To correct this shortcoming – to enable freedom without boundaries – cities and towns in the modern period developed means of surveillance.

Borderlessness led to the need for an internal policing regime, rather than simply an external one. Foucault writes:

An important problem for towns in the eighteenth century was allowing for surveillance, since the suppression of city walls made necessary by economic development meant that one could no longer close towns in the evening or closely supervise daily comings or goings, so that the insecurity of the towns was increased by the influx of the floating population of beggars, vagrants, delinquents, criminals, thieves, murderers, and so on, who might come, as everyone knows, from the country.[3]

Foucault captures a dialectic of motion and boundedness at the core of modern freedom. What Foucault understood was that the question facing political units was not whether to have walls, but where they would be situated. If not at the limit of the polity, than at the steps of one's door; if not at the edge of the state, then at the edge of the individual. Walzer makes a similar point in *Spheres of Justice*, namely that if you eliminate walls around states, you merely relocate them around cities: "To tear down the walls of the state is not ... to create a world without walls, but rather to create a thousand petty fortresses."[4] The same relationship is evident in contemporary Europe: the increased freedom of movement brought by the Schengen accords produced a need for high exterior walls, and a robust internal surveillance regime within, or as Didier Bigo remarks, "*some free movement of people* and goods but a *freedom under surveillance.*"[5]

The metaphor of Fortress Europe captures the general sentiments we have about borders and border walls. In fortresses, people on the inside are safe, they can move about. It is the people on the outside that are left in the cold. But is this really the metaphor that governs modern states? In fact, internal surveillance and restrictions on movement are increasing for everyone. The last years have seen a rise in data collection – surveillance – at all levels (global, domestic), with the same purpose of aiding the state in corralling globalized mobility. As David Lyon identifies, in the modern globalized world, two freedoms are put into contrast: freedom of movement, and freedom of anonymity (privacy): "If people wish to travel, or even see 'freedom of movement' as a right, then to engage that freedom identity must be demonstrated in ways that link individuation and control."[6] The tool of this endeavor is data, with ports and perimeters working together as part of a consolidated system of border security.

This chapter turns our attention to the ports of entry, especially after 9/11. At the ports, the move toward securitization is not embodied by images of walls and fences, but a related process of invasive data-driven security protocols. This chapter examines the securitization at the ports of entry specifically *within* the US, focusing on the shift toward risk-conscious policies designed to simultaneously "let in the good" and "keep out the bad."[7] Here too, metaphors are helpful: just as the changes at the perimeter turned *walls* into *moats*, the changes at the ports have turned *bridges* into *filters*. As DHS explains, its strategy is to

identify, document, and vet border travel and trade traffic in transit, as early as is necessary to determine risk and evaluate legitimacy. Once we have determined the risk of a particular person or shipment, we can prioritize our time and resources in order to expedite lower-risk traffic and focus resources on higher-risk traffic.[8]

Effective filtration is easy to demand but tricky to obtain, due to a central dilemma: if borders have more checks they impede trade; fewer checks diminish security. The solution is to increase the quality and selectivity of checks – i.e., create "smart" ports – such that the *good* is let in quickly, and only the *risky* are slowed down. Obtaining this balance requires filtering flows according to risk, a process that depends heavily on data – both biometric and biographic – captured at or in advance of border ports, and used to verify identities at the gate. In this way, filtration is derived from data management practices in which complex algorithms cull and interpret data to categorize travelers based on their expected "risk."

That ports of entry act as spaces of filtration is the result of their own remarkable evolution. Immediately after 9/11 port security meant increased invasive checks. This produced tremendous criticism of the heavy-handed methods of the TSA and outcry against the government's increasing reliance of data-based surveillance, alternately termed "dataveillance," the "surveillance-industrial complex," or the "identity-industrial complex."[9] However, just as with the perimeter, in subsequent years the "big bang theory" of port security came to be seen as ineffective. As a result, port securitization has undergone a major transition from "minimal security checks" to, immediately after 9/11, "more security checks for all," and finally to today's variant, "security checks for some more than others," via risk-based filtration. This is pursuant to the discussion of post-9/11 securitization writ large, but while the original push led to the restriction of flows, the new one embraces them.

In introducing this Part on ports, this chapter dedicates a lot of space to unpacking the basics of data usage in governance – and in particular, the parallel processes of *Classification, Filtration* and *Capture* that forge a link between border security and new data protocols. At the ports, this strategic shift is manifest in policies toward the capture and accommodation of data, which can be used in the separation of travel and cargo into risky and non-risky categories – the *politics of identification*. One example of this is Trusted Traveler-type programs, which gather data on prospective travelers and distinguish between them according to risk. In addition to this policy shift toward traveler filtering, there is also an associated infrastructural shift in ports, as they adapt to become locations of data capture, analysis and verification. Parallel to the perimeter, ports are also getting wider and deeper, taking on expansive new functions.

This empirical material raises large questions, beginning with the changing relationship between state and citizen, especially as part of the expanding project of state *rationalization* – or the management of a state by scientific principles, designed to maximize the state's capacity to control the totality of its subjects, to distinguish between them as individuals, and manage them with refined specificity. The development of the modern state was treated briefly in Chapter 1, but this discussion will expand upon the understanding presaged there, with Big Data considered its most recent, and in some sense most perfect variant. This is manifest in Justice Alito's remark that the surveillance power of data is like having a "tiny constable" on hand all the time.

This introduces a host of concerns, especially in terms of the relationship between new security protocols and freedom. One pertains to normalization. This is the idea that through filtration and categorization the state polices normal behavior, and penalizes forms of deviance. Another harm of this type of system can be best expressed as a form of invasion, the permeation of our innermost boundaries. In the creation of many data worlds, and data doubles – the composite of digital records that replicate the individual – there is no escape from being monitored by the state. Further, state rationalization engenders a world of totalizing institutions, which can have a dampening effect on human agency, or the capacity of an individual to self-shape, outside of the involvement of the state. This has ramifications not just for freedom, but also security – in this sense, our ability to feel secure in our everyday lives as citizens of a state.

Border Security *at the Ports of Entry* of the United States – 2001–2016

On September 11, 2001, nineteen terrorists turned airplanes into weapons, the greatest breach of port security in modern history. In several cases the airport filtration system, designed to prevent dangerous travelers from reaching the air, succeeded in flagging the potential offenders, but follow-up screening proved ineffective. In other cases, obvious candidates for screening simply slipped through. The mixture of the enormity of the attacks, and the obvious failure in existing security precipitated a total overhaul of US ports of entry – beginning with airports, but expanding to include all others.

The first pertinent law in this evolution, the Aviation and Transportation Security Act (ATSA), passed on November 19, 2001, established the Transportation Security Administration (TSA) charged with securing all forms of US transportation, including the civil aviation system, and all air carrier operations, foreign and domestic with service into and out of the US.[10] TSA's first task was to screen all passengers, baggage and cargo transported by aircraft. This seems banal today, however, previously screening was the responsibility of airlines, frequently outsourced to private contracting firms. In fact, until 1972, the Federal Aviation Administration did not require any screening of passengers at all – airport authorities actually were forbidden from overseeing internal checkpoints, which were considered the dominion of airline carriers. The new ATSA administration enforced in-person interviewing at airport checkpoints, first established as a trial in 2002. We are all familiar with the basic interrogation; ticket agents were legally obliged to ask:

Have any of the items you're traveling with been out of your immediate control since the time you packed them?

Has anyone unknown to you asked you to carry an item aboard the aircraft?[11]

Passengers were obliged to pass through metal detectors, with their carry-on subject to X-rays. The TSA also mandated cargo screening – an enormous endeavor, as to this point, cargo was almost entirely un-monitored.

In 2004, with the passage of the Intelligence Reform and Terrorism Prevention Act (IRTPA), DHS was empowered to compare traveler flight information with federal government watch lists – such as the No Fly list, or one of several terrorist watch lists. This was a central demand of the 9/11 Commission report, finally codified into law on October 28, 2008 as the Secure Flight Final Rule. This was a critical first step in the utilization of data toward determining whether travelers are "risky" or "not-risky."

This revolution in airport security was echoed in other ports of entry. Maritime ports received an enormous financial appropriation in January 2002 with the creation of the Port Security Grant Program (PSGP), which afforded subsidies to the bolstering of national seaports; continued appropriations were later codified into law as the Maritime Transportation Security Act (MTSA). In 2006, maritime port security was further augmented by the Security and Accountability For Every Port Act of 2006 (the "SAFE Port Act") – largely a response to the Dubai Ports World scandal, the prospective sale of port management rights at US ports to a company based in the United Arab Emirates. The sale fell through, but the controversy raised awareness over the degree to which foreign owners controlled US port assets. The SAFE Port Act enacted a number of regulations to protect US sovereignty over ports, and increase safety measures. This included the creation of the Transportation Worker Identification Credential (TWIC), an ID card that enabled the screening of all individuals working on US ports, the Container Security Initiative (CSI) which guaranteed the screening of all cargo at ports, and the enforcement of the Customs-Trade Partnership against Terrorism (C-TPAT).

All told, in the decade after 9/11 (2001–2011) the Port Security Grant Program, pulled in a remarkable and unprecedented 2.5 billion dollars for seaport security. One expert in maritime port security describes this evolution succinctly:

> Since 9/11 we have really changed the paradigm of how we look at cargo security. Facilities as well have a lot more security plans, and security officers – ten years ago, many ports did not even have security, they had their safety person and they kind of did security. Now most ports have a dedicated security force.[12]

The same rise is evident at land ports of entry. Since the passing of the American Recovery and Reinvestment Act of 2009, the US has invested over $400 million to renovate more than thirty ports of entry. However, this funding has been heavily skewed toward the US border with Canada. On the northern border, the number of CBP Officers at ports of entry increased from 2,721 officers in 2003 to approximately 3,700 officers in 2012. By contrast, the same focus on land ports has not materialized at US land ports with Mexico. Since the main concern with the southern land borders is the transit of drugs and migrants from Mexico, this is considered more the domain of the *perimeter* rather than the *ports*. As the former Attorney General of Arizona explains, on the US–Mexico border, perimeter security and port security are treated as zero sum, causing "the buildup of the Border Patrol at the expense of customs enforcement."[13]

Despite the immense investment in port security, concerns over port vulnerability were significant (and loudly voiced), during this initial phase, with most criticisms of port security focused on the TSA. For example, intra-agency audits have exposed how simple it is to bring weapons onto planes – including guns and bombs. One 2009 report revealed airport security failed in twenty-four out of thirty-two tests across the country – sneaking knives onto planes 70 percent of the time, bombs 60 percent, and guns 30 percent of the time; the following year, undercover checks by federal agents (aka "red team tests") at major airports, found that at Newark, bombs and guns were undetected twenty out of twenty-two times, at LAX fifty out of seventy, and O'Hare forty-five out of seventy-five.[14] All told, there was skepticism over whether the increased checks at airports had any positive impact on security.

While garnering less publicity, maritime ports have also received criticism. Initial exuberance of the possibility of full scanning of all cargo at seaports quickly dissipated, and in 2010 DHS Secretary Janet Napolitano claimed that hundred percent scanning was not feasible. As of 2012, while over two billion tons of freight cross US borders through our ports, less than three percent was scanned.[15] Further, there have been consistent breaches of supply chain procedures. According to an audit by the Office of the Inspector General, this is true both in terms of the initial validation process (who qualifies for secure transit) and subsequent validation and data maintenance.

At land borders, increased checks proved least feasible of all, due to economic costs. For example, at the US–Canada border in the immediate aftermath of 9/11 some accounts place the increased wait-times due to security measures as going from "one or two minutes to between 10 and 15 hours," with trucks backed up as much as thirty-six kilometers.[16] Similar costs were apparent at US–Mexico land ports. Remnants of this security exuberance exists to this day.

In short, the vast increase of funds, attention and manpower at the ports immediately after 9/11 did not necessarily provide favorable results. This has led to a considerable shift in strategy, away from "more scrutiny for all" to a "scrutiny for some more than others" approach – i.e., one that privileges risk assessment. There are two aspects of this risk strategy – *profiling* (increasing surveillance for the most risky) and *trusting* (decreasing surveillance for the least risky). Both of these processes require enormous amount of data – referred to as Big Data. This re-prioritization is radically transforming ports of entry.

Big Data & Biometrics – A Primer

Security at the ports of entry is driven by data (biometric and biographic) – so-called Big Data. Biometrics refers to the measurement of the human body – fingerprints, iris, face – and the translation of those measurements into unique data points. Big Data is the shorthand term for the massive accumulation of data in recent years, especially since the rise of social media, and full-force government efforts at data collection. According to the White House, Big Data can be understood as the "near-ubiquitous data collection where that data is being crunched at a speed increasingly approaching real-time."[17] More than any discrete "thing," Big Data represents a scale threshold. As one data analyst explains: "Last year we created over 1.8 zettabytes of information. Crudely put, we create as much information every two minutes as was created from the dawn of civilization up to 2003."[18] As of 2014 it is understood that the amount of extant data generated worldwide had reached four zettabytes.[19]

Another way to describe Big Data is through the so-called Three Vs, common in tech circles, which refers to the volume, velocity and variety of data, and which contribute to the rise of data's ubiquity and cheapness, and changes its fundamental character:

> For decades, there's been a fundamental tension between three attributes of databases. You can have the data fast; you can have it big; or you can have it varied. The catch is, you can't have all three at once ... [Today] analyzing data is trivially inexpensive. And when things become so cheap that they're practically free, big changes happen ... In the old, data-is-scarce model, companies had to decide what to collect first, and then collect it.[20]

Now we collect data first, and then ask questions later.

The data explosion is quite new, but the idea of collecting biometric data is not. The term "biometrics" was coined in the 1890s by one of the founders of statistics, and refers mainly to data derived from fingerprints. Facial recognition techniques had been used in law enforcement throughout the nineteenth century, beginning with sketches and then photographs, but the collection of fingerprints only began wholesale in the United States in 1904. Unlike body measurements (which could be precise but non-unique) and facial recognition (which could be unique but non-precise), fingerprints had the capacity to be both. For the last forty years, law enforcement has been dedicated to finding new forms of biometrics to capture, with the greatest breakthrough being the ability to analyze DNA, introduced in 1988.

Big Data also has a considerable history, if you take the long view. In some sense, the roots of Big Data lie in censuses, and agricultural tallies, which are ancient instruments. With the rise of more advanced forms of statistics in the seventeenth century, states began to measure polity-wide crime, marriage and suicide rates. The most familiar scientific study in this period was the natural experiment conducted by John Snow to test contaminated water in London. In the United States, data became a popular means of measuring economic efficiency, as in Frederick Winslow Taylor's use of a stopwatch to analyze floor output at Midvale Steel Works in Pennsylvania in 1911.

This said, it is no overstatement to say that we are living in an age of data revolution. This is because the Internet has become the site of nearly all forms of human interaction. We now carry the Internet with us wherever we go through phones, tablets, laptops, etc. These machines are two-way devices. They both bring the Internet to us, and also broadcast us – through data – back out into the world. The notion that technology is a data *site* is well known; we are only beginning to understand the fact that it is also a data *source*. That is, it is not merely receptive; it is *generative* – of our identities, our persons. There are many ways to describe these phenomena. One is to call it Internet 2.0, which highlights the idea that today the Internet is governed by so-called "User Generated Content," or that we are in a stage called the "Internet of Things," which emphasizes that increasingly technological devices communicate with each other.

A few more definitions are in order before proceeding. First, metadata. This refers to the transactions records about communications and documents, as opposed to their substantive content. Metadata is meaningful in that it is one of the means by which individuals shed data records, sometimes called "digital exhaust," or "trace data," that leaves behind more data records, such as geo-location. Second, the algorithm. This is a process, or set of rules, whereby computers can filter and analyze data according to categories and weights.[21]

So what is the point of Big Data? As far as the government is concerned, it makes the targeting of government services to citizens more precise – especially in sectors like health care and public safety. As we are primarily interested in questions of border security, here is how Homeland Security views Big Data:

Every day, two million passengers fly into, within, or over the United States. More than a million people enter the country by land. Verifying the identity of each person and determining whether he or she poses a threat falls to the Department of Homeland Security, which must process huge amounts of data in seconds to carry out its mission. The Department is not simply out to find the "needle in the haystack." Protecting the homeland often depends on finding the most critical needles across many haystacks – a classic big data problem.[22]

Data and the New Security Landscape

Predictably, government interest and investment in Big Data and biometrics burgeoned after 9/11, when data collection came to be seen as a panacea for patching holes in US immigration and border control. Speaking in 2013, Robert Mocny, Director of US-VISIT, described biometrics as the "ultimate identification tool across immigration and border security spectrums." He describes the evolution of US thinking as follows:

The tragic events of September 11th, 2001 raised awareness of gaps in what we collect, and how we collect and share information about foreign visitors …

And so, US-VISIT, the first large scale biometric identification program to support immigration and border management, was born. And now we have evolved into a biometric and biographic identity verification and analysis program. By infusing biometrics into the identity-screening process, we have changed – and I think revolutionized – immigration and border management on a global scale, provid[ing] actual, person-centric information and analysis to help decision-makers.[23]

US-VISIT employs two principle databases – or "identity verification systems," the Automated Biometric Identification System (IDENT) which collects biometric data, and the Arrival and Departure Information System (ADIS), which collects biographic data. The most important of these is IDENT, originally launched in 1995 by Border Patrol, as a means of stemming recidivism at the southwest border – mentioned in Chapter 2. This program has expanded to cover all aspects of border-crossings and immigration, providing identity information to departments throughout the government. Today, IDENT has over 150 million unique identities, and runs a watchlist of over 6.4 million people – including Known or Suspected Terrorists (KSTs), criminals, fugitives, immigrations violators and other "persons of interest" –verified by counter-IDs (over 450 million), as people are frequently encountered more than once. The numbers are awe-inspiring. As Patrick Nemeth, Deputy Assistant Director, US-VISIT, describes, they are "an identity services firm," involved in "production line biometrics."[24]

The second main database in DHS is ADIS, which is concerned with biographic data of people who travel into and out of the US, focused on their travel history and immigration status. As of 2013, ADIS has more than 270 million unique biographic identities, based on 1.9 billion encountered events – both banal ones, such as entries and exits, as well as over-extended visas or incompliance. There are two other biometric databases of note – the Department of Defense's ABIS and the Department of Justice's IAFIS (run by the FBI). New systems are being developed all the time, so that the state can match the new data capacities required. In 2012, two Big Data programs were launched by DHS, called Neptune and Cerberus, designed to be data aggregation sites – or "data lakes" – into which many different forms of unclassified information can be stored.

Just as there has been a landmark shift in the collection, management and storage of biometric data, there has also been a revolution in the sharing of data. This too is an outgrowth of 9/11, as the lack of data sharing within the government was considered largely to blame for the terrorist attack on US soil. One homeland security expert chronicles this evolution in intelligence as follows:

[Previously] the intelligence community's mantra was "need to know." The more important information was, the fewer people had access to it … Slowly we evolved from "need to know," to what became known as "need to share." Our great epiphany was to say: "if you need the information, and I've got the information, then by god, I should be sharing it with you to the best of my capabilities." Post 9/11, we have gone even farther than that, beyond "need to know" and "need to share," to "responsibility to provide." I need to give this information to you, whether you know you need it or not.[25]

Sharing within and across intelligence services in the US has become a popular buzzword, but it is easier said than done, as it requires the standardization of files and data entry protocols. This process is underway, and all current technologies funded by the federal government have interoperability in mind. Analysts variously call for systems that enable the "pattern-recognition of data," and tools that "normalize the data into readily searchable formats."[26] But standardization is no easy task. A report by the DHS Data Privacy and Integrity Advisory Committee explains the problem as being that different systems across the government "comprise a series of stovepipes, to support the unique functions of the distinct DHS components;" new DHS information-sharing projects are designed "to create a federated system."[27] Ideally, there would be an automated interface between systems, to make them quickly searchable, but right now sharing is described as "manual."[28] Standardization is essential because it enables coordinated matching – or what is called "back-end intelligence." This means running searches about individuals across several databases – domestically or internationally – to create a composite identity picture. In addition to matching prints or biometric records against other databases, standardization enables law enforcement officials to match records against watch lists. As one biometrics specialist describes, this process enables state officials to take these various search results and "stitch together a broader narrative."[29]

Data sharing is a growing reality within the US intelligence community, but it remains largely limited to fingerprints. Presently, state resources are being put toward the advancing other forms of biometric capture, such as iris and facial recognition – not to mention more far-fetched measures, such as gait, typeset or voice. The ideal, in the minds of most biometrics practitioners, is to use multiple methods of biometric matching to configure a subject – or what is called "multi-modal" biometrics. To this end, on December 31, 2012 a pilot program was launched bringing live-capture photos to the San Ysidro port, between San Diego and Tijuana, Mexico such that face, iris and fingers will all be captured and verified at the same time.

One senior official within the FBI technology division remarks that "the possibilities within biometrics are endless,"[30] as the biometrics "frontier is just developing."[31] What is essential for the argument leveled on these pages is that ports lie at the center of this strategy, as the sites at which data can be gathered, processed and applied.

Port Security and the *Politics of Identification*

The discussion that follows attempts to clarify the inner working of new securitized ports by breaking down the trends into three categories: *classification, filtration* and *capture*. *Classification* refers to the front-end processes, usually based off-site, that use algorithms and risk metrics to produce risk ratings. *Filtration* refers to the back-end policies that make use of this data at the port itself. *Capture* refers to the process whereby data is acquired, which is often off-site, but is increasingly part of the policies at the port itself.

Together, these facets comprise what I call *the politics of identification*, correcting an error in terminology common to both popular and scholarly discourse: we use the word *identification* to refer to the process of handing over documents at a border port or visa office, and say that documents such as passports *identify* us. This is incorrect. These procedures are part of a process called *identity verification*, or just *verification*. A photograph in a passport is compared to the face of the person presenting it to make sure that they are one and the same; a fingerprint scanner matches prints taken on site with those carried digitally on the ID chip. In addition to the relatively banal process of *verification*, there is a far more significant process afoot: *identification*, or the process of *creating identities*. This is the process performed in the databanks back at headquarters, where biometrics are matched onto individual data-records, alongside all other existing datapoints about the individual – this latter data is not just *biometric* but also *biographic*. *Identity* is thus the complex amalgam of biometrics, biographics, behavioral data, and social media and other forms of ready-made data; as such, it far exceeds the physical individual it putatively represents. Identity creation is the core of the identity infrastructure as it is here that risk ratings are produced – i.e. that an individual is flagged as a suspected terrorist, or linked to an illegal alien. In short: risky.

Identity creation is a growing field, with the goal of shaping robust identities from the clay provided by biometric and biographic data. A Department of Defense biometrics specialist explains that "total identity" includes all facets of identity including behavioral tendencies, and reputation – i.e. "what other people say about you, not what you say about yourself."[32] An expert in Big Data technologies describes the goal as going beyond the physical characteristics of an individual and toward cultivating "a 360 view of that individual."[33] This requires the bridging of biometric and biographic data. The goal is no longer simple authentication, but to paint a portrait of individual trustworthiness. This is pursuant to the "person-centric" view of security, considered the future of intelligence.

This person-centric view is possible exclusively because of the process of identity creation so described, as this data drives risk algorithms to determine who should be flagged and for what reasons – i.e. the process of *creating* identities, which are later to be *verified*. The goal of identity creation is, not just to describe identities but also to use existing data to model future behavior and create predictive risk assessments – i.e. "to predict events, based on patterns of behaviour,"[34] and to "to uncover, characterize, understand and potentially even predict threat-actors before they act."[35]

Classification

The ports are increasingly driven by data, with judgments parsed according to risk ratings. But what goes into a risk rating? The filtering of Big Data according to risk is a process known as classification, which is changing the nature of statecraft, due to the capacity to use Big Data to data mine. This is meaningful because now the state can find things about individuals that it *didn't even look for*. There are several steps in this process that warrant mention.

The first major capacity enabled by Big Data is *profiling* – a fact of which we are familiar in terms of consumer data, but less familiar (and perhaps less accepting) with regards to the state. As it has roots in consumer targeting, its helpful to detail how data can be broken down and categorized for the purposes of advertisements:

Data brokers aggregate purchase patterns, activities on a website, mobile, social media, ad network interactions, or direct customer support, and then further "enhance" it with information from public records or other commercially available sources. That information is used to develop a profile of a customer, whose activities or engagements can then be monitored to help the marketer pinpoint the message to send and the right moment to send it ... [Precise categories] identify populations for targeted advertising. Some of these categories include "Ethnic Second-City Strugglers," "Retiring on Empty: Singles," "Tough Start: Young Single Parents," "Credit Crunched: City Families," and "Rural and Barely Making It." These products include factual information about individuals as well as "modeled" elements inferred from other data.[36]

The same process happens politically with individual-level targeting, essentially data-driven discrimination. But here discrimination is a feature, not a bug – it is the essential way by which the good traffic is distinguished from the bad. Thus, data systems discriminate based on supposed "riskiness." This is something we should be wary about, given that these systems might also discriminate based on ascriptive characteristics of individuals (race, gender, etc.) irrespective of their place in risk matrices. For example, the US program E-verify has recently come under fire by the ACLU for categorizing minorities unfairly.[37]

This civil liberties angle will not be treated here – at least as regards intentional discrimination (a political problem). However, there is also *inadvertent* discrimination (a technological problem). This is prevalent with biometrics, especially those that use facial recognition software, in which race is an explicit target. As such we might doubt whether even inadvertent forms of discrimination are ever *actually* inadvertent. The reason we might question this goes back to the essential nature of algorithms, which is that while they may be scientific, they are still established by people. This point is captured well here:

> The steps taken by an algorithm are informed by the author's knowledge, motives, biases, and desired outcomes. The output of an algorithm may not reveal any of those elements, nor may it reveal the probability of a mistaken outcome, arbitrary choice, or the degree of uncertainty in the judgment it produces … The final computer-generated product or decision – used for everything from predicting behavior to denying opportunity – can mask prejudices while maintaining a patina of scientific objectivity.[38]

This concern is borne out by the sheer fact that data-based surveillance policies appear to target familiar subjects – immigrants, overstayers, drug users, welfare recipients, and of course anyone that could have any tie to terrorism (however distant). Data provides a more perfect means of distinguishing these forms of "others" from the rest of the "non-risky" population, but the actual practice is familiar from government policies for centuries – even internal programs, such as the ongoing war on drugs.

The second feature worth highlighting, and of far greater consequence (potentially), is that of *predictive analytics*, or the process by which different data sources are brought together to create a composite image of an individual, such that behaviors and preferences can be predicted. For example, the Chicago Police Department has developed a "heat list" which uses information held in police records to generate an index of people most likely to commit a violent crime. The Legislative Counsel of the ACLU discusses the problem with predictive profiling as follows: "The criteria for placement on the list are secret but reportedly go beyond indicators like criminal conviction, and raise real questions about racial bias in the selection process ... One person reported that a Chicago police commander showed up at his door to let him know the police would be watching him. He hadn't committed a crime or even recently interacted with police."[39] Predictive analytics is perhaps the most unique and interesting of the new features of Big Data. The civil liberties concerns raised here are manifold, and clearly present a threat to the vaunted notion of innocent-until-proven-guilty, as "the harvesting of data to try and ascertain who is likely to commit a crime places individuals who have done nothing wrong under suspicion."[40]

The problem of prediction – and police over-reach – is new vis-à-vis data. But it is also an old problem. For example, J. S. Mill expresses his concerns about the overreach of police doing preventative work, when he writes: "It is one of the undisputed functions of government to take precautions against crime before it has been committed, as well as to detect and punish it afterwards. The preventative function of government, however, is far more liable to be abused, to the prejudice of liberty, than the punitory function."[41] The normative significance of predictive analytics is treated below.

Filtration

Drawing on the *processes* treated above, this section outlines the *policies* that enable filtration, focusing on trusted traveler programs that gather data on travelers and categorize them according to risk-likelihood. These programs have existed in a localized capacity for some time; however, the government-wide expansion of trusted traveler programs was first placed before Congress in July 2010. In 2012, DHS published a set of objectives that prioritized the speedy and secure flow of people and goods – i.e. to "manage risk posed by people and goods in transit."[42] To accommodate these programs there is an associated infrastructural shift at ports, as they adapt to become locations of data capture (treated below), analysis and verification. Parallel to the perimeter, border ports are also getting wider, and deeper, and taking on vast new functions.

The logic of trusted traveler programs is twofold: expedite low-risk travel, to facilitate global commerce; increase screening and filtration of high-risk travel to prevent terrorism, and the passage of guns and drugs. Trusted traveler programs achieve both of these aims at once, as travel is reduced at regular gates, which allows officials to focus on preventing malfeasance. Participation in trusted traveler programs is voluntary, as applicants consent to providing personal information (biographic and biometric), which enable background checks by law enforcement officials to determine whether they are "low risk." In return, the successful applicant enjoys expedited processing at the port of entry. The central database cross-checked during the vetting process for trusted travelers is the Treasury Enforcement Communication System/Integrated Border Inspection System (TECS/IBIS), which includes data on previous law enforcement encounters, as well as access to numerous other databanks. Any individual deemed to be "high risk," is denied entry into the trusted traveler program, with their information kept on file for future scrutiny.[43]

In recent years, trusted traveler programs have expanded at an extraordinary rate. The original trusted traveler programs began as part of the Global Enrollment System (GES) of the former Immigration and Naturalization Service (INS), as early as March 1997. In 2002, as part of the Homeland Security Act, the GES was incorporated into CBP databases. The first wave of trusted traveler programs included Free And Secure Trade (FAST), Immigration and Naturalization Service Passenger Accelerated Service System (INSPASS), and Secure Electronic Network for Travelers Rapid Inspection (SENTRI) – each of which were localized programs, mediating traveler and cargo shipments at different points along the northern and southwest borders, as well as at specified air and maritime ports. Thus, standardization is a priority. The Terrorist Screening Database (TSDB) was recently created in order to make all authorities privy to the same information – what the Terrorist Screening Center (TSC) refers to as "one-stop shopping."[44] These new centralized filtration programs are aided by the new e-Passports, issued by the State Department in 2005, which carry the data to be cross-checked against the databanks.

The last few years has witnessed a veritable explosion of trusted traveler programs, with many millions now enrolled and has expanded to include programs whereby businesses too can agree to be vetted in exchange for expedited travel – programs known variously as "Trusted Shipper" or "Trusted Cargo." An exhaustive discussion of existing trusted traveler programs is unnecessary here. However, some examples are elucidating. One set of programs run by the TSA is Pre[check] and Secure Flight (they operate in tandem, as the former garners data, which the latter processes and checks). TSA Pre[check], launched in 2011, is a pre-screening initiative, which works not only with port administrations (CBP) but also frequent flyer programs from specific airlines; it is a fee-based program, in exchange for which approved travelers are not obliged to remove their shoes, and belts, nor liquids from their carry-on. TSA Pre[check] works alongside Secure Flight, a "behind-the-scenes watch list matching program" designed in accordance with the Intelligence Reform and Terrorism Prevention Act of 2004 (IRTPA), which enables the TSA to match individual travelers (based on data from US and foreign airlines) to federal watch lists.[45] As of November 2010, Secure Flight was operational for all international flights to or from the US. The goal is for these programs to expand to the point where expedited security lanes are as common as regular ones.

Capture

Thus far, this chapter has chronicled two contemporaneous trends: first, the realization after 9/11 that port security was woefully inadequate and that simply increasing the quantity of checks would be insufficient; second, that along with this awareness came enormous changes in capacity and political will toward the exploration of biometrics and data. These trends are mutually entwined. To make ports safe, travelers must be segmented by risk, a process driven by data-accumulation, much of which arrives in advance of the port itself. This is why *the ports depend on data-accumulation*. But outside of law enforcement and occasional military operations, the state can only gather data on people who want to travel into or out of the United States. Thus, nearly all biometric data is procured in advance of the border, or at the border, and verified at the port itself. This is why *data accumulation depends on the ports*.

The principle reason for the truth of this latter point is that, by and large, biometrics have to be captured *in situ*. Fingerprints obviously need one-to-one contact with a state official; even iris and face recognition must be within a fairly narrow range. Thus, accurate biometrics capture *has* to occur at the border, or in advance of the border (in the case of visas), and in either case it must be verified at the border. This is a technological point; but it is also a political one. The border is one of the few places where biometrics can be captured *legally*. Neither the FBI nor the DoD can collect biometric data from people that they do not already have cause to pursue. Thus, even the best technology is only useful at "contact points" – with ports of entry being the primary locations. To this end, even the military increasingly relies on the ports for biometrics. As one biometrics expert explains that from the DoD perspective, all modes of biometric capture "require some kind of cooperative contact ... whether you are taking fingerprints, or an iris, or photograph, maybe voice, maybe DNA. [You] can really only do it in set encounter points [such as an] international border."[46] The DoD is restricted because there are few military encounters that warrant biometric capture. The FBI is also limited, as unless US citizens are charged with a crime, they cannot be fingerprinted.

Thus, the entire system of data collection hinges greatly on the ports. This is our main filtration and data-verification point, and thus the locus of the shift in US strategy toward risk. And of course, this fact has brought upon material changes at the ports. To better evaluate risk at the port of entry – i.e. to attain the maximal amount of information about travelers before they get to the gate – the physical infrastructure must itself be expanded. This is not merely a matter of size or scale, but rather the structural redesign of ports space to accommodate risk-based filtration. This is not just prevalent at airports but also at land ports. The expansion we see at ports of entry occurs in two dimensions: they are getting "wider" – as in, they stretch farther along the perimeter – to enable a broader typology of lanes (as per trusted traveler), but also "thicker" – as in, expanding inland from the perimeter – to enable pre-screening in advance of the border itself. In the language of the US government, this is referred to as "layered security," which sees the increased layers of detection at ports of entry as "force multipliers." As one tech specialist explains, the most important future trend in bordering is "the ability to identify people at a distance … way beyond the line, before you get to the border;" another contends that the future of bordering lies in "pre-primary gates," where biometric identification is captured and processed in advance of the gate itself.[47]

Because of the great potential of ports of entry as sites of data accumulation, new technology is currently being developed to facilitate, not just new forms of biometric capture, but also those that work *remotely*. On this point, a central purchase of face- and iris-recognition is that it can be indirect, making it far less intrusive – i.e. non-cooperative. This is considered the cutting edge of biometrics, and comes with a host of normative concerns. After all, while there are legal prohibitions against *un*-cooperative capture, there is nothing that suggests against *non*-cooperative capture – as in the capture of facial images from remote cameras in a terminal. This is as much a concern over privacy as *anonymity*. Assuming *non-cooperative* biometric capture continues to take hold, then ports – especially *thick* ones, will only increase in importance. This is manifest in land ports with the example of automobiles. For example, Radio Frequency Identification (RFID) technology provides a reading of all information carried on identification cards within a considerable radius of the border, allowing CBP officials time to know if any suspected travelers are approaching, well in advance of the border. The goal now is not merely to have advanced databases of information available to border guards, but to have that information processed in the zone of crossing itself. An advertisement from a port technology firm crystallizes these points:

When a car pulls into a lane, a license plate reader captures the read license plate. As the vehicle proceeds it then encounters a driver camera, which takes a picture of the passengers. Next, the RFID antenna reads occupant RFID-enabled travel documents while a second license plate reader captures the front license plate and a scene camera takes a picture of the vehicle to assess its make and model. The system then sends the information to a backend system, which integrates with various databases from CBP, state Departments of Motor Vehicles (DMV), DOS, and other U.S. and international organization databases to retrieve data on both the passengers and the vehicle ... As a result of these various readers and integration with backend databases, the CBP officer has a wealth of information on the vehicle and its occupants as the vehicle reaches the primary inspection booth.[48]

The same can be said of individuals at airports. Examples of new traveler pre-screening technology designed for biometric capture include walk-through portals that capture images of the iris up to three meters away, while the traveler advances through layers of inspection. Technology firms also market portable biometric devices, such that CBP officials can rove through lines at the outer periphery of ports garnering information.[49]

As one biometric specialist within DoD remarks, current biometric capture devices that "conform to the model of collecting biometrics from cooperative individuals" are not sufficient. "The next generation of devices need to capture information from the full range of subjects, including un-cooperative and non-cooperative individuals."[50] For most biometrics experts the future lies in face recognition technology, as it enables the most accurate non-cooperative biometrics capture – or a "Face-Based 'Bad Guy' Lookout."[51]

Either way, the deeper the port, the more likely that either iris or face can be captured before the gate itself. There is little doubt that this is the way of the future. Moreover, it is here more than anywhere else that it is clear that – contra globalization-era thinking that the border was losing its relevance – borders are actually at the center of a geo-strategic shift toward individual-centric threat assessment that is occurring worldwide.

Data and Its Discontents

Before closing this section, it is worth mentioning a few of the problems facing Big Data. The most general concern about Big Data is a techno-logical one – misidentification – i.e. that an individual may be acciden-tally appended a risk rating that is incorrect, due to reasons out of their control and unbeknownst to them. At present, even the best biometric systems have a 90+ percent match-rate, which when scaled over hundreds of millions of people renders a non-trivial number of errors – not to mention errors in coding either in the front-end (data capture) or back-end (data processing) of the equation. A data specialist from the FBI was vocal on this point:

> We need better algorithms. Specifically, advanced algorithms with high reliability that scale to large data sets. Even with the reliability of 99.6% [the FBI] is convinced it might still be missing 720 identifications per day. What complicates these missing identifications is the amount of data we are dealing with – 99.6% reliability is pretty good when you are dealing with 100 people, but what about 100 million people? New algorithms must support large-scale [searches] to address big data.[52]

Another analyst I interviewed explains: "My fear is that the accidental dissemination of incorrect data could ruin someone's identity ... You are putting some confidence in that algorithm. None of them are perfect. They make mistakes."[53] Another describes the problems of specious connections: "There is a seductiveness to Big Data, being able to do easy link analysis that can actually occlude the real relationships they represent ... [we must be careful] because analysts make mistakes and false-positive linkages."[54] Systems are in place to solve such concerns – such as redress centers. But how often does we seek redress of risk ratings about which we are unaware?

A central concern over misidentification pertains to the question of context. Data sharing means taking particular pieces of data from one arena and applying it to another. Algorithms can establish connections between data-points, but cannot provide a holistic picture linking these different sources of information. Indeed, for sharing to truly be effective, databases have to be "data-source agnostic." In other words, if two databases are actually merged, and the sources fully trust each other, then the source of that data should in principle be irrelevant. However, such merging eliminates some of the most important aspects of the narrative that aid decision making about individual cases. As one analyst explains, biometric architecture enables the merging of two templates and providing a similarity score. This is helpful in that it merges disparate data points into a single identity, but the nature of this link itself is obscure: "The contextual stuff got stripped away a few layers ago ... What not many systems do is really indicate why you get that link. Who was responsible for it, what technology was used, what matching techniques were used, what was the confidence of that?[55]

There are technological solutions to some of these concerns, although their efficacy remains partial. One solution to concerns over misidentification is to at least protect privacy by removing personal information from data. This is referred to as the notion of "de-identification," or "anonymizing" – i.e. detaching personally identifiable information (PII), such that even those with access to databases cannot match data points to specific people. This seems like a reasonable solution: if PII is removed from data, what harm can it do to individuals? Perhaps nothing. The concern instead is that state practice is thus governed by a conflicting set of incentives: the more you cleanse data of PII, the more privacy is protected but the less useful it becomes. An analyst within the private sector raises this point:

We are still struggling over how to [use big data] … How do you take a huge dataset, and strip out all of the personal identifying information, anonymize it, sanitize it and still have it be useful, to be able to tell something?[56]

Further, this is only a partial solution, as technologies exist toward re-identification – such as by what is called "the 'mosaic effect,' whereby personally identifiable information can be derived or inferred from datasets that do not even include personal identifiers, bringing into focus a picture of who an individual is and what he or she likes."[57]

It would also be inaccurate to suggest that problems of misidentification are only *technological*, and not also *political*. At present, state algorithms are *too* sensitive, picking up hundreds of thousands of potential points of threat per day – far more than analysts within the government can process. At this point, given the glut of data, nearly anyone can be linked to potential threats in one way or another. As one Big Data expert explains: "an analyst these days has to be very, very sensitive to degrees of association on the Internet … you can link anyone to a bad actor in one or two degrees on the Internet."[58] The philosophy here is: catch more, even if you have to throw some back. From the vantage of the state, there is a tradeoff between accuracy (which takes time) and efficiency (which requires speed). This is made clear by the statements of Terrorist Screening Center Director Christopher Piehota, about the standards for American citizens being put onto a watchlist:

If we make the standards too high, we're going to miss people, potentially, who are suspected terrorists who may be in the planning or plotting phases, we will miss them … If we make it too low, then we will impact the privacy and the civil liberties of the public.[59]

This translates to a choice between what is best for citizens as individuals (liberty) and what is in the interests of the collective (security) – an issue revisited below.

Big Data and The State

This chapter raises large questions about the nature of state and citizen in this period of raised security, treating port security as part of the enduring problem of state *rationalization*. This story could be told in a number of ways, using any number of thinkers. This section focuses on the writings of Michel Foucault as he renders clearest the link between rationalization and security.

What does it mean for a state to be *rational*? Broadly, it is the management of state functions by scientific principles, designed to maximize the state's capacity to control the *totality* of its subjects, to distinguish between them as *individuals*, and manage them with refined specificity. The rational state embodies various processes of *differentiation*, whereby discrete items are distinguished and categorized, and *institutionalization*, or the process by which the state takes on the role of organizer, overseer and regulator. These lines of thought are brought together for Foucault in what he calls governmentality, which he defines as "the ensemble formed by institutions, procedures, analyses and reflections, calculations, and tactics that … has the population as its target, political economy as its major form of knowledge, and apparatuses of security as its essential technical instrument."[60] In this way, security is the engine of rational state power – especially in its more targeted form, "its capillary forms of existence, the point where power reaches into the very grain of individuals, touches their bodies, and inserts itself into their very actions and attitudes, their discourses, learning processes, and everyday lives."[61]

The modern state has always been interested in individualization. Starting in the sixteenth century, the state began to institutionalize the individuating capacity of Christianity, resulting in what Foucault calls "pastoral power," which focuses not merely on the community, but each individual within it. It is a kind of power that "cannot be exercised without knowing the inside of people's mind, without exploring their souls, without making them reveal their innermost secrets. It implies a knowledge of the conscience and an ability to direct it."[62] This process of statecraft, bent on the individuation of subjects, carried through into the eighteenth century, with religious vestiges increasingly being replaced by secular forms of authority (and especially policing), but which retained the aims of pastoralism:

We can see the state as a modern matrix of individualization, or a new form of pastoral power ... [Its objective] was a question no longer of leading people to their salvation in the next world but, rather, ensuring it in this world. And in this context, the word "salvation" takes on different meanings: health, well-being (that is, sufficient wealth, standard of living), security, protection against accidents ... Concurrently the officials of pastoral power increased. Sometimes this form of power was exerted by state apparatus or, in any case, by a public institution such as the police ... The multiplication of the aims and agents of pastoral power focused on the development of knowledge of man around two roles: one, globalizing and quantitative, concerning the population; the other, analytical, concerning the individual.[63]

This idea that the state shepherds – and polices – its population is immediately familiar. It is what we now take self-evidently to be government. Here again, rational power is at once totalizing and individuating.

The nineteenth and twentieth century forms of rationalization are borne out in myriad accounts of the rise of bureaucracy. Marx, for example, discusses bureaucracy as a totalizing form of political authority: "The bureaucracy asserts itself to be the final end of the state ... The aims of the state are transformed into aims of bureaus, or the aims of bureaus into the aims of the state. The bureaucracy is a circle from which no one can escape."[64] For Carl Schmitt, rationalization was the ultimate modern nightmare, specifically the death of the political at the hands of the state machine: "There must no longer be political problems, only organizational-technical and economic-sociological tasks ... The modern state seems to have actually become what Max Weber envisioned: a huge industrial plant."[65]

Returning to the problem of port security, the central point of interest is individuation. At the same time as the rational state seeks to control its entire population, it also seeks to divide it into individuals, and establish modes of control at the individual level. There are several aspects of this. The first is the process of *conditioning and creating subjects*. For Foucault, modern power:

applies itself to immediate everyday life, categorizes the individual, marks him by his own individuality, attaches him to his own identity, imposes a law of truth on him that he must recognize and others have to recognize in him. It is a form of power that makes individuals subjects. There are two meanings of the word "subject:" subject to someone else by control and dependence, and tied to his own identity by a conscience or self-knowledge. Both meanings suggest a form of power that subjugates and makes subject to.[66]

The principle mechanisms by which power turns humans into subjects are what he calls "dividing practices" in which the "the subject is either divided inside himself or divided from others. This process objectivizes him."[67] Examples in his work are familiar: madness and sanity; illness and health, etc. These divisions are ways in which heterogeneous subjects can be grouped, divided and controlled – to which list we can now add risky and non-risky. This process is what Foucault calls the "government of individualization," which "separates the individual, breaks his links with others, splits up community life, forces the individual back on himself, and ties him to his own identity in a constraining way."[68]

To achieve this end, the rational state targets the body – clearly manifest today in the state's pursuit of biometrics. Foucault calls this biopolitics, or "the set of mechanisms through which the basic biological features of the human species became the object of a political strategy, of a general strategy of power."[69] The biopolitical subject is one who can be effectively filtered into categories of safe and risky – and who can self-categorize. This, for Foucault, is the essence of the state's *power*. To turn rough, ungainly subjects into smooth manipulable subjects – much in the way that potters grind stone into clay, and then mold it into replicable shapes. Agamben, takes this point a step further, claiming that "*the production of a biopolitical body is the original activity of sovereign power*."[70]

The final point, and perhaps the most important, is that this form of government *normalizes* – an outcome of both totalizing power and individuating power. This comes out clearly in Foucault's discussion of discipline, which turns individuals into a manageable form:

> Discipline, of course, analyzes and breaks down; it breaks down individuals, places, time, movements, actions, and operations. It breaks them down into components such that they can be seen, on the one hand, and modified on the other … and finally, on the basis of this, it establishes the division between those considered unsuitable or incapable and the others. That is to say, on this basis it divides the normal from the abnormal. Disciplinary normalization consists first of all in positing a model, an optimal model that is constructed in terms of a certain result, and the operation of disciplinary normalization consists in trying to get people, movements, and actions to conform to this model.[71]

This sets up an interesting paradox vis-à-vis port security: we as individuals are reduced into our role in the population at the precise moment that we are, through increasingly advanced forms of identification, most individualized. Thus, it is the disciplining of a population, paradoxically, through regulated individuation.

This discussion of individuation brings to the fore the problem of risk, which repositions the unknown as the greatest threat to the system – even over and above the substance of the threat itself. This is what the disciplinary mechanism is designed to address. Foucault makes this clear with regards to the penal system:

The disciplinary mechanism is characterized by the fact that a third personage, the culprit, appears within the binary system of the code, and at the same time, outside the code, and outside the legislative act that establishes the law.[72]

This is the nature of being risky – riskiness is an undefined state, except for what it isn't (namely normal; safe). It is an anticipated thing, a state to come. But it can never be predicted, because the real risk is unknown. This is what Foucault means when he describes the culprit as being at once within the binary system of code, and also, simultaneously, outside of that code. We have allotted a space for the risky subject, but need the subject to appear before we can define what that is. To this end, he makes an interesting contrast between law and discipline, where law leaves room for that which is unknown to be allowable; for discipline, what is unknown is precisely the least allowable: "In the system of the law, what is undetermined is what is permitted; in the system of disciplinary regulation, what is determined is what one must do, and consequently everything else, being undetermined, is prohibited."[73] Thus, while in the sphere of law, one is innocent until guilty; in the sphere of discipline, one is guilty until innocent.

The rise of Big Data in security protocols renders this distinction appreciable as never before. It is discipline's perfect, distilled form. These notions of individuation, division and normalization are essential to understanding the concerns we might have about the securitized ports of entry.

Big Data and the Subject

The question now becomes, what does this mean for the citizen? *What type of citizen – and subject – does data produce?* This section will not treat the question of civil liberties or constitutional challenges – subjects treated carefully by the American Civil Liberties Union.[74] Instead, this section will discuss other ways we might go about understanding the complex relationship between data and freedom – and in particular the harms embedded in the *politics of identification.*

Freedom-as-Uniqueness

One harm of rationalization derives from *normalization,* borne of the processes of filtration and categorization. This role is built into data design, and has always been the goal of the rational state. John Torpey, in his *The Invention of the Passport,* explains that passports can be imprisoning, in that they "discourage people from choosing identities inconsistent with

those validated by the state," making people "prisoners of their identities."[75] Put another way, such documents condition the subject by
structuring what we consider to be the rational, or natural way of things.
How do we understand this normalization as a harm? Concerns are
frequently voiced in the canon in the language of *restriction*. For example, J. S. Mill decried the overwhelming capacity of the modern social
sphere "to maim by compression, like a Chinese lady's foot, every part
of human nature which stands out prominently, and tends to make the
person markedly dissimilar in outline to commonplace humanity."[76]
Similarly, Nietzsche describes modernity as the "social straitjacket" by
which man was "made calculable."[77]

The most thorough treatment of the harms of classificatory schemes –
distinction – comes out in the writings of Pierre Bourdieu. For him,
categorization is what makes possible cognition and selfhood, but also
self-restriction. This internalization of boundaries leads people to self-
restrict from certain goods because they believe "that's not for the likes
of us." Such people are consistently "defining themselves as the established order defines them, reproducing in their verdict on themselves
the verdict the economy pronounces on them, in a word, condemn-
ing themselves to what is in any case their lot, *ta heautou*, as Plato
put it, consenting to be what they have to be, 'modest', 'humble' and
'obscure'."[78]

The concern is that data forces people into patterns of identification,
conditioning who they can be according to the state imposed norm. This
instantiates the harm of both non- and mis-recognition. As Charles Taylor
explains, "people can suffer real damage, real distortion, if the people or
society around them mirror back to them a confining or demeaning or
contemptible picture of themselves. Nonrecognition or misrecognition
can inflict harm, can be a form of oppression, imprisoning someone in a
false, distorted, and reduced mode of being."[79] Harms to identity of this
sort are an ethical concern. It is through our identities that we come to
feel ourselves to be fulfilled and free.

Freedom-as-Quiet

Another harm of rationalization can be expressed as a form of invasion,
the permeation of our innermost boundaries. This is the deepest meaning of privacy – i.e. what it is about privacy that we find essential to protect, and devastating to lose; a place where individuals can be at home in
themselves. This is a sanctum, a place of quiet. In the dataverse, this is
precisely what is least plausible.

Privacy is a complex notion that escapes clear definition, but at base refers to something like that right to be "let alone," defending the private sphere from the public one.[80] This idea of freedom from state imposition is *negative*, understood, following Isaiah Berlin, as the "absence of interference beyond the shifting, but always recognizable, frontier."[81] This stipulation of a boundary is important. We need to feel that there is an external restraint – a frontier, the inside of which is safe – even if the binary itself is fictitious.

But data has finally collapsed the boundary between state and subject to the point where the subject is internally invaded. This is a full affront to privacy, which is not just a freedom from surveillance; it is a freedom to disappear into a realm of personal quiet. Hannah Arendt provides guidance here: in her *Human Condition* she describes how the Greek work for freedom (*shkole*) means quiet.[82] That is, you were free when you had quiet from the hustle of the world and could have time to contemplate. For the modern self, totally saturated by technology, such freedom is unimaginable.

This matter was also taken up by Freud, who diagnosed a number of concerns about modernity, including the lack of separation between the self and the social – a point he too expressed in the language of quiet: "against the suffering which may come upon one from human relationships the readiest safeguard is voluntary isolation ... The happiness which can be achieved along the path is, as we see, the happiness of quietness."[83] Being unable to do this can lead to madness. More recently, this quality of the data-world has been expressed in the language of *saturation* – a theme that came to prominence in the 1990s with the proliferation of our myriad identity profiles, "data doubles," which leads to "a *multiphrenic* condition, in which one begins to experience the vertigo of unlimited multiplicity."[84]

State rationalization engenders a world of totalizing institutions, which can have a dampening effect on human agency. This brings us back to another sense of privacy, which is the ability of an individual to self-shape without state involvement. It is the freedom from being *determined*.

Freedom-as-Security

This chapter presents a story of bureaucracy taken to its fullest. We live now in a society in which evermore institutions and state officials enjoy authority over citizens. Thus, we live at the whim of overbearing and at times arbitrary power. We have to beg officials to let us past borders, and to certify our forms, thus forcing us into positions of humiliation and defense. As such, another variant of this story pertains not to the disciplinary side of data policies, but rather a particular facet of its nature – namely that its deployment is (and can seem to be) arbitrary. With data we are stifled by an invisible hand of information, a hidden text, that is itself dominating. Following Petit, being subject to arbitrary power means "having to live at the mercy of another … [To] live in the shadow of the other's presence, even if no arm is raised against them."[85] This is important, since part of the point of data is that most of us move around as before – in fact, easier than before – and thus are in no way classically interfered with. But we are subjects of domination nonetheless. Arbitrary power is *over* you and *above* you, even if it is something you never see or feel.

Petit's critique of arbitrary power, and associated theory of non-domination is also one that gets at a deeper meaning of *security*. Drawing upon Machiavelli, Petit explains:

[The Roman plebs] sought protection or private security, so in general, Machiavelli says, people's eagerness for freedom comes of a desire, not to rule, but rather not to be ruled … What is the benefit to a person of living freely, living in security? Machiavelli answers: "the power of enjoying freely his possessions without any anxiety, of feeling no fear for the honor of his women and his children, or not being afraid for himself."[86]

Put in this light, new security protocols are themselves an inversion of security. Security should make us feel at ease; instead it makes us feel vulnerable. Otherwise put: to become *secure* vis-à-vis physical threats, we have to surrender security-qua-domination. But it is more perverse still. Since the first threat may never materialize, it is a fantasized fear to come, we are actually submitting to domination – are *insecure* qua domination, even though on any lived dimension, we may be just as physically secure as ever.

This gets at a tension intrinsic to the meaning of security. Security vis-à-vis the state of nature, draws from the concept of *safety* – on its own, a normative good. But security-*qua*-safety can also engage tradeoffs with individual liberty – here between individual security and collective security (*qua* safety). In this way, security for the polity necessitates individual insecurity (security here understood as *certainty* – the guarantee of rights). Relatedly, embedded in our notion of security is *comfort* – the way we come to feel at-home-in-ourselves. This is akin to the feeling of safety, but unmoored from physical harm. Stepping back, we might say that data creates a new securitized subject, who is at once secure (meaning safe), but insecure (meaning unmoored from his or herself). At what point is this sacrifice too much to accept?

Conclusion

Marx described the French revolution as a "giant broom" which swept away the past.[87] Data is the opposite: it is the vacuum by which everything is retained. We are only at the beginning stages of understanding how this revolution will work.

This chapter serves as an introduction to the new and unfurling ways in which data works in government, and in particular its role at the port of entry. Subsequent chapters will use this material to develop a more sustained critique of new practices at the ports. The problem of data is hard to place. But one would not be remiss in feeling it to be somewhat out of control. In this way, data today matches how Marx described capitalism as "like the sorcerer, who is no longer able to control the powers of the nether world whom he has called up by his spells."[88] The future of data is taken up in Chapter 7. Before this, Chapter 6 takes this analysis of data and extends it to the cross-border context, revealing the prevalence of data sharing in contemporary data governance and showing why this matters for politics – returning here to the question of sovereignty.

Notes

1 Hawley, Kip. "Why Airport Security Is Broken – and How to Fix It." *The Wall Street Journal*, April 15, 2012.
2 McCarter, Mickey. "TSA Launches Air Cargo Security Initiatives." *Homeland Security Today*, 2011.
3 Foucault, *Security, Territory, Population*, at 18.
4 Walzer, *Spheres of Justice*, at 38–9.
5 Bigo, "Frontier Controls in the European Union," in *Controlling Frontiers*, at 70.
6 Lyon, David. *Identifying Citizens: ID Cards as Surveillance*. Cambridge, UK: Polity Press, 2009, at 97.
7 Rockwell, Mark. "DHS Looks for 'Sweet Spot' to Balance Security and Economic Recovery." *Government Security News*, February 2012; Goodwin, Jacob. "Editorial: Security and Money." *Government Security News*, February 2012.
8 Department of Homeland Security (DHS). "Northern Border Strategy," 2012, at 11–12.
9 Amoore, Louise and Marieke de Goede. "Governance, Risk and Dataveillance in the War on Terror." *Crime, Law & Social Change* 43, no. 2 (2005): 149–73, at 151; American Civil Liberties Union, cited in Lyon, David. "Surveillance, Security and Social Sorting: Emerging Research Priorities." *International Criminal Justice Review* 17, no. 3 (2007): 161–70, at 165; Browne, "Digital Epidermalization" at 133.

10 This chapter is focused on international ports of entry – i.e. into and out of the USA. However, domestic airports were implicated by these policies as well.
11 Hawley, "Why Airport Security Is Broken – and How to Fix It."
12 Monteverde, Susan. "Navigating Maritime and Port Security." Remarks by Monteverde, Vice President for Government Relations, American Associations of Port Authorities. Counter Terror Expo Conference, Washington DC, May 17, 2012.
13 Goddard, "How to Fix a Broken Border."
14 De Vries, Lloyd. "Airport Security Fails Test." *CBS News*, February 11, 2009; Mosk, Matthew, Angela Hill and Timothy Fleming. "Gaping Holes in Airline Security: Loaded Gun Slips Past TSA Screeners." *ABC News*, December 16, 2010.
15 McCarter, Mickey. "Aviation, Port Security Bills Enjoy Bipartisan Support from House Lawmakers." *Homeland Security Today*, July 2, 2012.
16 Andreas, "The Mexicanization of the US–Canada Border," at 457.
17 "Fact Sheet: Big Data and Privacy Working Group Review." White House Office of the Press Secretary. News Release, May 1, 2014, https://www.whitehouse.gov/the-press-office/2014/05/01/fact-sheet-big-data-and-privacy-working-group-review.
18 Rohozinski, Rafal. "Big Data Analysis and Intelligence." Remarks by Rohozinski, Principal & CEO, the Secdev Group. Canadian Association of Defence and Security Industries (CADSI) SecureTech Conference, Ottawa, Canada, October 30, 2012.
19 Here is one rendering of what this is: "A zettabyte is 1,000,000,000,000,000,000,000 bytes … Imagine that every person in the United States took a digital photo every second of every day for over a month. All of those photos put together would equal about one zettabyte" ("Big Data: Seizing Opportunities and Preserving Values." White House Executive Office of the President, News Release, May 1, 2014, https://www.whitehouse.gov/sites/default/files/docs/big_data_privacy_report_may_1_2014.pdf, at 2).
20 Croll, Alistair. "Big Data Is Our Generation's Civil Rights Issue and We Don't Know It." *The O'Reilly Radar*, August 2, 2012.
21 "Big Data," 46.
22 Ibid., at 27.
23 Mocny, Robert. US-VISIT Priorities and Collaboration with Federal and International Partners and Private Industry – by Robert Mocny, Director US VISIT, DHS. Paper read at Biometrics for National Security and Law Enforcement, January 31, 2013, at Alexandria, VA.
24 Nemeth, Patrick. Interagency Biometric Collaboration – by Patrick Nemeth, Deputy Assistant Director, US-VISIT Identity Services, DHS. Paper read at Biometrics for National Security and Law Enforcement, January 30, 2013, at Alexandria, VA.
25 Bert Tussing, Director, Homeland Defense and Security, US Army War College. Personal interview, El Paso, TX, October 17, 2012.
26 Kalath, Jay. "Patrolling the Border: The New National Strategy." Remarks by Kalath, Vice President, General Manager, National Security Operations and

CTO, ARRAY Information Technology. Counter Terror Expo Conference, Washington DC, May 16, 2012; Munn, "Developing Human Domain Awareness."

27 Purcell, Richard. "Privacy Policy and Technology Recommendations for a Federated Information-Sharing System." 1–20: Department of Homeland Security Data Privacy and Integrity Advisory Committee, 2012, at 3.

28 Mocny, "US-VISIT Priorities."

29 Coleman, David. "Developing Biometrics for International Border Control." Remarks by Coleman, Product Manager, Novetta Mission Analytics. Biometrics for National Security and Law Enforcement Conference, Alexandria, VA, January 30, 2013.

30 Loudermilk, James. "Emerging Modalities: Future Directions in Identifications Technology." Remarks by Loudermilk, Senior Level Technologist, Science & Technology Branch, FBI. Biometrics for National Security and Law Enforcement Conference, Alexandria, VA, February 1, 2013.

31 Mocny, "US-VISIT Priorities."

32 Christopher Munn, Portfolio Lead, Biometrics, Office of the Under-Secretary of Defense for Intelligence (OUSDI). Personal interview, Alexandria, VA, January 31, 2013.

33 Shah, Rikin. "Biometrics Data and Apache Hadoop." Remarks by Shah, Big Data and Hadoop Strategist, Hortonworks. Biometrics for National Security and Law Enforcement Conference, Alexandria, VA, January 30, 2013.

34 Rohozinski, "Big Data Analysis and Intelligence."

35 Munn, personal interview.

36 "Big Data," at 44–5.

37 "Civil Rights and Big Data: Background Material." Leadership Conference on Civil and Human Rights & The Leadership Conference Education Fund, News Release, 2014, http://www.civilrights.org/press/2014/civil-rights-and-big-data.html.

38 "Big Data," at 46.

39 Calabrese, Chris. "When Big Data Becomes a Civil Rights Problem." news release, February 27, 2014, https://www.aclu.org/blog/free-future/when-big-data-becomes-civil-rights-problem?redirect=blog/technology-and-liberty-racial-justice-criminal-law-reform/when-big-data-becomes-civil-rights.

40 "Note on Big Data, Crime and Security: Civil Liberties, Data Protection and Privacy Concerns." *Statewatch*, April 3, 2014.

41 Mill, John Stuart. *On Liberty*. Edited by David Bromwich and George Kateb New Haven, CT: Yale University Press, 2003, at 158.

42 "Northern Border Strategy," at 11–12.

43 Scott, Sandra Faye. "Privacy Impact Assessment for the Global Enrollment System." 1–20: US Department of Homeland Security, 2006, at 6–9.

44 "Terrorist Screening Center: Frequently Asked Questions." FBI Terrorist Screening Center, 2012.

45 "Northern Border Strategy," at 12.

46 Coleman, "Developing Biometrics for International Border Control."

47 Interviews, Phoenix, AZ, March 6, 2012.

48 "U.S. Department of Homeland Security Ensures Secure and Efficient Borders with Western Hemisphere Travel Initiative (WHTI): Case Study." UNISYS, 2009, at 2–3.

49 For example: "SRI Sarnoff's handheld biometric system allows users to quickly enroll and identify subjects at a distance ... The [captured face image] is associated with Iris images in the data record. Once subjects are enrolled, the system verifies identity in less than one second. "Iris Recognition at a Distance and on the Move." SRI International Sarnoff, Iris on the Move Product Guide, 2012.

50 Boyd, John. "DoD Biometrics: Key Enabler for Identity Operations." Remarks by Boyd, Director, Defense Biometrics and Forensics, OSD." Biometrics for National Security and Law Enforcement Conference, Alexandria, VA, February 1, 2013.

51 Bell, Robert. "Canada–US Beyond the Border Initiative: Efficient Border Crossing for People – Innovate to Address Threats Early." Remarks by Bell, Director, Nextgen Id Inc. Canadian Association of Defence and Security Industries (CADSI) SecureTech Conference, Ottawa, Canada, October 30, 2012.

52 Boyd, "DoD Biometrics."

53 Michael Stone, Biometrics and Identity, Management, USNORTHCOM. Personal interview, El Paso, TX, October 16, 2012.

54 Rohozinski, "Big Data Analysis and Intelligence."

55 Ibid.

56 MacMahon, Dave. "Big Data Analysis and Intelligence." Remarks by MacMahon, Senior Engineer, Complex Security Program, Bell Canada. Canadian Association of Defence and Security Industries (CADSI) SecureTech Conference, Ottawa, Canada, October 30, 2012.

57 "Big Data," at 8.

58 Hakala, Uriah. "Big Data Analysis and Intelligence." Remarks by Hakala, Director Professional Services and Partner Enablement, Kapow Software. Canadian Association of Defence and Security Industries (CADSI) SecureTech Conference, Ottawa, Canada, October 30, 2012.

59 Quoted in Brown, Pamela and Mary Kay Mallonee. "First on CNN: Top U.S. Intel Official: Europe Not Taking Advantage of Terror Tracking Tools." CNN.com, April 7, 2016.

60 Foucault, Security, Territory, Population, at 108–9.

61 Foucault, Power/Knowledge, at 39.

62 Foucault, "The Subject and Power," in Power, at 333.

63 Ibid., at 334–5.

64 Marx, Karl. "Critique of the Gotha Project," in The Marx–Engels Reader.

65 Schmitt, Political Theology, at 65.

66 Foucault, "The Subject and Power," in Power, at 331.

67 Ibid., at 326–7.

68 Ibid., at 330.

69 Foucault, Security, Territory, Population, at 1.

70 Agamben, Giorgio. *Homo Sacer: Sovereign Power and Bare Life*. Translated by D. Heller-Roazen. Edited by W. Hamacher and D. E. Wellbery. Stanford, California: Stanford University Press, 1995 at 6.
71 Foucault, *Security, Territory, Population*, at 57.
72 Ibid., at 5.
73 Ibid., at 46.
74 "Big Data." American Civil Liberties Union News Release, February 27, 2014, https://www.aclu.org/issues/privacy-technology/surveillance-technologies/big-data.
75 Torpey, *The Invention of the Passport*, at 166.
76 Mill, *On Liberty*, at 134.
77 Nietzsche, Friedrich. *On the Genealogy of Morals and Ecce Homo*. Edited by Walter Kaufman New York: Vintage Books, 1989, at 59.
78 Bourdieu, Pierre. *Distinction: A Social Critique of the Judgement of Taste*. Translated by R. Nice. Cambridge, MA: Harvard University Press, 1984, at 471.
79 Taylor, Charles. "The Politics of Recognition." In *Multiculturalism: Examining the Politics of Recognition*, edited by Amy Gutmann. Princeton: Princeton University Press, 1994, at 25–6.
80 For a discussion of the "right to privacy" in the US, see "Big Data," at 16–17.
81 Berlin, "Two Concepts of Liberty," in *The Proper Study of Mankind*, at 199.
82 See e.g., Arendt, *The Human Condition*, at 14–15.
83 Freud, Sigmund. *Civilization and Its Discontents*. Translated by J. Strachey. Edited by P. Gay. New York: Norton & Co, 1961, at 27.
84 Gergen, Kenneth J. *The Saturated Self: Dilemmas of Identity in Contemporary Life*, New York: Basic Books, 2000, at 49.
85 Pettit, Philip. *Republicanism: A Theory of Freedom and Government*. Oxford: Oxford University Press, 1997, at 4–5.
86 Ibid., at 28.
87 Marx, "The Civil War in France," in *The Marx-Engels Reader*, at 629.
88 Marx and Engels, "The Communist Manifesto," in Ibid., at 478.

6   Sovereignty, Security and the *Politics of Trust*

It used to be that if you had a castle, you built a big wall around it and really didn't care what happened outside the castle as long as the wall stood up. Not anymore. You have to reach outside.
— Adam Hatfield, Public Safety Canada, 2012[1]

To enhance our risk management practices, we intend to continue planning together, organizing bi-national port of entry committees to coordinate planning and funding, building, expanding or modernizing shared border management facilities and border infrastructure where appropriate, and using information technology solutions.
— The White House, 2011[2]

Nothing is more antithetical to sovereignty than *trust*. This tension is brought forth in Derrida's exegesis that hospitality carries within it the concept of hostility. When the host opens the door to the guest, she is introducing vulnerability. She becomes the hostage of the guest, as the very notion of "hostage" carries within it the guarantee of "security, surety for the enemy lodged with the sovereign."[3] The same point can be made about data – and in particular, data sharing – what I call the *politics of trust*.

Port security is also a cross-border operation. This is only logical, as border ports – like perimeters – have two sides. It is far more efficient to jointly manage these spaces. The filtration mechanism is only as good as the data coming in and for the data to be good, as much information as possible must be known about travelers before they arrive. Trusted traveler programs represent an important first step in this data accession process, but they alone are insufficient; a more holistic data sharing arrangement is necessary. This chapter details the rise of cross-border data sharing policies – both at bilateral and multilateral levels – as well as radical changes in port management. In particular, ports have become increasingly jointly managed, such that entry functions of one side have aligned with the exit functions on another.

Cross-border data sharing is both a technological and a political question. Technologically the main obstacle to data sharing is standardization (or "harmonization"). Unstructured or differently structured data, cannot be processed by the same database without being re-structured in tandem. Given the evolving threat landscape in the post-9/11 era, there is a near consensus that it is increasingly dangerous for states to keep their data unstandardized. As one industry expert explains, today "we are wasting time sifting through that data, trying to look for threats."[4] Politically, the US has been pushing a system in which other countries come to imitate our data profiles. To this end, DHS has been providing technical support to countries, so that they capture biometric data that is compatible with our own databases. For example, Robert Mocny, Director of US-VISIT aims to cultivate a "growing international coalition of biometric users."[5] The White House advocates "active collaboration with the international community" in port security to protect the global supply chain, because – just like at the perimeter – the government "cannot achieve this alone."[6] Vic Toews, Minister, Public Safety Canada, concurs that cybersecurity requires "a collaborative approach."[7]

Drawing upon this empirical baseline, the principle arguments of this chapter are about sovereignty and the *politics of trust*. Changes at the ports of entry mirror those at the perimeter and thus are also creating a type of sovereignty that is heterogeneous – ports are becoming jointly managed spaces, with officials working "shoulder by shoulder." But, in addition to adding a dimension to the challenge to sovereignty-as-territoriality – discussed in Chapter 3 – the changes at the port also challenge the sovereign decision. This claim has three parts. First, ports are filtration devices drawing on information from national security databases. These databases produce risk evaluations based on algorithms, combining the many sources of data available on travelers to determine whether the individual should be admitted or rejected. Second, we are increasingly sharing information with other nations and deriving our own data from corporate and international sources. Third, once entered into the system and transferred into a risk-reading, most information about data (its origins, linkages) becomes obscure to users at the point of decision. Therefore, as far as the officials at the border port are concerned, these decisions are made based on information that increasingly may not be derived from sovereign sources and cannot be disaggregated or traced. Thus, while the choice occurs at the port, the predicates of that choice are based on information that is increasingly in heterogeneous state control. In relying on such sources, the sovereign is not stripped of choice; but the choice is stripped of sovereign exclusivity.

A second challenge to sovereignty comes from private or corporate sources. This means data that comes from the private sector – such as from mobile phone providers, credit card companies or Internet browsers – but also data that is *stored* and *processed* by the myriad tech companies that have contracts for government work. In these cases, the data is *national* but not *sovereign*. Thus, the same concerns about veracity, context and use arise – and with this, *trust*. This issue will only grow in importance due to collective concerns over cybersecurity. The conundrum is that cybersecurity requires that the state work *more* with private companies, not less. The challenge to sovereignty here is clear – mirroring the discussion above. Together these challenges amount to an evolving *politics of trust*, greatly antithetical to classic Westphalian sovereignty, which sees states as independent, self-contained units – akin to billiard balls. Instead, by its very nature trust introduces vulnerability, an inherent risk of collaboration. Otherwise put, modern data sharing arrangements are a calculated dependency. The wider the trust web gets – and there are only signs of further expansion – the more tenuous the trust relations.

The chapter closes by turning to questions of *citizenship*. New technologies of filtration used at ports of entry segment people not based on citizenship – membership in a polity – but based on risk scores. These risk determinations are citizenship-blind. Otherwise put: data filtration turns people into *de facto* non-citizens, even if they are *de jure* citizens. In doing so, it severs the political meaning of citizenship from its legal basis, further depleting the normative core of popular sovereignty. Further, co-bordering enables officials from two countries a say in constructing border policy, but this does not offer any protections to TCNs or the own-citizens (frequently minorities) it denominates as risky. With this in mind, the chapter proposes a new model of citizenship designed specifically for border crossers, suggesting that overlapping borders create not merely bilateral enforcement structures, but also an adjudicative wing situated at the ports of entry by which border crossers can seek and obtain representation. A *weak* version of this political administration would be bilateral, representing the interests and concerns of *citizens* of both neighboring states. But such an institution would be by definition partial, as it would enable representation of citizens of the two countries alone. A *strong* version of this system would require that states cede authority of cases involving TCNs – crossers of a border not their own – to international adjudication. Thus, it would ordain an international political institution specifically designed to oversee the management of bilateral borders, tasked with the representation, adjudication and treatment of migrants – acts already performed routinely at the border, but without international oversight.

Cross-Border Risk Assessment I – Trusted Traveler and Information-Sharing

This section discusses the rise of cross-border information sharing, especially as pertains to advance information. It looks first locally, at the expansion of the trusted traveler concept to the US' neighbors, Canada and Mexico. Second, the argument is brought to the international stage, still keeping mostly within the confines of bilateralism, but outlining possibilities for global agreements.

Trusted Traveler 2.0 – The Neighbors

The easiest inroad into this subject is the Beyond the Border Agreement with Canada – which, to date, represents the cutting edge of data sharing between the US and its neighboring states. Alongside the US, Canada has embraced the use of data at its borders, with a move toward advanced detection and automation, including at the ports themselves, with kiosks that can obtain and process data in advance of primary inspection. Much of this is in direct collaboration with the US – a process that began with Trusted Traveler. In fact, as intimated in Chapter 5, many trusted traveler programs were actually designed as joint, cross-border initiatives. Both CBP and the Canadian equivalent, CBSA, recognize NEXUS, FAST and WHTI identification for entry at all land and sea ports of entry. These are some of the most developed forms of trusted traveler programs, expanding rapidly, to the point where nearly all possible forms of transit between the US and Canada are equipped for trusted travel.

This development does not simply represent the expansion of trusted traveler via the incorporation of Canadian citizens into US programs. Rather, it is a far more comprehensive agreement toward data sharing. This is enabled first and foremost by the expansion of international data agreements between the US and Canada, most importantly regarding standardization. Much of this is driven by US policies toward exporting its data protocols. As one data engineer explains, Canada's model is "to look at what we have done in the US first" and then create "partner programs."[8] This coordination extends to many agencies within the government. For example, a DHS senior liaison is assigned to provide technical support to Citizenship and Immigration Canada (CIC) in their collection of biometrics to "ensure the interoperability of U.S. and

Canadian biometric repositories in the event of future data sharing."[9] As part of this plan, the CIC is looking into using US Citizenship and Immigration Services Application Support Centers to collect biometrics from Canadian citizens that are temporary residents in the US. Such merging of administrative functions at the ports only becomes possible with interoperable data.

Importantly, this is not just a US strategy – Canada considers it essential to their strategic outlook. Indeed, evidence of the truly bilateral nature of these new US–Canada initiatives lies in the fact that they are based to a large degree on *trust*. This is because the original data being entered into the system (on which all future vetting depends) is the responsibility of the attending officer alone. Thus, for example, in the case of data emanating from Canada, the Canadian officer is solely responsible for the veracity of the data input into the system, including the capture of biometrics and recording of biographic data. Throughout this process, Canadian officials maintain considerable access to this data – at all levels, including managers, system administrators, developers, etc. Of course, both the Canadian and US governments can vet the data collected by these programs. Continuing the example above, once the data is input into a shared databank, US access is enabled; should they decide scrutiny is warranted they can pursue it. However, their access is limited to the data already input, and is considered to be on a "need-to-know" basis.[10] In fact, the main point of vetting is to make sure that a person cleared by one metric, isn't flagged by another – it is not to question the data input of the partner nation.

Further afield, US–Canada data sharing is not limited to "trusted" programs. In fact, the central advance of information between the US and Canada pertains to new programs in electronic travel authorization for air travel. In the US, this is known as the Electronic System for Travel Authorization (or ESTA) founded in 2008. A Canadian version, modeled as a near exact copy of, and interchangeable with, the US system, known as the electronic Travel Authorization (or eTA) is being developed, at which point there will be a common US–Canada method of screening travelers between them. In the words of Neil Yeates, Deputy Minister, CIC, the goal is to create "a common Canada–US approach to screening travelers," in response to common "security threats to North America."[11] Indeed, while cooperation on traveler data is important, the future goal is a more complete opening of US databases to Canadian inquiry and vice-versa.

As with trusted traveler programs, there is increased data sharing on the commercial end as well. In 2009, DHS and Public Safety Canada (PS) agreed to integrate their C-TPAT and Partners in Protection (PIP) programs. In 2012, the Securing Maritime Activities through Risk-based Targeting (SMART) for Port Security Act (H.R.4251) builds upon the SAFE Port Act by allowing DHS to recognize other countries' Trusted Shipper Programs. Candice Miller (R-MI), chair of the House Subcommittee on Border and Maritime Security, explains the significance of this bill:

> Leveraging partnerships with private industry, as well as our international partners, is common sense and Trusted Shipper Programs, like the Customs Trade Partnership Against Terrorism ... [reduce] the amount of resources CBP needs to spend on looking at cargo shipments that we know the least about ... Our trusted allies like Canada and the European Union have programs similar to C-TPAT in place and this bill supports the concept of mutual recognition where the [DHS] secretary can accept other countries trusted shipper programs, when they provide an equal level of security.[12]

As one Canadian government official explains, the US and Canada are in the process of "developing a harmonized approach to screening inbound cargo" – mirroring the system in place with travelers – alongside "protocol standardization."[13] Today, the fact that the US and Canada share advanced trade data is considered the "new normal."[14]

As with perimeter management, the US and Mexico relationship is developing at a slower clip than its northern counterpart – or as one analyst explains "the handshake is weaker."[15] Nonetheless, there has been remarkable progress. For example, in 2010, Global Entry allowed Mexican nationals to enter its trusted traveler network; members of SENTRI, which includes Mexican nationals, were also allowed to enroll in Global Entry that same year. Mexico is also in the process of developing its own trusted traveler network, which, when operable, will be open to US citizens. This progress is largely due to the Merida Initiative. In 2010, Janet Napolitano and Mexican Interior Secretary Fernando Francisco Gómez-Mont signed an agreement to share electronic information of air travelers between the two countries, setting up a program called the Joint Security Program for Travelers (JSP). This remains far away from the progress with eTA in Canada, but they are clearly on the same track. Further, the same types of agreement are forming regarding trade as well. For example, Mexico has a program that mirrors C-TPAT, called NEEC, following along the Trusted Trader model. There is not yet mutual recognition between these programs or interoperable data platforms, but these are in the process of being developed.

US–Mexico interoperability lags considerably behind the agreements to the north; however, when placed in the perspective of broader US goals globally, it is clear that these will be integrated as well. Indeed, the move toward extending trusted traveler programs is already evidenced by the US partnership with the Netherlands Privium program; CBP has also recently struck agreements with the United Kingdom and Germany for the admission of their countries' citizens in the future. The global reach of data sharing agreements is treated below.

Expanding the Data-Sharing Web

That neighboring states increasingly pursue cooperative policies across their common borders is but a small part of a larger trend of global data sharing, enabled by the global standardization of data protocols. In such a network, members from the intelligence community of different states can communicate within the same database. This is a radical proposal – and still far away – but the rudiments are already in place. According to US-VISIT, due to data sharing partnerships with the international community, the US is now able to research the identities of 6,300 individuals, twelve of whom were identified as Known or Suspected Terrorists (KSTs). Because of these early successes, further data sharing agreements are at the forefront of the US agenda. Mocny explains:

I can't emphasize enough [how] important [it is] to share data with our friends and allies ... Working together we can ensure the integrity of our visa, border management and immigration systems. US-VISIT also provides technical assistance to other countries as they develop and employ biometric identity management capabilities ... Today, 60 countries around the world collect some form of biometrics, electronically from national identity programs, visa issuance or port of entry inspection ... We are rapidly collaborating with the world's authorities to increase the number of countries that use biometrics in screening for border management and to enrich US-VISIT's data repositories with actual biometric and biographic data.[16]

This move toward international data sharing is not confined to DHS. As one leading official within the Department of Defense explains, their current priority is to "continue to share relevant data with our international and multi-national partners and look for ways to expand these exchanges."[17] To this end, the DoD has completely flipped its technology acquisition priorities, seeking first systems that match international protocols, then US government ones, then finally those that align with existing DoD systems. Across units, the US army is coming to rely heavily on foreign partners for data-gathering, including by training foreign soldiers in the use of biometric technologies (through what they call their Sovereign Nation Exploitation Training program).

Returning to the question of port security, the US is presently engaged in a comprehensive scheme of multilateral data sharing regarding travelers. Data-sharing is most advanced in the so-called "Five Eyes" community – the US, the UK, Canada, Australia and New Zealand – which has agreed to a data sharing protocol on travelers who arrive at one of their shared borders seeking immigration benefits. As of 2016, the US and the UK also have agreements in place to share data on passengers in advance of their travel – once again part of what are referred to as Passenger Name Record (PNR) systems. The UK's system is called e-Borders. Similar types of engagement are in place with Australia and Canada. This initial commitment is in the process of expansion aimed at increased interoperability and the automation of joint data systems:

> [The "Five Eyes" has] a high-value data sharing protocol [allowing] for each of those countries [to] share biometrics on people who [seek] immigration benefits ... We are about to enter a new phase of that, instituting a communications pipeline – SRTB Secure – a real-time platform which will automate that process.[18]

A joint platform for real-time data exchange would fundamentally transform the functioning and efficiency of border ports. Moreover, unlike in the case of land-ports with neighboring states, under this model data sharing is truly global.

Certainly, the Five Eyes community represents a set of close allies; but this is only the beginning, as the US intends to expand data sharing agreements as far out as it can (with more proximate allies having the most access to US data). Looking first at the general level, the main partners with whom the US shares data remain the most developed nations. The principal database with which the US shares biometric and biographic data is RTID (Canada), but there is also a strong relationship with BMS (the EU) and Interpol. These international databases are linked-up via database matching. Farther afield, new initiatives include limited arrangements with nations in the Caribbean and Asia, and even China. The strongest data sharing agreements now exist regarding trade. At present, C-TPAT has more than 10,224 Certified Partners worldwide, with more than 19,700 on-site validations conducted in ninety-seven countries. More basic data sharing agreements are in place regarding information on air passengers with regional countries – including Argentina, Brazil, Chile, the Dominican Republic and Panama – a process that is increasingly becoming the global norm.

Another inroad into international data sharing comes via the Visa Waiver Program (VWP). Not all foreign travelers into the US require a visa; indeed, a large number of states (thirty-six at present) are part of the VWP. This presents both a challenge to data sharing and an opportunity. It is a challenge as there are numerous countries on this list with whom the United States enjoys only a weak alliance. Thus, letting individuals travel from these countries renders the state vulnerable. However, it also presents an opportunity, as it greatly increases the web of countries with whom some information is shared – and with whom data sharing practice might expand in the future.

The Visa Waiver Program was first established in 1986. Originally, nations qualified if they had a non-immigrant visa refusal rate of three percent or less. However, in the present data-hungry environment of national security, requirements have been raised considerably, beginning with the 9/11 Commission act (2007), which mandated that information sharing be part of this program (including watchlist information). Present requirements also include the issuance of machine-readable biometric passports. These demands are considerable and thus far only twenty-four of thirty-six nations have been able to comply, mostly due to domestic laws forbidding the sharing of personal information on its citizens. Roadblocks aside, the VWP presents an enormous opportunity for the US to increase the web of nations with which important data are shared. A central condition of being a Visa Waiver country is that there is a reciprocal exchange of biometric information with the United States, such that we assist partner states in their investigations and they assist us in ours. As Nemeth explains, while this type of biometric exchange "is still in its infancy … we are expecting this to be our largest growth industry for the next year or two."[19]

A second issue that highlights the expanding web of information sharing is the global supply chain. The question is: how do we trust goods arriving from foreign countries? Here too we rely on advanced information sharing, based on checks conducted at foreign ports of origin. Beginning with sea-ports, in 2007 the US began operating a cargo screening pilot in Hong Kong, called the Secure Freight Initiative (SFI) – in accordance with the requirements of the SAFE Port Act, which includes radiographic imaging and radiation scanning of cargo. In this model, all US-bound containers are scanned by computers and given a "confidence level" – akin to the type of risk-ratings familiar for travelers. If a package receives any score less than an "A," Hong Kong Customs and Excise (HKCE), which oversees port security, is empowered to conduct further scans and cargo searches. Under this system the sovereignty of the foreign port is not compromised, but US officials receive advance information on the material before it arrives. Along the same lines, in January 2008, CBP required that carriers electronically submit information on their cargo before it is brought into the US. Other regulations of this sort include the Twenty-Four Hour Advanced Cargo Rule, which requires all sea carriers to provide information on their loads twenty-four hours before they depart for the US. In 2010, the SFI, still in pilot, was extended to six countries where goods were considered to carry some risk – Pakistan, Honduras, Britain, Oman, Singapore and South Korea.

Because of the importance of airports to global port security, here global standards for cooperation are more advanced. US efforts here began in June 2006 with the National Strategy for Aviation Security. This was one of the most far reaching initiatives toward air security to date – moreover, it created a comprehensive plan for what is referred to as the "Air Domain," which is the global airspace, rather than merely US airspace. This National Strategy insists that air security is a global problem, for which there can only be a common solution:

Securing the Air Domain will not come from the United States acting alone, but through a coalition of nations maintaining a strong and united international front. The need for a strong and effective coalition is reinforced by the fact that most of the Air Domain is under no single nation's sovereignty or jurisdiction … international coordination, in concert with cooperative intelligence and information sharing among public and private entities, is required to protect and secure the Air Domain.[20]

This national strategy is building toward a Next Generation Air Transportation System (NGATS) – in which international cooperation plays a central role in cultivating "maximum domain awareness" or a system of operations, with information sharing, to protect the global airways, with open protection of all partners. This plan focuses on international coalitions to increase transparency within the aviation supply, with joint monitoring of aircraft and cargo from start to finish and to "encourage adoption of international standards and best practices [and] align regulation and enforcement measures." This is not simple coordination, but rather a much more involved form of interoperability that is "reinforced by joint interagency and international training and exercises to ensure a high rate of readiness."[21]

Similar processes are in place regarding air cargo, as the TSA wants to pre-screen all airline cargo before it reaches US soil, such as by setting up Certified Cargo Screening Facilities (CCSF) at airports overseas – essentially co-locating US inspectors abroad. This plan remains in its nascence, due to sovereignty concerns. However, in lieu of this more comprehensive plan, the TSA has taken to reviewing the facilities of foreign states, as part of the National Country Security Program (NCSP) and certify that their procedures are considered sufficient for US security – essentially setting up transparent screening processes among partner states, which they believe they can trust to screen cargo before arriving at US ports. The system is not perfect, but at present, the TSA is able to inspect about eighty percent of cargo on US-bound passenger flights largely by agreeing to engage countries in joint inspections. These programs are exceedingly popular and there will likely be even greater information sharing in the future. This is considerably easier with cargo than travelers, since "no package will ever complain about being profiled."[22]

This discussion has been US-centric; the global nature of cross-border agreements is treated in Chapter 7.

Cross-Border Risk Assessment II – State–State Cooperation and Co-Location

The sharing underway at ports of entry is in no way limited to data. Rather, it is part of a far more comprehensive collaboration between states regarding port security – i.e. a mutual pact toward the control of ports against non-state threats (terrorism, immigration, drugs, etc.). With this in mind we return to the physical ports, where there is increasing interest in the creation of "bi-national" or "shared" ports of entry that look very similar to the co-location at the perimeter, with officers on both sides jointly managing the ports, solving the problem of negotiating across jurisdiction. This type of joint planning and management solves one of the principal shortcomings of most ports, which is that while ports of entry are capable of monitoring *entry* into the country, they are not equipped to monitor *exit*.[23] The importance of an exit system was revealed after 9/11, as at least four of the nineteen hijackers were in the US on expired visas; additionally, almost half of all illegal immigrants (forty-five percent) entered legally and then stayed.[24] This is possible with collaboration alone, through what is known as a co-managed "entry-exit system" – a key demand of the 9/11 Commission report, which has yet to materialize. At present, US-VISIT electronically registers people when they arrive, but they can leave without any notification. DHS officials claim that monitoring exit would be too costly to implement.

Consequently, there is now a push toward next-generation integrated cross-border law enforcement at the ports. To understand the way this policy is commencing on the ground, it is best to begin with the US–Canada border where these types of changes are already taking effect. When Beyond the Border was announced, in February 2011, President Obama and Prime Minister Harper made clear that the border was a joint responsibility, committing the two states to develop an "integrated entry/exit system."[25] The White House describes the goal as follows:

To promote mobility between our two countries, we expect to work toward an integrated United States-Canada entry-exit system, including work toward the exchange of relevant entry information in the land environment so that documented entry into one country serves to verify exit from the other country.[26]

Interest in developing a cooperative strategy is not limited to travelers; rather, it includes the same type of cooperative strategy to operate on cargo, such that US and Canadian forces coordinate their screening methods and share programs and technology – essentially standing together as a unified guard to facilitate the rapid movement of secure goods. In the words of DHS, the two countries agreed to create "an integrated cargo security strategy that ensures compatible screening methods for goods and cargo before they depart foreign ports bound for either Canada or the United States."[27]

Initial mention of the idea of a joint entry/exit program preceded the Beyond the Borders Agreement – referred to then as the "Single Window Initiative." At the time this was discussed as an avenue for trade, described as "an opportunity to allow importers to submit all of the information it has to two governments in a more coherent way, into one single window."[28] It quickly became a policy for travelers as well, as the states realized that this was an ideal solution "for absconders – over-stayers – for example, who overstay their 90-day presence and try to go across the border into Canada."[29] Entry/exit verification was rolled out as a pilot at the US–Canada border in September 2012. While still in pilot, there is little question the US wants to expand and formalize the program.

An entry/exit scheme is also considered essential for trade, as it would enable the expedited clearance of cargo through "a single window" with clearance well in advance of the border itself. For this to be formalized as a policy, there would have to be a full harmonization of clearance processes. As a Canadian official explains:

We are looking at ways to harmonize how we do our targeting ... so the US trusts the way that we are doing our clearance aspect and they don't have to re-do the inspection, for example. So we want to clear it once, but have it pass through two inspections.[30]

The economic benefits of reduced examinations, inspections and wait times are considerable. However, politically, a lot of work remains before this would become policy. Indeed, there have been a few hitches about data sharing, as when Canada balked at giving up data on Canadian citizens to the US. This said, with the new Trudeau–Obama talks of 2016, these kinks appear to have been worked out, and now we might foresee even more data sharing on the horizon between the two countries. Further, in 2016, the two governments agreed to increase the number and capacity of pre-clearance sites, especially on land borders.[31]

What this amounts to is functional co-location at ports of entry, as the guiding principles behind the entry/exit policy include "operations conducted under the direction/management/laws of the host country," such that US and Canadian officers are "cross-designated to enforce host country laws," with "dedicated and co-located resources," under what is understood to be a "bi-national governance model."[32] To some degree this model follows on land what already exists at air and seaports. For example, at present eight Canadian airports in the US and Canada have assembled "committees that function with people on both sides of the border, providing pre-clearance services," a policy that is currently being expanded to twenty land ports as well.[33] At the seaports, the US and Canada have agreements in place such that if, "cargo comes through Vancouver, we won't screen you there, when you come across the border, because we are going to say we already screened you according to US requirements."[34]

But what is happening at land ports is truly new and exciting, giving border practitioners and analysts a lot to think about. For example, one border trade consultant foresees a future US–Canada port system in which there is but "one face at the border" that simply acts as a screen for traffic and that will "end duplicate inspection" at shared ports. If border ports become jointly managed, then there can be pre-load inspection far inland – as much as ten kilometers on either side – so that for all pre-cleared or low-risk traffic, there would be "clear travel at the 49th parallel" or "green laning" – i.e., "Check Once, Accept Twice."[35] This idea of a multiple-kilometer, cross-border pre-clearance area, puts the ports in direct conversation with the "zone" described at the perimeter in Chapter 2. If there were pre-checks in advance of the joint border, then the ports themselves could be little more than "remote supervised border points," with "remote capture" of travel documents and biometrics.[36] Another analyst takes this further:

[The future] is joint-borders ... if [the two sides] trust each other to do their examinations for them, then there is no reason I, being Canadian, couldn't do an examination on behalf of US customs ... It all can be done. They can be trained to carry out the laws in each location. Certain laws you can say are "North American" ... we are headed down that road, from the standpoint of dual jurisdictions ... You could imagine [a zone] with harmonized import data elements and classification codes ... In fact they have already completed a major review of the data requirements in both countries and are talking tri-laterally with Mexico [as part of] the Single Window Initiative (SWI).[37]

At that point: "why not CBSA/CBP officers at Land Border Ports?"[38] In other words, US and Canadian officials at the port train together and wear the same uniforms. Such a concept of dual-sovereign rule at the ports would be nothing short of radical.

It is easy to get excited about the US–Canada border, but it is questionable how much this can really teach us about an evolving geopolitical order – after all, the US and Canada are two highly developed English-speaking allies. But changes at the US–Mexico border are also afoot. At the federal level, there is certainly political will to work with Mexican counterparts at ports toward something like a joint management scheme. One CBP places the cooperative possibilities of the twenty-first Century Border Management Agreement in direct conversation with the US–Canada strategy:

How do we work together to secure our ports and borders and strengthen cooperation? ... standardized collections, integrating trusted-traveler and trade initiatives, single entry processes [the Single Window], bi-national coordination and in some cases exploring co-location strategies at our ports.[39]

The goals on the southwest border are the same as those on the northern – consolidated entry/exit program, standardization and even co-location – the only difference is the timeframe. But pilots here too are underway, designed to promote "better law enforcement cooperation than we have had in recent years."[40]

Beginning with the joint entry/exit concept, US interest in creating a collaborative agreement with the Mexican government began in 2010, after a failed DHS pilot system, which planted a US exit gate at the Nogales port of entry in Arizona, through which southbound travel would be screened. This project was, as Nogales Port Director Guadalupe Ramirez explains, an effort to catch criminals who sneak into the US to "do their business, but who then try to re-enter Mexico through the port."[41] This solo-attempt by the US at monitoring exit was considered inefficient; an effective system would require collaboration. But for collaboration to work, there had to be a significant amount of infrastructural development, so that border ports on both sides were up to the same technological standards. To this end, the US has invested a lot of technology into its southwest ports, some of which was provided to Mexico to upgrade their facilities and technological capacities. For example, in 2011, CBP revamped their southwest ports with new hand-held license plate readers at all 111 outbound lanes; Mexican authorities purchased the same technology for their own outbound lanes so that the system works in tandem. In addition, there is already data sharing between US and Mexican officials about the status of citizens within each other's databases. Functionally, this usually means that DHS provides Mexico with electronic criminal histories we have on Mexican nationals so that they can be apprehended should they reach the border. But the infrastructure is increasingly in place for this scheme to be expanded.

There are already US and Mexican officers working side by side at major ports of entry, such as San Ysidro, where as one former Border Patrol Chief describes:

CBP officers and Mexican Immigration are working shoulder by shoulder ... If somebody looks [suspicious] or is doing something wrong, they are in it together. They have the authority, we have the expertise. And we are building on their institutions, on their expertise by working hand in hand with different airports, seaports and landports.[42]

This degree of cooperation at the ports is expected to continue to expand in coming years.

In addition to working together toward the facilitation of travel, the US and Mexico have been engaged in a much larger project of widening their border ports in tandem to better allow for fast, secure trade. Perhaps the greatest advance on the US–Mexico border has been the development of jointly managed pre-clearance sites, to create expedited travel for un-risky goods before they reach the border itself. According to one border trade advocate, this pre-clearance model has actually advanced beyond what exists to the north. These pre-clearance sites remain pilots, but appear to be extremely effective:

We have three pilot programs. One in Laredo, one in Santa Teresa and one in Otay Mesa where we have US officers on Mexican soil and Mexican *adouanas* on US soil, pre-clearing products and services prior to their arrival at the border ... [This preclearance process] is starting. The infrastructure is being built ... In Laredo it will be an airport pre-clearance. You will have Mexican customs at Laredo airport, pre-clearing flights, freight into anywhere in the Republic of Mexico as a domestic flight. They will not have to clear customs again once they get there. In Santa Teresa you have a compound [where] you will have US offic-ers on Mexican soil, pre-clearing shipments that will bypass our ports of entry – they will go right through, in a special lane ... In Otay Mesa you will have US customs on one side of the facility and Mexican customs on the other side and meeting rooms in the middle.[43]

The analyst stresses that these policies are still at the planning stage, but there is optimism that they will be further developed in coming years. What is most important is that there is agreement about the concept. He continues: "Co-branded, co-operative ports of entry, where both organi-zations work side by side is ultimately the best solution ... I believe this to be the border of the future – where you have both agencies working together, under one roof, where they can literally walk to the next office and if there is a problem, they can get it solved immediately. It is the epitome [of] communication. It is the future."[44]

The pre-clearance model is very simple. Companies are vetted in their country of origin to get a rating of "low risk," which lets them travel through special pre-clearance lanes, rather than the regular ones, helping expedite low-risk travel. Farther afield, this model could even enable a dual-customs system. However, for these pilots to take the next step and be formalized into law they need extensive infrastructural development: for a border port to be dually managed it needs to be able to communicate with interoperable technology. And even more essentially, the two sides have to match – it does little to help traffic if one side of the border is wide, while the other is narrow.

Official relationships with Mexico at the ports remain less formal than with Canada. But this doesn't mean they don't exist on the ground – a fact revealed in interviews with local officials. As one agent from Homeland Security Investigations explains: "We deal with the Mexican Customs office, with Mexican Immigration, we deal with them quite often … We cross-designate state and local officers as customs officers, giving them the authority to work at the ports, with NEXUS at the ports." When asked about formal co-location, he was emphatic:

[Co-location] would be fantastic … We already have officers assigned to Mexico, who sit in Juarez and work with Mexican officers … [The goal] would be a Mexican law enforcement working in the United States as well as a US law enforcement officer working in Mexico … I think the US has seen the benefit of putting law enforcement officers in foreign countries, [of] sharing information and building those relationships to garner information from those countries to protect the United States … There is always a big [fear in Mexico] of the United States coming in and working in Mexico … Granted, we have that same fear, as you don't want them coming in for the wrong reasons. But working together? As long as it is shared information, we are good with that.[45]

And of course there is a regional dimension here – further discussed in Chapter 7.

Sovereignty and Trust

The Sovereign Decision

Borders are not merely sites of delineation, but of decisions – specifically vis-à-vis membership. This form of sovereignty is a variant of *decisionism* – a loaded term, derived from Carl Schmitt's famous definition of the sovereign as "he who decides on the exception," and the political as the distinction between friend and enemy.[46] I am not calling upon this broad notion here, only the particular aspect of the decision that pertains to the border – i.e. the authority of the state to decide on admission and membership in the polity. This aspect of decisionism sits at the core of sovereignty. Hannah Arendt remarks: "In the sphere of international law, it had always been true that sovereignty is nowhere more absolute than in matters of 'emigration, naturalization, nationality and expulsion'."[47] Kelsen argued that "every sovereign nation had the power to admit aliens only in such cases and upon such conditions as it might see fit to prescribe and to expel them at any time and for any reason."[48] Of course, there are limitations on the state's right to exclude aliens at its gate, due largely to "rules designed to protect human rights."[49] But these prohibitions are partial at best.

The argument here is that due to jointly managed ports, this aspect of the sovereign decision is becoming heterogeneous. The first two facets of this claim – that ports are increasingly driven by data and that this data is frequently derived from non-sovereign sources – have already been articulated at length in preceding sections. What is essential to establish here is the third facet, that this data cannot easily be disaggregated or traced. This has two components: first, at the level of the database; second, at the level of the officer at the ports. Beginning with the subject of centralized databases, the information stored in these databases is no longer clearly under the sole sovereign control of the United States. For example, when pressed about the origin of the data used in US databases, one security analyst I interviewed explained that the US' ability to distinguish bias was greatly limited:

When we used to collect data from national sensors … a centrally run set of intelligence institutions [would do] quality control of the data and then the data would feed the algorithms, which would feed the decision making process … If we are not using centrally controlled and collected data any more, how are we addressing the data quality issue? I would argue that we don't know how to do that yet … Is the sampling random? Is the data intentionally biased? Maybe the government of China is feeding us data to mislead us … Is there even a set of weights? How do we qualify certain sets of data over others? How do we deal with people influencing our data sets?[50]

The question is a critical one: in a Big Data world where data sharing is the name of the game, how does the state retain control over the information coded within that data?

This concern is not unique to DHS; it is endemic government-wide and is a natural outgrowth of information sharing. The same issues exist within the Department of Defense. For example, one biometrics specialist articulates concern over DoD databases and the variety of different sources of data from which they draw. How can you effectively match results from disparate sources (especially international ones)? Each time a government agency opens up its databases to sharing, it takes on risk:

[In today's threat environment] DoD is going to have to rely on partner missions a lot more. [We] are finally getting more tri-lateral data sharing. The question is, what is the impact of that going to be? ... DoD is used to collecting all of the data and managing all of the data and at every point in the process they have touched the data and know that it has got a good pedigree and understand why it is there. So, how can you move forward with assessing data that other people collect? How can we identify what the risks are when we share that data? ... As we look at more global operations, we have to accept that there is going to be errors in the identity resolution process. If there isn't some kind of way to audit those links, you can poison the system pretty quickly by having some bad merged records in there.[51]

Here again is a challenge to our classic conceptions of sovereign authority: as we increasingly share information, any single state loses some degree of control over the authenticity and veracity of its data. As more users gain access to shared databases, the more uncertainty is entered into the equation.

The risk of data infiltration is a serious issue. When asked about the risk that foreign partners flood US databases with questionable data, one DoD analyst replied:

That is certainly a risk with foreign partners. [For example], if we are going to initiate a sharing arrangement with the government of Zimbabwe, what is to say that they are not going to insert files [to bias our data]? We have to develop assessments for that which we don't really have in place yet ... If we are going to invite the government of Afghanistan to submit people to our biometric watchlist for the Department of Defense, one of the assessments has to be "is the current government just putting people on there that they want to target to have some sort of persistent surveillance and gain legitimacy by having it on our watchlist?" We are going to have to do our own due diligence to say "is the derogatory information that they are providing us something that we can corroborate?"[52]

Certainly, agencies like DoD and DHS are aware of these issues. But there is little to suggest they have been resolved.

Returning to the border, the second half to this equation pertains to the relationship of data and the port official. In a Big Data world, what information is available to the official at the port of entry? Can its attributes be sourced, disaggregated and analyzed at the border? Increasingly, the answer to these latter questions is no. As much as the Big Data revolution renders data sourcing obscure and heterogeneous, it also increasingly makes the decision-making capacity of the individual border guard obsolete. This is part of the design: border guards do not interpret the data, rather they use data already analyzed by algorithms that has been presented to them. It is not the job of the official to assess data quality or how risk-ratings were produced; the agent's job is to act upon the results. In this way, the logic is the same as when a cashier accepts payment with a credit card: they just trust that the card works, regardless of whether they understand the process. Looking farther afield, in the future, the port official "will have at the ready, fully analyzed pre-arrival information from both the carriers and the importers. They will be the gate keeper [who] will say 'enter' or 'don't enter' ... He is the last line of defense ... he shouldn't have to judge."[53] That the decision is made by the data, not the port official is essential to this design: it is a feature, not a bug.

The prioritization of data in port decision-making (over the judgment of port officials) is perpetuated by technology – especially those designed for remote capture. As travelers move through portals and submit to non-cooperative iris recognition, those whose biometrics indicates that they are on a watchlist are flagged for review; others pass without incident. Indeed, that algorithms produce risk-ratings, which are spit out to the individual user in a clear, uncomplicated fashion lies at the core of the way contemporary databases are set up. The goal of biometrics is in large part to reduce the amount of in-person identification and "automatically perform reliable person identification in unattended mode, often remotely."[54]

The design of this system is sensible: it would be impossible for an individual border guard to filter through all of the available information about a person and make a real-time decision. But what is of interest to the argument here is that not only is the source of data on which decisions of entry and exit are made obscure to the border official, but if that official did want to go back and look at the origins of a risk reading, this data is frequently unavailable – due, for example, to "anonymizing," discussed in Chapter 7. This point is crystallized via a technological example. In 2005 the State Department began issuing e-Passports that include embedded computer chips that store biographic and biometric data. By the very design of the system, the CBP officer at the border cannot verify the data inside the passport. This fact has led to concerns in policy circles about national security. Here is an example:

CBP does not have reasonable assurance that the e-Passport data being protected by the digital signature were written by the State Department because forgers or counterfeiters could simply generate the keys necessary to digitally sign the forged data and include their own certificate in the e-Passport for verification purposes ... Not being able to check the legitimacy of the document signer certificates affects [its] ability to verify the integrity and authenticity of computer chip data on any country's e-Passport ... [therefore] it does not have reasonable assurance that data signed by those countries were actually generated by the authorized passport issuance agency for that country.[55]

In short, in a Big Data universe, decisions made at the ports are increasingly *heterogeneous* in nature. This argument challenges the basic concept of the sovereign decision, or the state's right to decide on "emigration, naturalization, nationality and expulsion." Unpacking this point further, we face the same dichotomy here between authority (*de jure*) and control (*de facto*) challenges as discussed in Chapter 3, with challenges at the ports pertaining almost exclusively to control. The state's authority to determine matters of inclusion and exclusion at the ports remains intact; however, the state's capacity to do so is radically delimited. In relying on heterogeneous sources, the decision is stripped of sovereign exclusivity.

What is most remarkable about this evolution in port management is that this is a trade-off that the state is willing to make. As with the perimeter, the state is willing to cede certain aspects of sovereignty for the sake of security. This is a central paradox of contemporary cross-border relations: whereas in the past security and sovereignty were conceptually aligned, in today's world, to protect national security a state actually has to cede some sovereign control over its borders. As one former UK official puts it:

We are operating in a transnational medium. There are huge benefits from this transnationality. But, we have a sovereign need to make sure that the things we care most about are secure. How do we meet that need? We may meet a lot of it not by sovereign measures, but by collaborative international measures ... You have to [choose over which domains] you want to be absolutely sovereign; you may not be sovereign [over others].[56]

In other words, for the sake of security, the sovereign state increasingly relies on non-sovereign means – in this case, collaboration, sharing and *trust*.

The Corporate Challenge

If the above discussion treats the problem of the *foreign* sourcing of data, this section looks at the *corporate* sourcing of data. This means data that comes from the private sector – such as from mobile phone providers, credit card companies or Internet browsers – but also data that is *stored* and *processed* by the myriad tech companies that have contracts for government work. In these cases, the data is *national* but not *sovereign*. Thus, the same concerns about veracity, context and use arise – and so, *trust*.

The reliance of the state on private data is riddled throughout the preceding empirical discussion. The most notable example of this was the public feud between the FBI and Apple, centering on the question of encryption, considered the embodiment of the trend "toward burden shifting by governments to private sector technology companies for different aspects of law enforcement and foreign intelligence surveillance."[57] But this is an issue that goes much farther down into less sexy forms of interaction, such as how most of the US trusted shipper programs work by having private companies self-screen their packages and report their own data to the state; it is also these same private companies that run background checks on personnel who handle cargo and set screening procedures. This issue will only grow in importance due to collective concerns over cybersecurity. The conundrum is that cybersecurity requires that the state work *more* with private companies, not less. This co-dependency is articulated here:

There is no silver bullet solution and there is no one particular organization – it is not just the private sector, it is not just the public sector – it truly is a collaboration … [cybersecurity] is beyond the capabilities of the nation-state *in and of itself* … Everybody sees a little different piece of the picture. So the criticality of sharing information can't be understated.[58]

The White House itself is unequivocal about the importance of private data for cybersecurity: "The federal government's collaboration with private sector partners to use big data in programs, pilots and research for both cybersecurity and protecting critical infrastructure can help strengthen our resilience and cyber defenses, especially as more cyber threat data is shared."[59]

Like most things in politics, the idea of some form of outsourcing of state functions to private entities is not new. For example, in the Middle Ages many sovereign tasks were performed by private entities, including tasks ranging from the coining of money to the setting of weight standards. This version of sovereignty, that includes the use of private corporations, is called delegation. The outsourcing of government functions to private entities is also considered a central aspect of globalization, to the point where state functions are "substitutable and may be assumed by external agencies, by private companies and by a range of transnational actors."[60] But even if the outsourcing of some forms of state function to private sources is not new, certainly the scale here is. This has been the source of a lot of critical attention in recent years – as in the conflict between Apple and the FBI. The essential question posed by this case is as follows: what happens when the state demands data from private companies – can they say no? Corporations have split incentives. If they encrypt their data, they protect the privacy of their users; but encrypted data cannot be used by the state, thus potentially compromising security. Once again: the liberty–security tradeoff. This has led some companies, notably Apple, to use data that they cannot themselves de-encrypt, making it so that they do not have to choose. In short: encryption keeps the Internet dark, which has the consequence of paradoxically helping out both privacy and terrorism. Here is an account:

[Encryption and anonymity] help whistle-blowers, dissidents and other at-risk individuals to exercise their fundamental rights … But anonymity technology can also help paedophiles, drug dealers and other criminals who use the "darknet." European governments are calling for a ban on encryption, especially after the latest attacks in Paris. They argue that encryption hinders the fight against terrorism and organised crime … But encryption keeps government out of the citizen's personal affairs, whether or not that business is legitimate. In the great trade-off between privacy and security, privacy activists have found unexpected allies in US technology companies.[61]

This means that there are strange bedfellows: law transgressors and privacy seekers both share a desire to be hidden from the state. You can't protect the one without the other.

The challenge to sovereignty here is clear – mirroring the discussion above. But two additional points warrant mention. First, the state's reliance on private data heralds a shift in balance away from the state and toward private corporations in terms of data accession. The state is delimited by legal restrictions, especially the Privacy Act of 1974, which do not apply to the private sector. Naturally, restrictions on the state have minimal purchase if they do not exist in the private collection of data – after all, while the state cannot collect this information, it can use it in its law enforcement practice. Most importantly, however, this leads to an uncomfortable dependency of state law enforcement practice on private sources. Second, to add a final layer to this puzzle, the threats to sovereignty from *foreign* and *corporate* sources are frequently one and the same, as when data emerges from foreign corporations. As a distilling example of this, GazIntech LLC, a Russian company, provides European states with much of their biometric tech. Their product, "'BioID' Systems" is the chief technology used in determining the border crossing between Russia and Finland – i.e. into the EU.[62]

Joint Ports – Considering Citizens and Aliens

The discussion so far has been focused on binational ports and what this means for *states*. But how do these changes implicate *individuals*? This section will treat the subject using the language of citizenship. The first part of the discussion will focus on the problem of *own citizens* (i.e. citizens of one or either of the linked states). It looks at the potential harms of sharing information on *own* border crossers, as well as the more broad challenges presented by data-driven port regimes. The second part focuses on the problem of Third Country Nationals (TCNs) or those individuals that arrive at another nation's door. This section closes by offering a new speculative model of citizenship, to ameliorate some of the concerns raised here, with a special focus on the problem of TCNs.

Data, Filtration and the Citizen

Do jointly administered ports of entry create new opportunities for domination? Certainly there is cause for alarm, especially as regards the question of data sharing. If data is shared between countries, how is it to be protected and maintained? Can shared data ever be truly secure from hacking? Sharing data internationally raises a number of concerns – many of which are true of all forms of data sharing (including internally). Just because it was ethical to obtain and process biometric data in one context, doesn't mean that it is necessarily ethical for this data to be shared and used in a different setting. This is a general point, given that there is a constant risk that data collected in one place will be misinterpreted in another:

> When information is shared outside the component that originally collected it, there is increased potential for misunderstanding its relevance and context, introducing inaccuracies and allowing it to become outdated. Furthermore, the quality of the new information product obtained by combining data on an individual from multiple components is dependent on that of its sources, with any shortcomings potentially multiplied and magnified by the act of combination.[63]

Here concerns over accuracy and privacy overlap: if sharing might lead to misinterpretation, state security interests are as much in peril as civil liberties.

But beyond these technical points about the risks of data sharing, is there something in particular about cross-border sharing the concerns us? Does it bother us, normatively, that another country might have access to information about us? Why? It seems to go against our interests in privacy – but the same can be said about our own state surveillance. So what is unique about the harm of shared data? One answer is that data sharing becomes dangerous when countries lose control over that data, leading to the abuse of their citizens. One example here is the Maher Arar case in which incorrect information, shared by Canada with the US led to the arrest and torture of a Canadian citizen.[64] Points to this effect were also raised by Jennifer Stoddart, former Canadian Privacy Commissioner, who when asked about the sharing of biometric data, remarked that it would bring us "ever closer to the bleak reality of a 'surveillance society'."[65] This once again introduces a trade-off between security and liberty. Another concern pertains to government priorities. Does cross-border data sharing forge compromises? For example, would states privilege gathering information on others, over protecting information of *own* citizens? This is a natural concern surrounding data sharing, as it explicitly entails compromising the data privacy of individual citizens for the sake of the security of the collective. It would seem these concerns can only assuaged by robust national oversight of citizens' data by *own* states.

These concerns about joint port administration come on the heels of broader concerns about the effect of data-driven filtration mechanisms on *citizenship*. Put succinctly: new technologies of filtration used at ports of entry segment people not based on citizenship but on risk scores. Certainly, filtration is nothing new and in fact corresponds to what we would expect to see at a border whereby distinction is made between inside and outside. Such distinctions affirm our priors about sovereignty. The more radical and interesting development has come in terms of *internal* surveillance, or the distinction *between* citizens (members of the polity) and the distinction of wanted and unwanted travelers *irrespective* of citizenship.

This point can be illustrated by returning to the example of trusted traveler programs such as NEXUS, which segments travel according to a two-track system of passage: movement for the global "good" and security-checks for the global "bad." These risk determinations are themselves citizenship-blind. To use a vulgar example, an Arab-American might face greater difficulty entering the US at JFK than a British business traveler. This is participant to a devaluing of citizenship based on risk. The following quotation from Peter Graham, a Director of IBM's global division, puts this in relief:

In the long term we think the travel experience could be very different and border controls more efficient. The business traveller who flies most months would be a member of their nearest airport's frequent traveller scheme. They would pass through most airports almost without stopping until they reached the aircraft, facilitated by the Airport and the Airline. The foreign business traveller who comes to Europe regularly would have a Biometric Residence Permit and when using it would go through the same light touch process as a European citizen.[66]

Otherwise put: data filtration turns people into *de facto* non-citizens, even if they are *de jure* citizens. In doing so, it severs the political meaning of citizenship from its legal basis, further depleting the normative core of popular sovereignty: namely, that citizens are at one with the state, that they determine its character and author its laws.

This argument builds upon numerous other critiques of citizenship, especially those linking the problematics of travel and class – such as notions of "SUV citizenship," or "Gulfstream citizenship."[67] Indeed, trusted traveler programs do not merely enable security stratification, but can be linked into class privileges, as they let members "park closer to the departure hall and use fast check-in counters."[68] The point is that in these circumstances, what matters is not that you are a citizen, but what status of citizen you are – in short, the very form of "second-class" citizenship that we have done our best to eradicate *within* states and yet perpetuate and even reify *between* them. This confirms Zygmunt Bauman's observation that the global era is based on the ability of states to distinguish variable rights to mobility based on the unspoken distinction between "tourists" and "vagabonds."[69] Bigo picks up on these themes, especially how third world travelers are *always already suspect* due to their potential to become immigrants and are thus evaluated as "virtual invaders."[70] Amoore points out the trade-off between security and freedom at the core of contemporary citizenship, such that individuals "verify a credible and secure identity and trade this for mobility."[71]

This type of class analysis of citizenship and global mobility is common and highlights the part of the story with which we are familiar – citizenship is not class-blind. What is of interest is that new forms of data-filtration add an element – risk – that cannot be reduced to class. Indeed, the greatest enemies of the state are frequently the wealthiest. To return to the earlier example, the type of risk-rating produced by an Arab-American with links to vastly wealthy Islamic charities is not identical to the class profiling we have come to expect with non-white Americans in general (or immigrants in Europe).

This amounts to a discrete challenge to citizenship. It is now manifest (what was perhaps always known, but more invisible) that there are *graduated scales* of citizens. The highest position – the most mobile – is essentially stateless in that they are itinerant and welcome wherever they go. This is a total inversion of the "statelessness" that Hannah Arendt describes in *Origins of Totalitarianism*. In the present form, global travelers are stateless not because they no state, but because they are not *bound* to any particular state. They are welcome everywhere. For this global few, the world is their state. Once one receives the global stamp of "acceptable," mobility becomes a right. For those deemed unacceptable, it is at best a privilege, if it is even tenable at all.

It is at the border that these distinctions are made *visible* and *permanent*. Never is this more evident for the traveler than when entering one's own state. What determines whether you are "welcomed" at the border is *not* your passport, it is the complex constellation of codes and content that lays therewithin. This is part of the anxiety we feel at the border, regardless of whether we are coming home or going abroad, whether we are citizens or strangers. This aligns with Derrida's insight – brought up at the outset to this chapter – that hospitality always carries within it a form of hostility;[72] except, here the hostility does not face outward, it faces inward. At the border, even as a citizen, you feel you are an incomplete member, needing hospitality from your own state.

The point here is that what was good about states – whatever else was bad about them – was that they *at least* protected their citizens. This appears to no longer be true.

The TCN Problem – a New Model of Citizenship

Co-Bordering enables officials from two countries a say in constructing border policy. While this might make border policy less coercive to the neighboring state and its citizens, it does not offer any protections to immigrants and travelers from other states (i.e. Third Country Nationals or TCNs) or the own-citizens (minorities) it denominates as risky. With this in mind, this section offers a new model of citizenship designed specifically for border-crossers, suggesting that overlapping borders create not merely bilateral management and enforcement structures, but also an adjudicative wing situated at ports of entry by which border crossers can seek and obtain representation. A *weak* version of this political administration would be bilateral, representing the interests and concerns of *citizens* of both neighboring states. But such an institution would be by definition *partial* as it would enable representation of citizens of the two countries alone. The degree to which this type of structure would assist in the representation of border-crossers would vary by context – at some ports, the predominant immigrant population is from one neighbor to the other (for example at the US–Mexico border); in other cases, local migrants are less common (US–Canada). In either case, it would still be weak.

A *strong* version of this system would require that states cede authority of cases involving TCNs – crossers of a border not their own – to international adjudication. Thus, it would ordain an international political institution specifically designed to oversee the management of bilateral borders, governed by principles of subsidiarity. This would be a physical institution at the border tied to an international deliberative body, positioned and staffed according to need. It would be tasked with the representation, adjudication and treatment of migrants – acts already performed routinely at the border, but without international oversight. An additional purchase of an international body would be to mediate between neighbors over disputes. This need not be simply over questions of migration, but even over security policy, errors and incursions and so forth. As these borders are *bilaterally* run, decisions might by definition be split.

The degree to which an international border administration would be endowed with authority is a question of sovereignty. In its *weak* form, a bi- or multilateral border commission will make little challenge to sovereignty, with states remaining the final arbiters of questions of entry and exit; nonetheless, an international body might offer additional channels for the redress and ultimate placement of immigrants stuck at borders – where currently no institutions are in place to guarantee their fair treatment. In its *strong* form, the international body would have greater authority in adjudicating such concerns – and thus, the more likely the appeals will fit the demands of justice. Suffice it to say that institutional authority on the border mirrors that at the global level, with international organizations possessing varying degrees of authority over sovereign states.

With this rough sketch outlined, the question is what it would achieve. At the very least, international institutions mediating border claims of targeted own-citizens third-party migrants might protect against human rights infringement. As TCNs are by definition without representation, this is the type of population that a strictly territorial law is poorly equipped to address (and which a world governance structure would be too bloated to manage). However, a system of bilaterally run borders, with international oversight, would provide institutional protection of arguably the world's most vulnerable population – targeted minorities and migrants at a border that is not their own – a human rights concern *par excellence*.

Certainly, this system would also assuage some concerns about representation. For example, Arash Abizadeh argues that borders cannot be unilaterally controlled due to the inevitability of coercion, and thus must be run via some system of multilateralism.[73] The model detailed here, with its vertically nested jurisdictions at the border such that members of neighboring states have *shared* voice over policy and TCNs enjoy institutional protection, might satisfy his concerns. In this rubric, the states whose members are most directly and consistently affected by the border (neighbors) share *authorship* over border policy; whereas those with transient concerns (migrants) have an umbrella of protection. As such, this model can be seen as an extension of Abizadeh's aim to structurally represent those coerced (contra the *externality* problem).

Bilaterally run and internationally overseen ports would also become more *transparent* – an important means by which changes to *state* sovereignty may come to match demands of *popular* sovereignty. Indeed, creating a structure for the representation and protection of border-crossers at the border satisfies a lot of our desires for what a just border might look like. In this rubric, the state preserves the essential qualities of self-determination, as they are still ultimate adjudicators of who is entitled to enter onto their soil. But these demands for self-determination do not come at the expense of institutional transparency and mechanisms for the representation of border crossers. Finally, if properly specified, such a system might offer a solution to the problem of distributing refugees and asylum seekers. Problematically, certain countries bear the brunt, by dint of the location of their borders. What we would want is some global distribution mechanism. This is precisely what international adjudicative bodies at bilateral ports of entry could facilitate.

Conclusion

Ports of entry are changing. Just as, at the perimeter, the US and its neighbors are beginning to collaborate at their shared ports of entry – even going so far as to co-locate forces on either side of the line. This move is borne of a shared need for risk-based adjudication of admission, engendering a regime of cross-border data sharing and interoperability between states at levels heretofore unimagined. The implications of this process are significant, especially as pertains to our evolving notion of state sovereignty. As with the perimeter, sovereignty at the ports is increasingly *heterogeneous*, with overlapping spheres of management. But the problem of data is truly a global one, warranting a rethinking far beyond the parameters of bilaterally run ports. This is not simply a question of citizenship and sovereignty, but at core, the future of human rights protection in a data-centric world. These far-reaching concerns are addressed in Chapter 7.

Notes

1 Hatfield, Adam. The Cyber Threat: The Way Forward – Panel Discussion by Adam Hatfield, Director, Technical Advice, Public Safety Canada, National Cyber Security Paper read at Canadian Association of Defence and Security Industries (CADSI) SecureTech Conference, October 30, 2012, at Ottawa Convention Centre, Ottawa, Canada.

2 Declaration by President Obama and Prime Minister Harper of Canada – Beyond the Border. The White House, Office of the Press Secretary.

3 Derrida, "Hostipitality," 2011, at 9.

4 Jay Kalath, CEO, Allied Mission Group LLC. Personal interview, Washington DC, May 16, 2012.

5 Mocny, "US-VISIT Priorities."

6 "The National Strategy for Global Supply Chain Security." The Office of the White House, 2012, at i.

7 Toews, Vic. Keynote Speech by Honorable Vic Toews, Minister, Public Safety Canada. Paper read at Canadian Association of Defence and Security Industries (CADSI) SecureTech Conference, October 30, 2012, at Ottawa Convention Centre, Ottawa, Canada.

8 Kalath, "Patrolling the Border."

9 Department of Homeland Security (DHS). "Northern Border Strategy," 2012, at 17.

10 Scott, "Privacy Impact Assessment for the Global Enrollment System," at 12.

11 Yeates, Neil. "Plenary Address," by Yeates, Deputy Minister, Citizenship and Immigration Canada." Canadian Association of Defence and Security Industries (CADSI) SecureTech Conference, Ottawa, Canada, October 31, 2012.

12 Quoted on Kimery, Anthony. "House Passes SMART Port Security Act." *Homeland Security Today*, June 28, 2012.

13 Meunier, Pierre. Canada–US Beyond the Border Initiative: Efficient Border Crossing for People – Innovate to Address Threats Early – Panel Discussion by Mr. Pierre Meunier, Head, Borders & Critical Infrastructure, DRDC Centre Security Science Paper read at Canadian Association of Defence and Security Industries (CADSI) SecureTech Conference, October 30, 2012, at Ottawa Convention Centre, Ottawa, Canada.

14 Dydynsky, Oryst. "Canada–US Beyond the Border Initiative: Expedited Cargo Clearance." Remarks by Dydynsky, Cross Border and Regulatory Affairs, Descartes Customs Compliance. Canadian Association of Defence and Security Industries (CADSI) SecureTech Conference, Ottawa, Canada, October 31, 2012.

15 Jay Kalath, CEO, Allied Mission Group LLC. Personal interview, Washington DC, May 16, 2012.

16 Mocny, "US-VISIT Priorities."

17 Boyd, John. DoD Biometrics: Key Enabler for Identity Operations – by John Boyd, Director, Defense Biometrics and Forensics, OSD. Paper read at Biometrics for National Security and Law Enforcement, February 1, 2013, at Alexandria, VA.

18 Nemeth, Patrick. Interagency Biometric Collaboration – by Patrick Nemeth, Deputy Assistant Director, US-VISIT Identity Services, DHS. Paper read at Biometrics for National Security and Law Enforcement, January 30, 2013, at Alexandria, VA.

19 Ibid.

20 National Strategy for Aviation Security. 2007. National Security Presidential Directive (NSPD) 47, 1–29, at 16.

21 Ibid., at 21, 19.
22 Mike Rogers, chairman of the Homeland Security Subcommittee on Transportation Security, quoted in McCarter, "TSA Launches Air Cargo Security Initiatives."
23 Exit is a problem for land and sea ports, but not airports, due to the quantity of data available.
24 McCarter, Mickey. "Reconsider US-VISIT Exit Tests: GAO Finds US-VISIT Exit Trials Unsatisfactory." *Homeland Security Today*, August 11, 2010.
25 Phillips, "Canada–US Beyond the Border Initiative."
26 "Declaration by President Obama and Prime Minister Harper of Canada – Beyond the Border."
27 "Northern Border Strategy," at 13.
28 Xavier, Caroline. "Bi-Lateral Cooperation: Joint Operational Efforts, US–Canada." Remarks by Xavier, Director General, Canadian Border Security Agency. Border Security Expo, Phoenix, AZ, March 12, 2013.
29 Alvarez, "Emerging Threats and DHS's Western Hemisphere Strategy to Combat Transnational Crime."
30 Xavier, "Bi-Lateral Cooperation."
31 Bronskill, Jim. "Canada, U.S. To Share Border Security Data." *The Canadian Press*, March 10, 2016.
32 Quoted in Phillips, "Canada–US Beyond the Border Initiative."
33 Wallin, "Plenary Address."
34 Interview, Washington DC, May 17, 2012.
35 Phillips, "Canada–US Beyond the Border Initiative."
36 Bell, Robert. Canada–US Beyond the Border Initiative: Efficient Border Crossing for People – Innovate to Address Threats Early – Panel Discussion by Mr. Bob Bell, Director, NextGen ID Inc. Paper read at Canadian Association of Defence and Security Industries (CADSI) SecureTech Conference, October 30, 2012, at Ottawa Convention Centre, Ottawa, Canada.
37 Dydynsky, Oryst. Cross Border and Regulatory Affairs Consultant, Descartes Customs Compliance. Personal interview, Ottawa, Canada, October 31, 2012. Updated, January 22, 2017.
38 Phillips, "Canada–US Beyond the Border Initiative."
39 Merriam, Mitchell. "Bi-Lateral Cooperation: Joint Operational Efforts, US–Canada." Remarks by Merriam, Deputy Commander, CBP Joint Field Command, Arizona. Border Security Expo, Phoenix, AZ, March 12, 2013.
40 Alvarez, "Emerging Threats and DHS's Western Hemisphere Strategy to Combat Transnational Crime."
41 Quoted in Kimery, Anthony. "A Day in the Life of Nogales." *Homeland Security Today*, September 1, 2010.
42 Gilbert, "Cooperative Efforts between Mexico, Canada and the U.S. in Law Enforcement and Prosecution."
43 Nelson Balido, Border Trade Alliance. Personal interview, El Paso, Texas, October 16, 2012. Updated March 5, 2017.
44 Ibid.
45 Interview, El Paso, Texas, October 16, 2012.

46 Schmitt, *Political Theology*, at 5; Schmitt, Carl. *The Concept of the Political* Translated by George Schwab. Chicago: University of Chicago Press, 1996 [1932].
47 Arendt, *The Origins of Totalitarianism*, at 278.
48 Cited in Ugur, Mehmet. "Freedom of Movement vs. Exclusion: A Reinterpretation of the 'Insider'–'Outsider' Divide in the European Union." *International Migration Review* 29 (4): 964–99, 1995, at 995.
49 Robert Plender, cited in ibid, at 995.
50 Interview, Washington DC, May 16, 2012.
51 Coleman, "Developing Biometrics for International Border Control."
52 Munn, personal interview.
53 Dydynsky, personal interview.
54 Jain, Anil K. "Biometric Recognition." Lecture given at Michigan State University, 2011. Available at http://biometrics.cse.msu.edu, at 14.
55 From Barkakati, Nabajyoti. "Border Security: Better Usage of Electronic Passport Security Features Could Improve Fraud Detection." 1–45: United States Government Accountability Office, Report to Congressional Requestors, GAO-10–96, 2010, at 19–20.
56 Sir David Pepper, former Director, Government Communications Headquarters, UK and Chair of the Defence Science and Technology Laboratory (DSTL). Personal Interview, Ottawa, Canada, October 31, 2012.
57 Donahoe, Eileen. "So Software Has Eaten the World: What Does It Mean for Human Rights, Security & Governance?" *Human Rights Watch*, March 22, 2016.
58 Turner, Dean. "The Cyber Threat: The Way Forward." Remarks by Turner, Director, Global Intelligence Network, Symantec Canada. Canadian Association of Defence and Security Industries (CADSI) SecureTech Conference, Ottawa, Canada, October 30, 2012.
59 "Big Data: Seizing Opportunities and Preserving Values," at 66.
60 Hurrell, *On Global Order*, at 116–17.
61 Mortera-Martinez, Camino "Big Data, Big Brother? How to Secure Europeans' Safety and Privacy." news release, December, 2015, https://www.cer.org.uk/sites/default/files/pb_CMM_bigbrother_4dec15.pdf.
62 Yury Kerekesh; cited in "European Union Border Security," *Government Gazette*, March 2013.
63 Purcell, Richard. "Privacy Policy and Technology Recommendations for a Federated Information-Sharing System." Department of Homeland Security Data Privacy and Integrity Advisory Committee, 2012.
64 Walkom, Thomas "Trudeau Quietly Agrees to Share Info on Canadians with U.S." *The Star*, March 13, 2016.
65 Ling, Justin. "Canada Is Going to Start Handing over Even More Data About Travelers to the US." *Vice News*, March 14, 2016.
66 Peter Graham, Global Director, Immigration, Border and Transportation Security, IBM Global Business Services; cited in *Government Gazette* 2013.
67 Sparke, Matthew. "A Neoliberal Nexus: Economy, Security and the Biopolitics of Citizenship on the Border." *Political Geography* 25 (2): 151–80, 2006, at 156. See also, Lyon, *Identifying Citizens*.
68 Jain, "Biometric Recognition," at 31.

69 Bauman, *Globalization*.
70 Bigo, "Frontier Controls in the European Union," in *Controlling Frontiers*, at 62–3.
71 Amoore, Louise. "Governing by Identity." In *Playing the Identity Card: Surveillance, Security and Identification in Global Perspective*. London: Routledge, 2008, at 28.
72 Derrida, "Hostipitality."
73 See e.g., Abizadeh, "Democratic Theory and Border Coercion."

7 Into the Digital Dark: Data, the Global Firewall and the Future of Security

There is a problem in that we tend to be technofetishists. Big data is very alluring. It draws us in. It seems to give us answers to questions with authority. But it can be wrong.
– Rafal Rohozinski, SecDev Group, 2012.[1]

Data is the new oil. Beyond collecting information, it also means gathering power ... Every government has become dataholic.
– Joana Varon Ferraz, Center of Technology and Society, Brazil.[2]

In 1991, two events simultaneously occurred: the Soviet Union fell and the World Wide Web was born. This juxtaposition was momentous, taken as a harbinger for peace and the victory of liberal values worldwide.[3] But with the benefit of hindsight, another conclusion obtains: while the Internet promised to protect democracy from authoritarianism, it has also enabled democracies to become more authoritarian. The link between securitized democracy and authoritarianism is staggering. This is borne out in a remark about the Stasi:

The Stasi dreamed of computers combining and cross-referencing all the data they had collected to tease out new information they would otherwise have missed. Computers were faster than humans, more precise ... In the 1970s and 80s, however, the technology was just not there and with the fall of the Berlin Wall in 1989 the Stasi was no more. But as we enter a world in which we all produce so much more data and in which computers are able to do more with it [we might ask]: what might the Stasis of today or tomorrow be able to do with technology?[4]

We have come a long way. In 1991, the Russian state could only tap 300 phone lines simultaneously.[5] These days, local police departments have access to more powerful tools of surveillance than those used during the Cold War.[6]

Global politics is dominated by mobility, the movement of people and goods that liberal principles support, but states cannot control. This is not just a matter of immigration and terrorism; it is also about the meteoric

204

rise of business travel and tourism, an important factor in the global challenge of border security. The principle solution to this glut of mobility is for states to collaborate through the sharing of data. This chapter chronicles this global move toward bilateral port administrations and data sharing. The empirical portion reveals collaborative port security and data sharing to be a global phenomenon. Thereafter, it turns toward a more careful exploration of data usage in the EU. Data sharing is an obvious solution to matters of cross-border concern and sits at the center of the global agenda, with many convinced that a comprehensive system will eventually be established. As Sir David Pepper, former Director of UK Government Communications, explains: "[Every] country has to recognize that it cannot deal with [Cybersecurity] alone and in isolation."[7] How this takes shape will greatly inform the future of global governance.

With this global picture painted, the chapter turns toward normative questions. There are numerous possible benefits of a transnational digital public space for world citizens and human rights. In so far as it might come to pass, it will grow out of innovative data platforms that enable micro-targeting of information to subnational and transnational communities. These are mechanisms by which people in different corners of the world might find the fora in which to critically engage. Indeed, one of the lessons of the Arab Spring was that data could bring world attention to harm, and activists worldwide could be gathered together toward common ends. But another lesson was that states can use data too, frequently as a means of repression. Indeed, with the rise of data we have seen new and unheralded means by which the democratic participation of citizens can be curtailed and discrimination perpetuated. Rather than being antithetical to democracies, these practices increasingly appear to be essential to them. In fact, both liberal and non-liberal states increasingly use data against their own citizens. Thus, we need to ask how data can be mobilized *in response* to state co-option and think critically about how and under what conditions couter-publics might become meaningful instruments in the reclaiming of an autonomous public sphere.

Thereafter the chapter engages in a forward-looking discussion about a new global bipolarity forming around data. Global divisions are a given: there will always be an "other," a constitutive outside. But the character of these distinctions varies wildly. In this chapter, I explore a new form of othering on the global stage – a global *firewall*, or the bifurcation of the globe along data capacity. Increasingly, states that have data on their citizens are able to align forces and trust each other, whereas those that are data "dark" are vilified and excluded. This bifurcation raises a number of points. The first and clearest, pertains to dehumanization – namely, in making the "others" barbarian, we make them less than human. This poses a challenge to Human Rights, which would be at risk of becoming a limited concept, such that where there is no data, there are no rights. Further, the firewall threatens to perpetuate global inequality, as those who are down and out – in the digital dark, so to speak – have no means of escaping that predicament. This kind of authority also revisits concerns over neo-imperialism, in this case by a decentered data community – in short, a *digital imperium*.

The chapter concludes with a more careful look at the threats intrinsic to the rise of data, and in particular how new forms of data usage may foretell the future of statecraft. The first concern pertains to the "digital land grab." More data is being collected today than at any point in human history, a trend that will likely continue. This raises complicated rights claims – vis-à-vis storage and the quasi-permanence of records – and greatly changes the relations between individuals, as well as embattled notions such as *consent* and *privacy*. A second concern is that people will lose the will to resist forms of data encroachment, due to the banality of data. In particular, the concern is that we will become unable to see the kinds of discrimination embedded in new data policies. A final point pertains to what I call *pixilation* – a natural outcome of individuation and targeted data collection. A central aim of this book is to identify the grand strategic shift away from a focus on nation-states and sub-state actors and toward the individual. But what if this foretells the end of the individual too, now at the expense of the sub-individual, composed of data points?

A Global Problem

Data, Port Security and Global Bilateralism

Collaborative port security and data sharing is a global phenomenon. One case that illustrates how binational port security is at the front of the world's agenda is the UN Mission in Haiti (MINUSTAH), which has assisted in reconstructing the Haiti–Dominican border after the devastating earthquake of 2010. In addition to humanitarian relief, the mission has revised customs and immigration laws between the two states and facilitated the signing of a Memorandum of Agreement (MOA) between the two countries to streamline the importation of aid. This case is particularly interesting, as the UN had the chance to re-conceptualize the border policy from scratch, choosing to propose a port of entry system that is mutually run and maintained. A leading official from the Border Management Unit for MINUSTAH explains their present strategy:

The vision is to have a common border at the ports of entry ... Not to have Haitian ports of entry and Dominican ports of entry, with some land in the middle, the idea is to have one common place ... We are trying to create a table, where all of the stakeholders of the border sit together ... a harmonized system on the island.[8]

The goal has yet to be realized, but the fact that the UN used its mission to re-design border spaces is telling. Indeed, Haiti is a model for the future – "a laboratory" – to test the efficacy of including border management as part of capacity building missions. On this point, the UN also put together a "One Stop Border Port" in East Timor.

Following up on some of the cases introduced in Chapter 4, there are similar trends in East Africa. In 2004, the EAC agreed upon a Customs Union Treaty, which brought forth common customs laws and procedures, as well as a common external tariff. These changes were participant to a broader move toward the creation of an EU-like "Common Market Protocol" which was agreed in 2009. These changes radically transformed the behavior of the ports. The EAC is becoming a Single Customs Territory – such that you pay a single tax/tariff when you enter the collective region. Collaborative border management is designed "to facilitate inter-agency co-operation and co-ordination for smooth and easy transiting across entry/exit points."[9] The EAC signed a One Stop Border Post agreement in 2006, whereby neighboring states co-manage their border ports. It has taken a long time to materialize, but right now a "One Stop" border post between Ethiopia and Kenya is in its final stages of completion. Several additional border posts between Kenya and Uganda/Tanzania, are under construction. As one Kenyan official explains, this amounts to co-location at the ports, mediated by a common legal frame:

We are trying to eliminate the fact that currently there are two border authorities ... So we put the exporting country's officers [in] the same office with the receiving countries ... it is a jointly managed border and it is legislated as a zone. Currently for these countries we have a common law, which is the East African Customs Management Act [which enables] the One Stop Border Post, which will now give powers to [one country's officer] to execute his responsibilities in another country.[10]

At the ports there is also a data exchange system in place called RADDEX – the Revenue Authorities Data Exchange – in operation since 2009 in Uganda, Kenya and Tanzania, but soon to be expanded across the EAC. This system keeps all data about cross-border traffic and trade in a format that is interoperable with all three countries, enabling real-time coordination over potential threats, because, as another

Kenyan official explains: "all of the agencies need to be able to get access into the database."[11]

Also following on the heels of some of the research introduced in Chapter 4, some of the same cross border developments are afoot in port security in South Africa. In terms of port security, there is a move toward embracing pre-processing schemes, including more advanced development of border ports to enable advanced RFID capabilities and even expedited traveler and trusted shipper systems. These resolutions are part of a broader binational scheme whereby South Africa and its neighbors agree to merge their ports into a single entry/exit system – akin to the one at the US–Canada border – called the One Stop Border Post Initiative (OSB). As one South African trade analyst explains: "we can't act without each other ... We [need] synchronization on border issues. It is no good having an efficient side of Zimbabwe and an inefficient side of South Africa."[12]

South Africa is also in the process of expanding its use of data and bio-metrics at ports of entry. A one SANDF colonel mused: "The European union is trying to fight the issue [of immigration] with data ... In the modern digital world, you cannot exist without a digital presence. Why is it not feasible of trying to control all of this immigration by track-ing the behavior of this data, within the database?"[13] The South African government is currently in the process of creating data-standardization procedures in its own systems, with the hope of exporting these protocols with neighboring states. As one data analyst explains: "Governments of neighboring countries need to agree on certain standards, certain proce-dures, certain ways of doing things."[14]

Australia is another interesting example because it is an island, far from most population centers – two conditions which make biometrics and data sharing essential, especially regarding advanced traveler infor-mation. They use an electronic travel card system that gives Australian authorities advance warning of traveler details before they arrive on Australian soil, a fact enabled by the long flight times to the continent. As Janette Haughton, a prominent official in the Australian Department of Immigration and Citizenship, explains, this enables a "risk-tiered approach to identity ... where we have a range of concentric circles around Australia and we are pushing [the border] further and further out, [and] are doing more and more checks before the person hits our shores."[15] This is a very advanced form of "defense-in-depth."

Australia relies on data sharing perhaps as much as any state in the world. What this does, just as with any system of data sharing, is place *trust* at the center of port management. In 2002 Australia instituted a

Smart Gate program that allows for risk-based adjudication of entry. This enabled faster travel for those deemed unrisky and more scrutiny on those that appear to pose the highest risk:

> With countries where you have confidence in the biometric enrollment process and the document that has been presented, such as a passport where you trust their enrollment process for the passport, you trust that the document is secure, that the chip is secure and that you are then able to use that process for people who you consider to be low-risk.[16]

How does Australia verify identities? In cases where they do not trust the country of origin, they complete further investigation. But due to a strain on resources, when they trust the country of origin, they also trust the claimed identity. This brings this discussion back to the themes treated in Chapter 6. From the state's perspective, trust solves problems of vulnerability; but this is paradoxical, as trust also introduces vulnerability.

Data-Sharing and the Politics of Trust – the European Case

The epicenter of data securitization outside the US is in Europe, especially in recent years. Prior to 9/11 the only data systems that collected information on Third Country Nationals (TCNs) in Europe were the Schengen Information System (SIS) and Eurodac. These were primarily concerned with issues of migration. However, after 9/11 a "second generation" data system was established (SIS II) for the purpose of consolidating counter-terrorism and border security policies. Another data system, the Visa Information System assisted in border security. These data measures took on new urgency after the 2004 Madrid Bombings, at which point the European Council resolved to move toward interoperability between border security databases, aimed at improving data sharing from member states.[17] The 2007 London bombings further extended this call for consolidated, centralized control over the data necessary for collective EU border security, rather than relying on member states alone.

Today, similar kinds of collection systems are in place in Europe as in the US. For example, there are programs to collect data prior to its need or use by authorities – as with Eurodac, or the EU-wide program of collecting the fingerprints of asylum seekers. There are also metadata collection programs, as with the Data Retention Directive, currently under evaluation by the European Court of Justice (ECJ). There are also myriad systems using technology to track refugees (including by recruiting locals and duping travelers). And as with the US, the aim of these programs is to track people before they arrive – another data version of defense-in-depth. Here is an account:

European governments keen to bring the refugee crisis under control are considering using apps, biometrics and smart cards to attempt to manage refugees before they leave countries with border crossings into the EU ... For those who do reach Europe, a smartcard ID system could be used to control access to food and accommodation, under one proposal. Another suggestion is to tempt refugees to download tracking apps on their smartphones by offering helpful information about sea crossings and conditions in different EU countries.[18]

As in the US, the problem of turning people – citizens and aliens alike – into suspicious subjects raises concerns by civil liberties watchdogs. For example, in the UK there have been concerns raised over predictive policing and surveillance programs designed to "legalize mass global surveillance by UK security agencies and allow extraterritorial hacking of computers, phones and networks."[19] In France, anti-terrorism laws raise "issues of compatibility with the rights to free movement, to the presumption of innocence and to free expression."[20]

And of course, one of the main stories of the past few years has been the re-establishing of Europe's internal borders – including with states collaborating with each other to bar the transit of migrants. One variant of this new bordered reality within Europe is that the EU Commission is using its borders once again as sites for data acquisition. Indeed, in 2016 the EU revisited a proposal for an "Entry–Exit" system, so that states collaborate on their mutual frontiers, especially as regards the arrival of third-country nationals, so that they can restrict irregular migration and address the challenge of visa overstayers.[21] Renate Weber, a Member of the European Parliament Committee on Civil Liberties, Justice and Home Affairs describes some components of the European "smart borders" system:

The "Entry–Exit System" will lead to the fingerprinting of all third-country nationals entering the European Union, significantly expanding the EU's biometric information systems and increasing the amount of personal data accessible to law enforcement and security agencies. The "Registered Traveller Programme," under which business and other frequent travellers would benefit from faster crossings, will institutionalize a two-tier border control system in the EU based on crude indicators such as wealth, nationality, employer and travel history. In envisaging the gradual replacement of border guards with "Automated Border Control" gates, the planned "smart borders" proposals may also pave the way for increased surveillance of EU citizens, whose movements could easily be recorded and stored in future.[22]

The goal is for a system to be in place by 2020.

This said, matters of sovereignty continue to bedevil European attempts at data sharing. In 2005, the Prum Convention – sometimes known as Schengen III – was unsuccessful in implementing a pan-European security regime (centered on the sharing of fingerprints and license plate numbers). As the UK's Home Office stated in a report, the "gap created by lack of implementation by some Member States ... [allows criminals] to continue offending across borders," a fact that was especially true because EU police forces could not easily share fingerprints.[23] As with any system, partial buy-in is minimally effective. It will only really take off if other European countries agree to share data more robustly. The problem of intelligence sharing in Europe is widely recognized. As a result of keeping up their sovereign fortresses, European states ironically end up relying heavily on the US – a paradoxical variant of the *politics of trust*. For example, a 2016 editorial in the *New York Times* remarked:

There is no central intelligence service. Indeed, most European governments rely heavily on the United States for intelligence and share data with the C.I.A. or the F.B.I. that they would not share with other Europeans ... Democracies must always find balance between security and freedoms, but the need for Europe to abandon attitudes and structures that impede counterterrorism cooperation could not be more acute.[24]

Some forms of intelligence sharing are very robust, as between Britain, Germany and the Netherlands. But as a general rule, governments refuse to share even simple information – thereby making it considerably harder to predict and preempt terrorist attacks (which requires connecting the dots between different databases). Indeed, the EU totally understands that it needs to create forms of cooperation and data sharing (and in particular, intelligence sharing) that mirror the US. So far, however, this has not transpired (largely due to concerns over sovereignty). On this point, Rob Wainwright, director of Europol, critiques the system in Europe by saying there is a "fragmented intelligence picture" that is not well equipped to manage a "dispersed community of suspected terrorists."[25] Indeed, part of the problem is that bilateral agreements are very strong, and thus "some of the biggest member-states prefer their well-established bilateral agreements."[26]

The important thing is the fact that even when states are able to push past sovereignty concerns, they get log-jammed based on privacy concerns – two of the trade-offs that have been discussed throughout this book. On this point, Stefano Stefanini, of the Atlantic Council remarked: "there is not enough sharing of intelligence to counter this kind of terrorism ... It is obvious that the EU has to accept some trade-off on privacy for security."[27] Regarding the sovereignty trade-off, another EU diplomat remarked: "By nature, it is difficult to get secret services to share information ... No one wants to share their own intelligence."[28] And here is a crystal-clear remark on the data-protection security trade-off: after the 2016 Brussels bombings German Interior Minister Thomas de Maizière remarked, "Data protection is nice ... But in times of crisis – and we are in times of crisis – security has priority."[29]

Despite these challenges, there is near consensus on the need for more data sharing, including within the EU. In a recent poll of seventy-eight European and American political elites, the main priority was to heighten intelligence sharing and thus eliminate the stovepipes between "stupid, national, proud" governments and replace them with "a classified intelligence-sharing network as in NATO."[30] But even in a poll like this, the question of civil liberties remains divisive, with nearly the same number of respondents claiming that increased data sharing should not go along with compromises of individual rights. As one respondent remarked: "Personal freedoms must be sacrosanct ... Upholding our values is at the very core of what Europe means. Citizens must be free to move and work freely and free to speak their minds without fear of reprisal."[31] But one interesting outcome of all this is that there is a pragmatism to the "we must curtail civil liberties side" of the coin: namely, that perhaps it is better to do it at a Europe-wide level, rather than let member states do it.

There is a lot of advice presently being doled out about what the EU should do. Analysts variously claim that the EU should share intelligence, centralize intelligence structures (even to the point of creating something like an FBI) and pool resources toward the common aim of border security.[32] The US has been pushing for more data sharing and is concerned that the EU doesn't do enough with the data they are provided. To this point, in 2016, Terrorist Screening Center Director Christopher Piehota criticized Europe for not doing enough to screen travelers before they arrive on US soil:

It's concerning that our partners don't use all of our data ... We provide them with tools. We provide them with support and I would find it concerning that they don't use these tools to help screen for their own aviation security, maritime security, border screening, visas, things like that for travel.[33]

Data is only as good as its usage. Even if the US has the best data on suspected terrorists or illegal migrants, they can only stop them if European countries make good use of the data. But if the US favors security, the EU has countered with concerns over liberty. The US and the EU dispute over data sharing – "Safe Harbour" – remains unresolved as the ECJ declared that the US did not provide sufficient protection for EU data. At the time of writing, debates are ongoing.[34]

The Emerging Multilateralism

Data sharing is an obvious solution to matters of cross-border concern; but it remains very hard. As such, it is worth saying a few words here about the bridge between bilateral sharing and more multilateral arrangements. After all, unlike with the perimeter, which by its very nature is bilateral, there is no structural reason that cross-border governance at ports of entry cannot embrace a global administration – or at least a dominant regional one. Here is one account of how a web of multilateral sharing might grow out of bilateral agreements, focused on the case of bilateral sharing in Europe:

> [In Europe] there are lots of bi-lateral [agreements] ... The question now becomes: How do you broaden bi-laterals into a multi-lateral web? ... Such arrangements take time to put in place because they are based on trust. And you don't suddenly say "hey guys, lets trust each other" ... It will take a period of years before you can get a real level of trust.[35]

An example of how bilateral data sharing arrangements can grow into multilateral ones is evident regarding collective efforts toward cyberse-curity – which has become a priority in national administrations around the globe. For example, right now countries are acting on their own to protect vulnerable data – such as by setting up nation-level Computer Emergency Response Teams (CERTs) that can respond in the case of cyber-warfare and hacking. However, no global system exists, and these national solutions are increasingly considered insufficient given the magnitude of the threat. As one expert puts it, "national sovereignty is one thing, but in cyber-space collective responsibility can't be avoided;" another adds, "until we can pool our data ... we are playing chess with only half the pieces."[36] This type of thinking has come to the point of being an international consensus – that cybersecurity is bigger than any one nation and that the only comprehensive protection lies at the global level. An official from Public Safety Canada remarks: "Is the challenge beyond any one nation-state? ... Yes it is, because it is not the role of any one nation state to address this problem. Cybersecurity is a shared responsibility. We say this a lot, but it is true ... no one organization can fix this problem. We need to work together."[37]

But this is easier said than done. Right now, nearly all preventative measures on cybersecurity remain at the national or bilateral level. Indeed, even the US, normally sure of its ability to handle global problems on its own, has been pretty forthcoming about the insufficiency of such responses. One Washington DC consultant remarks:

The US is engaging primarily at a bilateral level, which is always easier than broader, multi-state international engagement … but in order to make a difference, all countries have to take responsibility for what's happening in their own infrastructure and the only way to achieve that is through international organizations. We have to agree in the G20, NATO and the UN about what is acceptable.[38]

Certainly there are models for multilateral agreements, as with the Five Eyes, discussed earlier. The point here is simply to show the increased interest in multilateral data sharing solutions to cross-border problems – even if the morass between bilateral and multilateral agreements remains hard to bridge. Michael Allen, former staff director of the House Intelligence Committee, explains these needs as follows: "There's a general recognition among intelligence professionals that the services have to cooperate more and that the US should take the lead in bringing them together."[39]

The most comprehensive attempt at creating a schema for global protection of cyber information came at the Budapest Convention on Cyber-Crime introduced by the Council of Europe in 2001. At this convention, the US, Japan and Canada agreed that authorities in one country should be able to pursue criminals in another. However, the agreement failed to garner significant support; Russia, for example, argued instead for a UN treaty that would respect national sovereignty. Since then, there have been numerous attempts at establishing international governance of cyberspace, but they have met with similar barriers. For example, in 2010 the UN held an International Telecomunications Union Conference in Mexico, which discussed the prospects of a "cyber peace treaty." However, there has yet to be an agreement about the rules.

Consequently, right now existing agreements are either national, bilateral or regional – such as with the Five Eyes community. In NATO's 2010 summit in Lisbon, cyber-security was a central issue, with NATO pledging to enhance its capabilities so as to respond to breaches in cyber-security and bringing all NATO members under a common umbrella of cyber protection. NATO members currently agree that member nations are expected to share cyber information with each other, with NATO providing a support system. The organization also determines what kind of information is to be shared, as well as what can be disseminated to non-member nations. However, NATO itself is unable to intervene across sovereign lines.

A similar drive toward global data sharing exists within Europe. Elly Plooij-Van Gorsel, Founding Chair of the European Internet Foundation (EIF) explains: "Cyber-attacks are borderless, so we have to cooperate and coordinate, starting with the EU."[40] But here too, sharing remains limited. To start, there are still intra-European concerns over standardization – although this problem is presently being addressed. There are longer-term goals of their being a single EU identity database (as there is in the US), but this remains incomplete. Moreover, there is also awareness that a strictly European solution is insufficient. The head of the technical department of the EU's European Network and Information Security Agency (ENISA), Steve Purser remarked: "Everything is globally connected. A European approach doesn't make sense unless aligned to the approach of international partners."[41]

Can these bilateral and regional forms of data sharing expand into a global arrangement? Perhaps, although global data sharing remains inchoate. The problem is simple: a centralized system would be efficient and enable better oversight; but it also requires more trust. At present, data sharing is de-centralized, operating mostly on a bilateral basis. Some lip service is paid toward the consolidation of data, but this remains far afield. The more likely scenario is a web of bilateral agreements sufficiently well coordinated as to make up for the inefficiencies of duplication.

Normative Considerations – Introducing the Global Firewall

There are numerous normative concerns inherent to global data sharing. This section will introduce a new concept – the global firewall – but before this a few words of overview are warranted. That data is used for nefarious purposes comes as no surprise in non-liberal states; however, as evidenced by the material presented in Chapter 5, it is increasingly common in liberal ones too. Further, following on the material in Chapter 6 and in this chapter, we might ask whether there is something deleterious about the way liberal states use and disseminate data technologies to foreign regimes – and thus, whether our data protocols are now going to let autocratic states be more brutal than ever.

Authoritarian states already use data to monitor their populations – through complex forms of censorship, information restriction and monitoring. It is no surprise that they have taken very quickly to data. This relationship is doubly problematic, as in most less-developed societies, the state's capacity to use data for state purposes far outflanks the civilian capacity to use technology toward their own protection. As a result, the same digital revolution that may be liberating in the West may be devastating for many of the world's citizens, who are likely experiencing restricted freedoms and a receding democracy. One particularly clear example of this is China and the rise of so-called "digital authoritarianism," where older forms of social control are mixed with new data-driven forms of surveillance and repression. As an example of the sophisticated nature of Chinese data usage, the state predicates credit ratings on an algorithmically derived mix of factors, which includes not just financial merit, but also assigns "citizenship scores" based on "patriotic criteria."[42] Another example of China's authoritarian counter-democracy toolkit: during pro-democracy rallies in Hong Kong in 2015, the state disseminated an app to protestors alleging to help them organize but which actually sent their messages and their locations to state officials on the mainland.[43]

In the case of China, technology is clearly utilized in contravention of human rights. But this is not simply a Chinese problem, as the West has had a large role in producing the technology used by autocratic regimes (and in selling and distributing it). But beyond this role as technology purveyor, we might think our role is a more important one. It is up to us to act as model societies in terms of data usage. Insofar as we in the West have been using data as a means of technological oppression, what signal do we send the rest of the world?

There are real challenges to human rights in the data era. It is up to us to develop new frameworks to rein in the invasive aspects of data and harness it as a tool for the good. We need norms against sharing data with certain kinds of regimes. We also need mechanisms to protect individuals, regardless of where that sharing may occur. These are important subjects, but outside the remit of this book.

The Global Firewall – Defining the Concept

The idea of collaborating, *trusting*, states has the potential to be a positive force in geopolitics. But, we must be careful what we wish for. There is also an ugly underbelly to trust in that it unfolds in concentric rings of proximity and familiarity. This begins with proximate allies, as with the Five Eyes community – majority white, English-speaking states – and extends outward with waning strength. Finally, the circle of inclusion stops in areas in which data is absent. This is what David Coleman, a data analyst I interviewed, refers to as the global firewall – with data sharing allies on the inside and other states outside. This firewall is here taken to mean the virtual "wall" erected between the community of nations that shares data at the expense and exclusion of those that don't. Such a

scheme maximizes data security, but at the expense of a new stratification of the world. He described the unfurling world order as follows:

The question is what is the perimeter of what you consider trustworthy? ...
[In the West] there is truly a cloud of identity artifacts out there that holds you
accountable for who you are ... More and more, if you are investigating someone from inside the identity firewall, they are going to live in a culture where you
can investigate them, where their country has a credit-reporting agency, similar
things to Lexus-Nexus and the credit reporters. We are basically setting up this
visa waiver firewall. It is not quite as free as the Schengen region, but it is a little
bit broader. If you are in this [domain] you can move pretty easily; but it is really
hard to get into it if you are coming from a tribal area or some place where your
identity is purely social and it is not stored in any electronic media.[44]

The firewall is a barrier of distinction and membership, but also isolation
and vilification. Inside the firewall, there is verifiable data; outside, there
is either unstructured data, or none at all, signaling untrustworthiness
and unverifiability. This is the new great threat: not calculable risk, but
the unknown. When asking if this perpetuated a global caste hierarchy, he
replied that we are "ghettoizing the world."[45]

This mirrors in important ways the analysis provided by Arendt in
Origins of Totalitarianism about the problem of stateless peoples after
World War I. What Arendt was concerned about was that stateless people
have a lack of identification. The power of the ID for Arendt is here
explained: "the loss of citizenship deprived people not only of protection,
but also of all clearly established, officially recognized identity, a fact for
which their eternal feverish efforts to obtain at least birth certificates
from the country that denationalized them was a very exact symbol."[46]
Today the dataless are doubly vulnerable. They do not have ID (the old
problem) and what they do have is unverifiable (the new one). This discussion feeds back into the importance of retaining citizenship (treated
in Chapter 6).

Division, Empire and the New Barbarians

Previous chapters discussed security in the language of rationality – and
the formation of the so-called perfectly rational state. Does the firewall
not represent a perfectly "rational" global order? Embedded in this point
is a longstanding fear of a certain kind of imperialism always at the heart
of liberal global projects. Perhaps the best expression of this point is what
Onora O'Neill has referred to as the "dark side of human rights," namely
that human rights include within them a tendency of "extending the
power of states over non-state actors and human individuals ... establishing systems of control and discipline that extend into the remotest

corners of life."[47] If data is good – and rational – than the rationalized order is better than the pre-rational ones. This is the very logic by which we might legitimate our superiority. This idea of reducing the world to a structural form of identity and difference in many ways mirrors the old division of the world into civilization and barbarism.

This history is long and tortured. Aristotle thought that the Greeks were naturally free and barbarians were naturally slaves, justifying the mastery of the uncivilized by the civilized. Rousseau was adamant about the importance of the maturity of states, as some peoples were not ready for liberty. Mill argued that barbarian peoples can be ruled despotically, as only civilized ones can rule themselves: "Despotism is a legitimate mode of government in dealing with barbarians … Liberty, as a principle, has no application to any state of things anterior to the time when mankind have become capable of being improved by free and equal discussion."[48]

The bifurcation of the globe along the lines of data communities raises a number of concerns. The first, and clearest, pertains to the problem of dehumanization – namely, in making the "other" into a barbarian, we make them less than human. In this way, the firewall gives substance to the concern that modernity has an "exterior" a form of permanent dispossessed. So what happens to people on the wrong side of the firewall? In some deep sense, they are returned to a state of savageness, i.e., they are reduced to bare humanity, because nothing else – state, national community, language, religion, etc. – can help them. This is a state of profound vulnerability. In this way, it follows Agamben's remark that the essence of politics lies in the politicization of bare life:

> The fundamental categorical pair of Western politics is not that of friend/enemy but that of bare life/political existence, *zoel bios*, exclusion/inclusion. There is politics because man is the living being who, in language, separates and opposes himself to his own bare life and, at the same time, maintains himself in relation to that bare life in an inclusive exclusion.[49]

Is this not what the firewall does? On *our* side of the firewall is civilization and politics; on *their* side is just life as such.

By this way of thinking, people without data trails would not really count any longer *as people*. Consequently, human rights would come to pertain only to the sphere of humans about whom information is known. Within the firewall, all humans would have rights, but where there is no data, there would be no rights. Borrowing from Orwell, we might say that, vis-à-vis human rights, some people would be more equal than others. And worse, this would be structural and come to be as real as Apartheid, or any other form of segregation with which we are familiar.

The language of dehumanization brings us back to the question of neo-colonialism – in this case regarding the harms of labeling, as once given such a label, it is hard to break. One reason for this is that any rebel acts will only be read through the guise of their supposed barbarianism. Indeed, we have a long history of using international law to reify state violence, vilify non-state forms of violence and recast them as terror. Hurrell explains that state attempts to legalize their own acts of war against each other required forging a distinction with private violence, such that "pirates (and, of course, more recently terrorists) were enemies of all humankind, *hostis humani generi.*"[50] Following Talal Asad, this is why we are particularly incensed by suicide violence, as opposed to violence in the name of the state.[51]

This argument mirrors those on labeling – or the ways in which colonial subjects were subjugated by and struggled against, the classifications cast upon them by the colonial powers. As Mary Louise Pratt explains, this led to a kind of madness, as colonial subjects strove to define themselves both in opposition to the label, but also without respect to it (a logical impossibility).[52] Because it is data that is doing the defining, and data defines the means by which the new colonial) shackles can be broken, a similar kind of labeling is perpetuated here. The problem is not just that the dataless are excluded, but also that we essentially rob them of the capacity to be included – after all, how can they prove their worth to us, if they have no data trail? Without data, by what metric can innocence even be established? Here again, it is not the lack of ID, but the fact that whatever IDs exist cannot be verified.

The firewall division of the globe perpetuates difference and inequality by disincentivizing states to intervene in the dark spots. In this way, the global firewall will only perpetuate the scourge of distance (as a facet of otherness). Distance matters when the conditions of power between master (center) and subject (periphery) get so distant that the subjects of that power become unknown and unknowable (to the center). Or, in Butler's terms, when their lives become so distant as to be considered *ungrievable.* This is the core normative harm at the heart of peripherality, – a condition we should aim to defeat, through integration. Pogge makes this point about distance in economic terms:

We live in extreme isolation from severe poverty. We do not know anyone earning less than $30 for a 72-hour week of hard, monotonous labor. The one-third of human beings who die from poverty-related causes includes no one we have ever spent time with ... If we had such people as friends or neighbors, we would think harder about world poverty and work harder to help end this ongoing catastrophe.[53]

This isolation that Pogge describes is very meaningful for this argument. The problem isn't just that "we" will never meet "them." It is that absent data, we won't even know who "they" are. They will be as if dead to us: mute, bound, in the dark. If Pogge is right, this isolation is part of the reason we in the West can justify inequality. By creating institutions that perpetuate isolation, we also perpetuate that injustice.

Data also perpetuates inequality within states, especially those that are on the bubble. These societies have considerable upper- and middle-classes that travel and have cutting edge data profiles and would like to be on the "right" side of the firewall. So how do they get there? According to Coleman, they must either "bifurcate their societies into two castes," or "invest a significant amount into bringing their poor classes into the electronic light."[54] It is no surprise that they usually chose the former, thereby exacerbating internal divisions. In this case, "the lack of electronic identity doesn't cause the ghettoization, but it reinforces it."[55]

The global firewall may also generate barriers to mobility for large swaths of the world. This lack of movement seems particularly oppressive in part because of what it says about the people themselves, which is that by dint of their place of birth they are *inherently risky*. Didier Bigo makes a similar point in his discussion of inequalities vis-à-vis immigration, and the fact that tourists from poor countries cannot enjoy the leisure of travel, as they are treated as though they are *already suspect*.[56] He is discussing this issue vis-à-vis immigration to Europe. But we don't need to restrict our view in this way.

Before closing, it is worth saying a few words about sovereignty. If we follow Agamben, isn't this global bipolar division an expression of sovereignty? After all, for him it is through the moment of the biopolitical decision that the whole sovereign order is itself created. Sovereignty in this sense has a lot in common with the idea of banishment – sovereign is he who determines who is to be banished to exterior. Agamben follows Jean-Luc Nancy's suggestion to look at the word "ban" in terms of understanding the exception:

The relation of exception is a relation of ban. He who has been banned is not, in fact, simply set outside the law and made indifferent to it but rather *abandoned* by it, that is, exposed and threatened on the threshold in which life and law, outside and inside, become indistinguishable. It is literally not possible to say whether the one who has been banned is outside or inside the juridical order.[57]

Here we return to the semantic problem of understanding what to call imperial authority – especially in this case, where the empire has no metropole. What we have is the rule by a decentered data-technical community – a *digital imperium*. This type of authority is once again a means of banishment or exclusion, but now from an amorphous, poly-headed data empire, tasked with a new decision: who gets to be included in the community of light.

This remains speculative. Insofar as we accept such a division of the world, the question facing theorists is how to create institutional structures toward the best realization of our values. Multipolarity, regionalism and networked forms of collaboration once again appear to be an important route to solvency. But perhaps this is naïve. It is hard to really imagine, at this early stage, what it would look like, the segregation of the world into light and dark, and the kind of power this would engender. As data lets states be less geo-located, the potential sites of their projected power multiply. Why would a state's motive – in the event that it is concerning, say, to control peoples' data or restrict their digital speech for the sake of order or stability – not extend outside of borders? If states are increasingly imperial, so too are their data capacities and interests. Once the black box of sovereignty is penetrated, it isn't merely light that is let in, it is darkness that is let out.

Data and the Future of Security

Before closing, a couple of future trends in data usage warrant attention. One should always be wary of predictions. But we are clearly at the forefront of a revolution and it is important to consider threats that loom on the horizon. As one cybersecurity expert explains: "we are the first generation that can be tracked from birth to our deathbeds, where we are, what we do, who we communicate with, what are our interests ... It feels like we're in a massive experiment done on mankind."[58]

The "Digital Land Grab"

More data is being collected today than at any point in human history. The White House refers to this as "structural over-collection," and offers the following admonition about the future: "The potential future value of data is driving a digital land grab, shifting the priorities of organizations to collect and harness as much data as possible."[59] We have to accept that more data will be collected every year. The key task facing theorists is how to find principles that match this over-collection, rather than spend time hoping the data deluge will be dammed.

A number of issues spring from this trend, especially as pertains to storage. In the past, states had limited capacity to keep records. Today, all documents can be retained, copied, disseminated, all at nearly no cost to the state. Further, data is being generated at unimaginable rates. This

is not just a problem within the state; people leave traces on the Internet
that remain quasi-permanent, even if the people themselves change and
the circumstances around that data change too. This leads to a new set
of rights concerns, such as the "right to be forgotten" and the corollary
concept that even people who have "nothing to hide" may want the right
to hide it.[60] This is not just the problem of "Big Brother" but of "Little
Brother," which arises through data-generating instruments outside of
the state, as with the "internet of things" or the superabundance of apps.
This foretells, perhaps, *the end of privacy* – following on the proclama-
tion by founder and CEO of Facebook, Mark Zuckerberg that in our era
"privacy is not a social norm." Relatedly, it appears also to presage the
end of consent as a meaningful principle in politics, or as the White House
puts it, there are "instances where the notice and consent framework
threatens to be overcome,"[61] such as in the collection of data that is non-
cooperative, as with apps.

But what is perhaps most interesting about the question of data and
privacy pertains not to the state-subject relationship, but the intersubjective one. One of the complicated aspects of privacy is that the decisions
of some citizens greatly influences the lives of others – because if a lot of
people disclose information about themselves, it turns those people who
choose not to into a kind of suspect. As one analyst has argued,

My decision to disclose personal information, even if I disclose it only to my
insurance company, will inevitably have implications for other people, many of
them less well off. People who say that tracking their fitness or location [through
their smartphone, for example] is merely an affirmative choice from which they
can opt out have little knowledge of how institutions think. Once there are
enough early adopters who self-track – and most of them are likely to gain something from it – those who refuse will no longer be seen as just quirky individuals
exercising their autonomy. No, they will be considered deviants with something
to hide.[62]

This compounds the existing trend of vigilantism, or the move for citizens to take it upon themselves to enforce the law. With data, many different types of actors claim the authority of the state. Louise Amoore
explains this problem well: "The constant demand for identification
operates as though it already had juridical status. Not only the state,
but the security guard, the biometrics software engineer, the ticket sales
clerk, even the citizen, acquires the power of policing the security policy
... [What matters is] not strictly the requirement to produce identification *per se*, but rather the profound uncertainty as to the authority of the
demand. Who is authorized to ask 'identify yourself?' What is the basis of
that authority?"[63] This raises the question of source – i.e., from whom do
we seek protection? Increasingly the answer is *from each other*.

The Banality of Data

Another fear is that people are losing the will to resist forms of data encroachment, due to the banality of data. Two concerns about state transgression obtain. The first is that while citizens are wary about giving over their data to the government, they are generally happy to breach their own privacy through the publication of photographs on social media sites or offering up data to private corporations. But, given the increased reliance of the state on private companies and data, this should offer no solace, and indeed are increasingly one and the same (a fact most citizens do not appreciate). The second aspect is that citizens generally accept relinquishing privacy when they believe this to be essential to stopping terror. But how can this truly be established – it will never be clear whether security attacks were actually foiled because of specific privacy breaches? As we become inured to data – and the state use of individual data – the concern is that we will be less capable of erecting institutional barriers to defend against abuse.

Another outcome of this trend is that we will increasingly become incapable of seeing the kinds of discrimination embedded in new data policies. Given the nature of data accumulation, this means that "small biases have the potential to become cumulative, affecting a wide range of outcomes for certain disadvantaged groups."[64] Thus, the discrimination we see at present has the capacity to ossify and thus become both more permanent and more overbearing.

The sum of this is that Big Data has the potential to radically skew the balance between the state and citizens. In democracies, the people are supposed to be sovereign over the state, which acts in their service. The people should watch over the state – not vice-versa. This is an essential aspect of democratic legitimacy, currently in the process of being upended. The seriousness of this point is made manifest by Rousseau: "The essence of the body politic consists in the harmony of obedience and liberty; and the words *subject* and *sovereign* are identical correlatives, whose meaning is combined in the single word 'citizen'."[65] The key is the *harmony* of obedience and liberty. It doesn't sustain if we are more obedient than we are free.

The Birth of the Pixelated Subject

A central theme of this book pertains to individuation – a natural outcome of targeted data collection. Data systems now can merge biometric data with biographic material, for the purpose of creating a "360 degree" profile. Indeed, there has been a grand strategic shift *away from a focus on nation-states and sub-state actors and toward the individual.* This move need not be harmful – indeed, the primacy of the individual is also at the center of human rights norms. But what if this foretells the end of the individual too, now at the expense of the sub-individual, a subject composed of data points? The point here is not the *enumerated* subject – this was the problem of modernity. Now the problem is the *pixelated* subject. A subject composed of so many data points that the individual is no longer a meaningful category, except as the aggregation of those datapoints in the way a photograph is an aggregation of pixels.

Given the fact of pixelation, we have a lot more work to do to understand the role of rights in a data universe. Generally, we understand rights as boundaries around persons, or "defenses erected round individuals."[66] Do these boundaries protect not just the person but also their data double? Does the data double have certain rights, but not all? Which are they and how are they derived?

Conclusion

> Perseus wore a magic cap so that the monsters he hunted down might not see him. We draw the magic cap down over our eyes and ears so as to deny that there are any monsters.
> – Marx, *Capital* I, Preface to the First Edition [1867].[67]

Writing in the eighteenth century, Rousseau remarked that the perversion of democracy was *ochlocracy*, or rule by mob.[68] Perhaps Rousseau had it wrong – when democracy is perverted, it is ruled by machines. It is the *tyranny of the algorithm* we should fear, the purest form of bureaucracy. Indeed, perhaps the greatest question facing the study of politics today is whether states come to control data, or data comes to control states.

This book has detailed numerous reasons for concern about the trends to come. But there is no reason for defeatism. There are many policy correctives generated from within the civil liberties community about matters of injustice arising from data – such as auditing tools to ensure proper protocols are followed and that specific populations are not unfairly targeted or profiled, especially by automated decision-making structures.[69] Such legal protections are important, but we have to be vigilant. Indeed, we might surmise that *as the state securitizes, law is less and less potent as a form of resistance to power.* We should also be wary that solutions will come from within Big Data itself or improved data analyzing systems – the answer to the ills of bureaucracy is rarely more bureaucracy.

Marx invoked the myth of Perseus slaying Medusa as a clarion call; my purpose is the same here. While it is foolish to prognosticate in politics, it is just as foolish to observe trends and make no effort to shape them in a way that is socially responsible. It is time to face the monster; the stakes are too high to hide our eyes any longer.

Notes

1 Rohozinski, "Big Data Analysis and Intelligence."
2 Joana Varon Ferraz, researcher at the Center of Technology and Society, Brazil; cited in Eubanks 2014.
3 Corera, Gordon. "Will Big Data Lead to Big Brother?" *BBC News* (November 17, 2015). I am grateful to this article for calling this juxtaposition to my attention.
4 Ibid.
5 Ibid.
6 "Big Data: Seizing Opportunities and Preserving Values," at 49–50.
7 Pepper, Sir David. "The Cyber Threat: The Way Forward." Remarks by Pepper, former Director, Government Communications Headquarters, UK and Chair of the Defence Science and Technology Laboratory (DSTL), Canadian Association of Defence and Security Industries (CADSI) SecureTech Conference, Ottawa, Canada, October 30, 2012.
8 Rocco Messina, Acting Chief of Border Management Unit, MINUSTAH. Personal interview, El Paso, TX, October 17, 2012.
9 Nganga, Kamau. Case Study: The Kenyan Experience at our Border Stations – by Kamau Nganga, Deputy Commissioner, Kenya Revenue Authority. Paper read at Border Management Southern Africa, January 22, 2013, at Pretoria, South Africa.
10 Personal interview, Pretoria, South Africa, January 22, 2013.
11 Personal interview, Pretoria, South Africa, January 22, 2013.
12 Wylie, Phillip. "Improving Cross Border Trade at the Border." Remarks by Wylie, Founder, Andevi Trading, Executive Consultant to South African Association of Freight Forwarders. Border Management Southern Africa Conference, Pretoria, South Africa, January 23, 2013.
13 Interview, Pretoria, South Africa, January 23, 2013.
14 van der Schyf, Ockert. Remarks by van der Schyf, Head of Marketing, Sub-Saharan Africa, SAAB. Border Management Southern Africa Conference, Pretoria, South Africa, January 23, 2013.
15 Haughton, Janette. "Managing Borders Using Biometrics." Remarks by Haughton, Regional Director for the Americas, Australian Department of Immigration and Citizenship. Biometrics for National Security and Law Enforcement Conference, Alexandria, VA, January 30, 2013.
16 Ibid.
17 Boswell, Christina. "Migration Control in Europe after 9/11: Explaining the Absence of Securitization." *Journal of Common Market Studies* 45 (3), 2007: 589–610, at 602.
18 Taylor, Diane and Emma Graham-Harrison. "EU Asks Tech Firms to Pitch Refugee Tracking Systems." *The Guardian*, February 18, 2016.

19 Donahoe, Eileen. "Digital Disruption of Human Rights." *Human Rights Watch*, March 25, 2016.
20 Ibid.
21 Baczynska, Gabriela. "EU Executive to Present Steps to Tighten External Border Controls." April 6, 2016.
22 Cited in "European Union Border Security," *Government Gazette*, March 2013.
23 Foster, Peter. "European Cross-Border Security Years Away, Experts Warn." *The Telegraph*, March 23, 2016.
24 "Editorial: Europe's Urgent Security Challenge." *The New York Times*, April 11, 2016.
25 Brown and Mallonee, "First on CNN."
26 Mortera-Martinez, "Big Data, Big Brother?"
27 Cited in Dendrinou, Viktoria. "Brussels Attacks Expose Europe's Scant Progress on Security." *The Wall Street Journal*, March 24, 2016.
28 Cited in Ibid.
29 Ibid.
30 Chadwick, Vincent. "Policymakers: Share Intel but Don't Betray Liberty." *Politico.eu*, April 7, 2016.
31 Ibid.
32 See e.g. Soufan, Ali. "Opinion: Terrorists Cross Borders with Ease. It's Vital That Intelligence Does Too." *The Guardian*, March 24, 2016.
33 Brown and Mallonee, "First on CNN."
34 Mortera-Martinez, "Big Data, Big Brother?"
35 Pepper, Sir David, former Director, Government Communications Headquarters, UK and Chair of the Defence Science and Technology Laboratory (DSTL). Personal Interview, Ottawa, Canada, October 31, 2012.
36 Grauman, Brigid. "Cyber-Security: The Vexed Question of Global Rules." 1–103: Security & Defence Agenda, 2012, at 23; Phyllis Schneck, Chief Technology Officer for Public Sector at McAfee, quoted on Grauman, "Cyber-Security," at 8.
37 Hatfield, Adam. "The Cyber Threat: The Way Forward." Remarks by Hatfield, Director, Technical Advice, Public Safety Canada, National Cyber Security. Canadian Association of Defence and Security Industries (CADSI) SecureTech Conference, Ottawa, Canada, October 30, 2012.
38 Melissa Hathaway, quoted on Grauman, "Cyber-Security," at 85.
39 Cited on Ignatius, David. "Brussels Shows Europe's Shockingly Dysfunctional Approach to Security." *The Washington Post*, March 22, 2016.
40 Quoted on Grauman, "Cyber-Security," at 73.
41 Quoted on ibid., at 23.
42 Donahoe, "Digital Disruption of Human Rights."
43 Corera, "Will Big Data Lead to Big Brother?"
44 David Coleman, Senior Director and Product Manager, Novetta Mission Analytics. Personal interview, Alexandria, VA, January 30, 2013.
45 Ibid.
46 Arendt, *The Origins of Totalitarianism*, at 287.
47 O'Neill, Onora. "The Dark Side of Human Rights." *International Affairs* 81, no. 2 (2005): 427–39, at 439.

48 Mill, *On Liberty*, at 81.
49 Agamben, *Homo Sacer*, at 8.
50 Hurrell, *On Global Order*, at 51.
51 Asad, Talal. *On Suicide Bombing*. New York: Columbia University Press, 2007.
52 Pratt, Mary Louise. *Imperial Eyes: Travel Writing and Transculturation*. New York: Routledge. Original edition, 2008, at 235–6.
53 Pogge, Thomas. *World Poverty and Human Rights*. Second ed. Malden, MA: Polity Press, 2008, at 4–5.
54 David Coleman, Senior Director and Product Manager, Novetta Mission Analytics. Personal interview, Alexandria, VA, January 30, 2013. Updated, January 23, 2017.
55 Ibid.
56 Bigo, "Frontier Controls in the European Union," in *Controlling Frontiers*, at 63.
57 Agamben, *Homo Sacer*, at 28–9.
58 Mikko Hypponen; cited in Corera, "Will Big Data Lead to Big Brother?"
59 "Big Data: Seizing Opportunities and Preserving Values," at 53–4.
60 Mortera-Martinez, "Big Data, Big Brother?"
61 "Big Data: Seizing Opportunities and Preserving Values," at 56.
62 Evgeny Morozov, cited in "Note on Big Data, Crime and Security: Civil Liberties, Data Protection and Privacy Concerns." *Statewatch*, April 3, 2014.
63 Amoore, "Governing by Identity," at 21–2.
64 "Big Data: Seizing Opportunities and Preserving Values," at 58–9.
65 Rousseau, "The Social Contract," in *The Basic Political Writings*, at 196.
66 Freeden, Michael. *Rights*. Minneapolis: University of Minnesota Press, 1991, at 43.
67 Marx, Karl. *Capital, Volume 1*. Translated by Ben Fowkes. London: Penguin, 1990 [1867], at 91.
68 Rousseau, "The Social Contract," in *The Basic Political Writings*, at 193.
69 For arguments like these, see: "Civil Rights Principles for the Era of Big Data." Leadership Conference on Civil and Human Rights & The Leadership Conference Education Fund, 2014, http://www.civilrights.org/press/2014/civil-rights-principles-big-data.html.

References

"2012–2016 Border Patrol National Strategy" US Border Patrol Press Release, 2012.

"244 Million International Migrants Living Abroad Worldwide, New Un Statistics Reveal." United Nations Sustainable Development, 2016. www .un.org/sustainabledevelopment/blog/2016/01/244-million-international-migrants-living-abroad-worldwide-new-un-statistics-reveal/.

Abizadeh, Arash. "Democratic Theory and Border Coercion: No Right to Unilaterally Control Your Own Borders." *Political Theory* 36 (1):37–65, at 2008.

Agamben, Giorgio. *Homo Sacer: Sovereign Power and Bare Life*. Translated by D. Heller-Roazen. Edited by W. Hamacher and D. E. Wellbery. Stanford, California: Stanford University Press, 1995.

State of Exception. Translated by K. Attell. Chicago: University of Chicago Press, 2005.

Amoore, Louise. "Governing by Identity." In *Playing the Identity Card: Surveillance, Security and Identification in Global Perspective*. London: Routledge, 2004.

Amoore, Louise, and Marieke de Goede. "Governance, Risk and Dataveillance in the War on Terror." *Crime, Law & Social Change* 43 (2):149–73, 2005.

Anderson, Benedict. *Imagined Communities: Reflections on the Origin and Spread of Nationalism*. New York: Verso, 2006.

Anderson, Malcolm. *Frontiers: Territory and State Formation in the Modern World*. Cambridge: Polity Press, 1996.

Andreas, Peter. "The Mexicanization of the US-Canada Border: Assymetrical Interdependence in a Changing Security Context." *International Journal* 60 (2):449–462, 2008.

Ansell, Christopher K. "Territoriality, Authority and Democracy." In *Restructuring Territoriality: Europe and the United States Compared*, edited by C. K. Ansell and G. D. Palma. Cambridge, UK: Cambridge University Press, 2004.

Anzaldúa, Gloria. *Borderlands: The New Mestiza*. San Francisco: Aunt Lute Books, 2007.

Arendt, Hannah. *The Origins of Totalitarianism*. New York: Harcourt, 1976.

The Human Condition. Chicago: University of Chicago Press, 1998.

Aristotle. *The Politics and the Constitution of Athens*. edited by S. Everson. Cambridge: Cambridge University Press, 1996.

Asad, Talal. *On Suicide Bombing*. New York: Columbia University Press, 2007.

Baczynska, Gabriela. "EU Executive to Present Steps to Tighten External Border Controls." *Reuters*, April 6, 2016, http://uk.reuters.com/article/uk-europe-migrants-eu-borders-idUKKCN0X30BO

Barkakati, Nabajyoti. "Border Security: Better Usage of Electronic Passport Security Features Could Improve Fraud Detection." United States Government Accountability Office, Report to Congressional Requestors, GAO-10-96, 2010.

Baubock, Rainer. "Global Justice, Freedom of Movement and Democratic Citizenship." *Archives of European Sociology* 1:1–31, 2009.

Bauman, Zygmunt. *Globalization: The Human Consequences.* New York: Columbia University Press, 1998.

Beitz, Charles R. *The Idea of Human Rights.* Oxford: Oxford University Press, 2009.

Bekdil, Burak Ege. "Turkey to Shop for Border Security Equipment." *Defense News*, September 5, 2015.

Benhabib, Seyla. *The Claims of Culture: Equality and Diversity in the Global Era.* Princeton: Princeton University Press, 2002.

Dignity in Adversity: Human Rights in Troubled Times. Cambridge, UK: Polity Press, 2011.

Berlin, Isaiah. "Two Concepts of Liberty." In *The Proper Study of Mankind: An Anthology of Essays*, edited by Henry Hardy and Roger Hausheer. New York: Farrar, Straus and Giroux, 2000.

"Big Data." American Civil Liberties News Release, February 27, 2014, https://www.aclu.org/issues/privacy-technology/surveillance-technologies/big-data.

"Big Data: Seizing Opportunities and Preserving Values." White House Executive Office of the President, News Release, May 1, 2014, https://www.whitehouse.gov/sites/default/files/docs/big_data_privacy_report_may_1_2014.pdf.

Bigo, Didier. "Globalization of In-Security: The Field of the Professionals of Unease Management and the Ban-opticon." *Traces: A Multilingual Journal of Cultural Theory* 4:109–57, 2004.

"Frontier Controls in the European Union: Who is in Control?" In *Controlling Frontiers: Free Movement Into and Within Europe*, edited by D. Bigo and E. Guild. Chippenham, Wiltshire: Ashgate Publishing Company, 2005.

Boswell, Christina. "Migration Control in Europe after 9/11: Explaining the Absence of Securitization." *Journal of Common Market Studies* 45 (3):589–610, 2007.

Bourdieu, Pierre. *Distinction: A Social Critique of the Judgement of Taste.* Translated by R. Nice. Cambridge, MA: Harvard University Press, 1984.

Outline of a Theory of Practice. Translated by R. Nice. Edited by E. Gellner, J. Goody, S. Gudeman, M. Herzfeld and J. Parry, *Cambridge Studies in Social and Cultural Anthropology.* Cambridge, UK: Cambridge University Press, 2003.

Bronskill, Jim. "Canada, U.S. To Share Border Security Data." *The Canadian Press*, March 10, 2016.

Brown, Pamela, and Mary Kay Mallonee. "First on Cnn: Top U.S. Intel Official: Europe Not Taking Advantage of Terror Tracking Tools." *CNN.com*, April 7, 2016.

Brown, Wendy. *Walled States, Waning Sovereignty*. Cambrige, MA: Zone Books, 2010.

Browne, Simone. "Digital Epidermalization: Race, Identity and Biometrics." *Critical Sociology* 36 (1):131–50, 2010.

Brunkhorst, Hauke. "Globalizing Democracy without a State: Weak Public, Strong Public, Global Constitutionalism." *Millenium: Journal of International Studies* 31 (3):675–90, 2002.

Buchanan, Allen. "The Making and Unmaking of Boundaries: What Liberalism Has to Say." In *States, Nations, and Borders: The Ethics of Making Boundaries*, edited by A. Buchanan and M. Moore. Cambridge: Cambridge University Press, 2003.

Buchanan, Allen, and Margaret Moore. "Introduction: The Making and Unmaking of Boundaries." In *States, Nations, and Borders: The Ethics of Making Boundaries*, edited by A. Buchanan and M. Moore. Cambridge: Cambridge University Press, 2003.

Burbank, Jane, and Frederick Cooper. *Empires in World History: Power and the Politics of Difference*. Princeton: Princeton University Press, 2010.

Butler, Judith. *Frames of War: When Is Life Grievable?* London: Verso Books, 2010.

Calabrese, Chris. "When Big Data Becomes a Civil Rights Problem." news release, February 27, 2014, https://www.aclu.org/blog/free-future/when-big-data-becomes-civil-rights-problem?redirect=blog/technology-and-liberty-racial-justice-criminal-law-reform/when-big-data-becomes-civil-rights.

Callahan, Mary Ellen, and Wesley Wark. "Privacy and Information Sharing: The Search for an Intelligent Border." In *One Issue Two Voices*: Woodrow Wilson International Center for Scholars, 2010.

Carens, Joseph H. "Aliens and Citizens: The Case for Open Borders." *Review of Politics* 49 (2):251–73, 1987.

Immigrants and the Right to Stay. Cambridge, MA: The MIT Press, 2010.

Castells, Manuel. *The Rise of the Network Society*. Malden, MA: Blackwell, 2000.

Cavallero, Eric. "Global Federative Democracy." *Metaphilosophy* 40 (1):43–64, 2009.

Ceyhan, Ayse. "Technologization of Security: Management of Uncertainty and Risk in the Age of Biometrics." *Surveillance & Society* 5 (2):102–23, 2008.

Chadwick, Vincent. "Policymakers: Share Intel but Don't Betray Liberty." *Politico.eu*, April 7, 2016.

"Civil Rights and Big Data: Background Material." Leadership Conference on Civil and Human Rights & The Leadership Conference Education Fund, News Release, 2014, www.civilrights.org/press/2014/civil-rights-and-big-data.html.

Cochrane. ClearVu: The Invisible Wall. Cochrane USA, Product Guide, 2012.

Cochrane USA: Perimeter Security Barrier Specialist. Cochrane USA, Product Guide, 2012.

Cohen, Jean L. "Sovereign Equality vs. Imperial Right: The Battle over the "New World Order." *Constellations* 13 (4):485–505, 2006.

Globalization and Sovereignty: Rethinking Legality, Legitimacy, and Constitutionalism. Cambridge: Cambridge University Press, 2012.

Connolly, William. *Identity/Difference: Democratic Negotiations of Political Paradox.* Minneapolis: University of Minnesota Press, 2012.

Costa, Antonio Mario. The Globalization of Crime: A Transnational Organized Crime Threat Assessment. United Nations Office on Drugs and Crime (UNODC), 2010.

De Vries, Lloyd. "Airport Security Fails Test." *CBS News,* February 11, 2009.

Declaration by President Obama and Prime Minister Harper of Canada – Beyond the Border. 2011. The White House, Office of the Press Secretary.

Derrida, Jacques. "Hostipitality." *Angelaki* 5 (3):3–18, 2000.

On Cosmopolitanism and Forgiveness. Translated by M. Dooley and M. Hughes. Edited by S. Critchley and R. Kearney, *Thinking in Action.* New York: Routledge, 2001.

Di Palma, Giuseppe. "Postscript: What Inefficient History and Malleable Practices Say about Nation-States and Supranational Democracy When Territoriality is No Longer Exclusive." In *Restructuring Territoriality: Europe and the United States Compared,* edited by C. K. Ansell and G. D. Palma. Cambridge, UK: Cambridge University Press, 2004.

Donahoe, Eileen. "So Software Has Eaten the World: What Does It Mean for Human Rights, Security & Governance?" *Human Rights Watch,* March 22, 2016.

"Digital Disruption of Human Rights." *Human Rights Watch,* March 25, 2016.

Doyle, Michael. *Empires.* Ithaca: Cornell University Press, 1986.

DRS Technologies Advertisement. *Homeland Security Today,* March, 5, 2012.

"Editorial: Europe's Urgent Security Challenge." *The New York Times,* April 11, 2016.

Elden, Stuart. *The Birth of Territory.* Chicago: University of Chicago Press, 2013.

Eubanks, Virginia. "Want to Predict the Future of Surveillance? Ask Poor Communities." *The American Prospect,* January 15, 2014.

"European Union Border Security," *Government Gazette,* March 2013.

Fabre, Cecile. *Justice in a Changing World.* Cambridge, UK: Polity Press, 2007.

"Fact Sheet: Big Data and Privacy Working Group Review." White House Office of the Press Secretary. News Release, May 1, 2014, https://www.whitehouse.gov/the-press-office/2014/05/01/fact-sheet-big-data-and-privacy-working-group-review.

Febvre, Lucien. *A Geographical Introduction to History.* Westport, CT: Greenwood Press, 1974.

Finnegan, Philip. "Analyst's Notebook: FLIR + ICx = New Opportunities." *Homeland Security Today* June 8, 2012.

Finnegan, Philip, and Peter Barnes. "Homeland Security Today's Top 25 of 2011." *Homeland Security Today,* April 24–29, 2012.

Foucault, Michel. *Power/Knowledge: Selected Interviews & Other Writings 1972–1977.* Translated by C. Gordon, L. Marshall, J. Mepham and K. Soper. Edited by C. Gordon. New York: Pantheon Books, 1980.

"The Subject and Power." In *Power,* edited by James D. Faubion, 326–48. New York: The New Press, 2000.

Security, Territory, Population: Lectures at the College de France, 1977–1978. Translated by G. Burchell. Edited by M. Senellart. New York: Picador, 2007.

Foster, Peter. "European Cross-Border Security Years Away, Experts Warn." *The Telegraph*, March 23, 2016.

Fraser, Nancy. *Scales of Justice: Reimagining Political Space in a Globalizing World*. New York: Columbia University Press, 2009.

Fraser, Nancy, and Axel Honneth. *Redistribution or Recognition? A Political-Philosophical Exchange*. New York: Verso, 2003.

Freeden, Michael. *Rights*. Minneapolis: University of Minnesota Press, 1991.

Freud, Sigmund. *Civilization and Its Discontents*. Translated by J. Strachey. Edited by P. Gay. New York: Norton & Co, 1961.

Fuller, Gillian. "Welcome to Windows 2.1: Motion Aesthetics at the Airport." In *Politics at the Airport*, edited by M. B. Salter. Minneapolis: University of Minneapolis Press, 2008.

Ganapathy, Nirmala. "US, India Move Towards Sharing Logistics." *Strait Times*, April 13, 2016.

Gergen, Kenneth J. *The Saturated Self: Dilemmas of Identity in Contemporary Life*, New York: Basic Books, 2000.

Gidda, Mirren. "As Routes to Europe Close, Refugees Are Starting to Consider One of the Oldest and Deadliest Crossings." *Newsweek*, April 12, 2016.

Giddens, Anthony. *The Nation-State and Violence: Volume Two of A Contemporary Critique of Historical Materialism*. Berkeley, CA: University of California Press, 1987.

Goddard, Terry. "How to Fix a Broken Border: A Three Part Series." In *Perspectives*: Immigration Policy Center, 2012.

Goodin, Robert E. "Enfranchising All Affected Interests, and Its Alternatives." *Philosophy & Public Affairs* 25 (1), 2007.

Goodwin, Jacob. "Editorial: Security and Money." *Government Security News*, February, 2012.

"With SBInet behind it, CBP develops a new procurement strategy." *Government Security News*, February 26, 2012.

Grauman, Brigid. "Cyber-Security: The Vexed Question of Global Rules." Security & Defence Agenda. Available at: www.mcafee.com/us/resources/reports/rp-sda-cyber-security.pdf, 2012.

Grene, David. "Introduction" to *Herodotus: The History*, Chicago: University of Chicago Press, 1987, at 14.

Habermas, Jurgen. "Three Normative Models of Democracy." In *Democracy and Difference: Contesting the Boundaries of the Political*, edited by Seyla Benhabib, 21–30. Princeton: Princeton University Press, 1996.

The Inclusion of the Other: Studies in Political Theory. Edited by C. Cronin and P. D. Greif. Cambridge: MIT Press, 1998.

Hardin, Peter. "Eyes in the Skies." *Richmond Times-Dispatch*, October 30, 2003.

Hawley, Kip. "Why Airport Security Is Broken – And How To Fix It." *The Wall Street Journal*, April 15, 2012.

Heidegger, Martin. "Building Dwelling Thinking." In *Basic Writings: From Being and Time (1927) to The Task of Thinking (1964)*, edited by D. F. Krell. London: Routledge, 1993.

Held, David. *Democracy and the Global Order*. Palo Alto: Stanford University Press, 1995.

Models of Democracy. Cambridge, UK: Polity, 2006.

Honig, Bonnie. *Democracy and the Foreigner.* Princeton: Princeton University Press, 2001.

Hovsepian, Marcel. "Frontlines: Border Security Strategy Remains Myopic." *Homeland Security Today,* January 2, 2011.

Hurrell, Andrew. "International Law and the Making and Unmaking of Boundaries." In *States, Nations, and Borders: The Ethics of Making Boundaries,* edited by A. Buchanan and M. Moore. Cambridge: Cambridge University Press, 2003.

On Global Order: Power, Values, and the Constitution of International Society. Oxford: Oxford University Press, 2007.

Huysmans, Jef. "The European Union and the Securitization of Migration." *Journal of Common Market Studies* 38 (5):751–77, 2000.

Ignatius, David. "Brussels Shows Europe's Shockingly Dysfunctional Approach to Security." *The Washington Post,* March 22, 2016.

Iris Recognition at a Distance and on the Move. SRI International Sarnoff, Iris on the Move Product Guide, 2012.

Jain, Anil K. "Biometric Recognition." *Lecture* at Michigan State University. Available at: http://biometrics.cse.msu.edu. (Last Accessed: September 11, 2011), 2011.

Johnson, Jeh. "Statement by Secretary Jeh C. Johnson on Southwest Border Security." news release, March 9, 2016, https://www.dhs.gov/news/2016/03/09/statement-secretary-jeh-c-johnson-southwest-border-security.

Keene, Edward. *International Political Thought: A Historical Introduction* Cambridge, UK: Polity Press, 2005.

Khalidi, Rashid. *Palestinian Identity: The Construction of Modern National Consciousness.* New York: Columbia University Press, 1997.

Kimery, Anthony. "A Day in the Life of Nogales." *Homeland Security Today,* September 1, 2010.

"Northern Border Intel-Sharing Deficient, Fed Audit, Officials Say". *Homeland Security Today,* March 8, 2011.

"House Passes SMART Port Security Act." *Homeland Security Today,* June 28, 2012.

"First In-Depth Inside Look at Border Patrol's New National Strategy, Issues and Implementation." *Homeland Security Today,* May 7, 2012.

Kostiuk, Christine. "Bill C-60: Keeping Canadians Safe (Protecting Borders) Act." *Parliamentary Information and Research Service Legislative Summary LS-670E,* 2010.

Krasner, Stephen D. *Sovereignty: Organized Hypocrisy.* Princeton: Princeton University Press, 1999.

"Problematic Sovereignty." In *Problematic Sovereignty: Contested Rules and Political Possibilities,* edited by S. D. Krasner. New York: Columbia University Press, 2001.

Kuper, Andrew. *Democracy Beyond Borders: Justice and Representation in Global Institutions.* Oxford: Oxford University Press, 2004.

Kymlicka, Will. *Multicultural Citizenship: A Liberal Theory of Minority Rights.* Oxford, UK: Oxford University Press, 1995.

References   235

"Territorial Boundaries: A Liberal-Egalitarian Perspective." In *Boundaries and Justice. Diverse Ethical Perspectives*, edited by D. Miller and S. H. Hashmi. Princeton: Princeton University Press, 2001.

National Responsibility and Global Justice. Oxford: Oxford University Press, 2007.

Kymlicka, Will. *Contemporary Political Philosophy: An Introduction*. Oxford: Oxford University Press, 2002.

Laborde, Cecile. *Critical Republicanism*. Oxford: Oxford University Press, 2008.

Lacey, Marc. "Arizona Officials, Fed Up With U.S. Efforts, Seek Donations to Build Border Fence." *The New York Times*, July 20, 2011, A16.

Lattimore, Owen. *Inner Asian Frontiers of China*. Boston: Beacon Press, 1951.

Leggiere, Philip. "Beyond the One-Way Alert." *Homeland Security Today*, March, 10–11, 2012.

Leonard, Sarah. "The Creation of FRONTEX and the Politics of Institutionalisation in the EU External Borders Policy." *Journal of Contemporary European Research* 5 (3):371–88, 2009.

Ling, Justin. "Canada Is Going to Start Handing over Even More Data About Travelers to the US." *Vice News*, March 14, 2016.

Locke, John. *Two Treatises of Government*. Cambridge: Cambridge University Press, 2014.

Luttwak, Edward. *The Grand Strategy of the Roman Empire: From the First Century A.D. To the Third*. London: Weidenfeld & Nicholson, 1976.

Lyon, David. "Surveillance, Security and Social Sorting: Emerging Research Priorities." *International Criminal Justice Review* 17 (3):161–70, 2007.

Identifying Citizens: ID Cards as Surveillance. Cambridge, UK: Polity Press, 2009.

Machiavelli, Niccolo. *The Prince*. edited by H. C. Mansfield. Chicago: University of Chicago Press, 1996.

Discourses on Livy. Translated by Ninian Hill. Mineola, NY: Dover Publications, [1531], 2007.

Maier, Charles S. *Among Empires: American Ascendancy and its Predecessors*. Cambridge, MA: Harvard University Press, 2006.

Manent, Pierre. *A World Beyond Politics a Defense of the Nation-State*. Princeton: Princeton University Press, 2006.

Marx, Karl. *The Marx-Engels Reader*. edited by Robert C. Tucker. New York: W. W. Norton & Company, 1978.

Capital, Volume 1. Translated by Ben Fowkes. London: Penguin Classics, 1990.

McCarter, Mickey. "287(G) Vital To Immigration Reform: Ex-chief of ICE calls for More Flexibility to Enforce Law." *Homeland Security Today*, November 12, 2009.

"CBP Chief Lists 7 Principles For Agency's Success: Bersin Says Facilitating Trade as Important as Preventing Terror." *Homeland Security Today*, October 15, 2010.

"DHS Programs Under Review Get No Funding: Cargo Screening? SBInet? General Aviation? Under Review." *Homeland Security Today*, February 25, 2010.

"Napolitano Outlines DHS Priorities for 2010: At Top: Aviation, Borders, Information Sharing, Immigration Reform." *Homeland Security Today*, January 27, 2010.

"Reconsider US-VISIT Exit Tests: GAO Finds US-VISIT Exit Trials Unsatisfactory." *Homeland Security Today* August 11, 2010.

"Disagreements Over Virtual Fence Decision." *Homeland Security Today*, 2011.

"TSA Launches Air Cargo Security Initiatives." *Homeland Security Today*, 2011.

"Aviation, Port Security Bills Enjoy Bipartisan Support from House Lawmakers." *Homeland Security Today*, July 2, 2012.

"Governor of Puerto Rico Calls for US Caribbean Border Initiative To Combat Drug Cartels." *Homeland Security Today*, June 22, 2012.

"Bersin Steps Down as CBP Chief, Returns to DHS International Affairs." *Homeland Security Today* January 3, 2012.

Mill, John Stuart. *On Liberty*. Edited by David Bromwich and George Kateb. New Haven, CT: Yale University Press, 2003.

Miller, David. *Citizenship and National Identity*. Cambridge: Polity Press, 2000.

"Political Philosophy for Earthlings." In *Political Theory: Methods and Approaches*, edited by David Leopold and Marc Stears, 29–48. Oxford: Oxford University Press, 2008.

"Debatable Lands." *International Theory* 6, no. 1 (March): 104–21, 2014.

Mortera-Martinez, Camino "Big Data, Big Brother? How to Secure Europeans' Safety and Privacy." news release, December, 2015, https://www.cer.org.uk/sites/default/files/pb_CMM_bigbrother_4dec15.pdf.

Mosk, Matthew, Angela Hill, and Timothy Fleming. Gaping Holes in Airline Security: Loaded Gun Slips Past TSA Screeners. *ABC News*, December 16, 2010.

Muir, Richard. *Modern Political Geography*. New York: Palgrave Macmillan, 1975.

Muller, Benjamin J. "Travelers, Borders, Dangers: Locating the Political at the Biometric Border." In *Politics at the Airport*, edited by M. B. Salter. Minneapolis: University of Minneapolis Press, 2008.

"National Strategy for Aviation Security." *National Security Presidential Directive (NSPD)* 47, 2007.

"The National Strategy for Global Supply Chain Security." *The Office of the White House*, 2012.

Neal, Andrew W. "Securitization and Risk at the EU Border: The Origins of FRONTEX." *Journal of Common Market Studies* 47 (2):333–56, 2009.

Nicolaïdis, Kalypso. "Europe's Ends." In *The Meanings of Europe: Changes and Exchanges of a Contested Concept* edited by Claudia Wiesner and Mieke Schmidt-Gleim, 236–57. London: Routledge, 2014.

Nietzsche, Friedrich. *On the Genealogy of Morals and Ecce Homo*. Edited by Walter Kaufman New York: Vintage Books, 1989.

Untimely Meditations. Edited by Daniel Breazeale. Cambridge: Cambridge University Press, 1999.

Nikala, Oscar. "Tunisia to Install Surveillance Gear on New Libyan Border Wall." *DefenseNews*, February 19, 2016.

"Northern Border Strategy." *Department of Homeland Security (DHS) Press Release*, 2012.

"Note on Big Data, Crime and Security: Civil Liberties, Data Protection and Privacy Concerns." *Statewatch*, April 3, 2014.

Nowrasteh, Alex, and Patrick G. Eddington. "How Effective Is Border Security?" *Cato Institute Online*, March 4, 2016.

Ohmae, Kenichi. *The End of the Nation State: The Rise of Regional Economies.* New York: Free Press Paperbacks, 1995.

O'Neill, Onora. "The Dark Side of Human Rights." *International Affairs* 81, no. 2 (2005): 427–39.

Owen, David. "Editor's Note." In *On Global Citizenship: James Tully in Dialogue.* London, UK: Bloomsbury Academic, 2014.

Patrick, J. Michael. "The Economic Cost of Border Security: The Case of the Texas-Mexico Border and the US Visit Program." In *Borderlands: Comparing Border Security in North America and Europe,* edited by E. Brunet-Jailly. Ottawa: University of Ottawa Press, 2007.

Payan, Tony, and Amanda Vasquez. "The Cost of Homeland Security." In *Borderlands: Comparing Border Security in North America and Europe,* edited by E. Brunet-Jailly. Ottawa: University of Ottawa Press, 2007.

Piccone, Paul. "General Introduction." In *The Essential Frankfurt School Reader,* edited by A. Arato and E. Gebhardt. New York: Continuum Publishing, 2000.

Plato. *Complete Works.* Indianapolis: Hackett Publishing Company, 1997.

Pogge, Thomas. "Cosmopolitanism and Sovereignty." *Ethics* 103:48–75, 1992.

World Poverty and Human Rights. Second ed. Malden, MA: Polity Press, 2008.

Poggi, Gianfranco. *The State: Its Nature, Development and Prospects.* Stanford: Stanford University Press, 1990.

Pratt, Mary Louise. *Imperial Eyes: Travel Writing and Transculturation.* New York: Routledge, 2008.

Purcell, Richard. "Privacy Policy and Technology Recommendations for a Federated Information-Sharing System." *Department of Homeland Security Data Privacy and Integrity Advisory Committee,* 2012.

Raghuvashani, Vivek. "Indian Defense Minister to Visit China, Discuss Boundary." *DefenseNews*, March 16, 2016.

Rawls, John. *The Law of Peoples.* Cambridge, MA: Harvard University Press, 1999.

Richardson, J. S. "Imperium Romanum: Empire and the Language of Power." *The Journal of Roman Studies* 81 (1991): 1–9.

"Risk Analysis for 2016." Frontex Press Release, March 26, 2016, frontex.europa.eu/assets/Publications/Risk_Analysis/Annula_Risk_Analysis_2016.pdf.

Rockwell, Mark. "DHS Looks for 'Sweet Spot' to Balance Security and Economic Recovery." *Government Security News*, February, 2012.

Rosenblum, Marc R. "Border Security: Immigration Enforcement Between Ports of Entry." In *Congressional Research Service Report for Congress 7–5700,* 2012.

Rousseau, Jean-Jacques. *The Basic Political Writings.* Edited by D. A. Cress. Indianapolis: Hackett, 1987.

Ruggie, John Gerard. "Territoriality and Beyond: Problematizing Modernity in International Relations." *International Organization* 47 (1):139–74, 1993.

Rushdie, Salman. *Step Across This Line: Collected Non-Fiction 1992–2002.* London: Vintage, 2003.

Sahlins, Peter. *Boundaries: The Making of France and Spain in the Pyrenees.* Berkeley: University of California Press, 1989.

Sandel, Michael. *Liberalism and the Limits of Justice.* Oxford: Oxford University Press, 1982.

Sassen, Saskia. *Territory, Authority, Rights: From Medieval To Global Assemblages.* Princeton: Princeton University Press, 2006.

"Borders, Walls, and Crumbling Sovereignty." *Political Theory* 40 (1):116–22, 2012.

Schmitt, Carl. *The Concept of the Political* Translated by G. Schwab. Chicago: University of Chicago Press, 1996.

Political Theology: Four Chapters on the Concept of Sovereignty. Translated by G. Schwab. Chicago: University of Chicago Press, 2005.

The Nomos of the Earth in the International Law of the Jus Publicum Europaeum. Translated by G. L. Ulmen. New York: Telos Press Publishing, 2006.

Scott, James C. *Seeing Like a State: How Certain Schemes to Improve the Human Condition Have Failed.* New Haven, CT: Yale University Press, 1998.

The Art of Not Being Governed. New Haven: Yale University Press, 2009.

Scott, Sandra Faye. "Privacy Impact Assessment for the Global Enrollment System." *US Department of Homeland Security,* 2006.

Shachar, Ayelet. *The Birthright Lottery: Citizenship and Global Inequality.* Cambridge, MA: Harvard University Press, 2009.

Silverberg, David. "10 Years After 9/11." *Homeland Security Today,* September 8, 2011.

Soufan, Ali. "Opinion: Terrorists Cross Borders with Ease. It's Vital That Intelligence Does Too." *The Guardian,* March 24, 2016.

Sparke, Matthew. "A Neoliberal Nexus: Economy, Security and the Biopolitics of Citizenship on the Border." *Political Geography* 25 (2):151–80, 2006.

Spruyt, Hendrik. *The Sovereign State and Its Competitors: An Analysis of Systems Change.* Princeton: Princeton University Press, 1994.

Taylor, Charles. "The Politics of Recognition." In *Multiculturalism: Examining the Politics of Recognition,* edited by Amy Gutmann. Princeton: Princeton University Press, 1994.

Terrorist Screening Center: Frequently Asked Questions. 2012. Federal Bureau of Investigations, Terrorist Screening Center.

Torpey, John. *The Invention of the Passport: Surveillance, Citizenship, and the State.* Cambridge, UK: Cambridge University Press, 2000.

Triandafyllidou, Anna. "Governing Migrant Smuggling: A Criminality Approach Is Not Sufficient." *openDemocracy.net,* April 6, 2016.

Tully, James. *On Global Citizenship: James Tully in Dialogue.* London, UK: Bloomsbury Academic, 2014.

US Department of Homeland Security Ensures Secure and Efficient Borders with Western Hemisphere Travel Initiative (WHTI): Case Study. 2009. Unisys.

Ugur, Mehmet. "Freedom of Movement vs. Exclusion: A Reinterpretation of the 'Insider'-'Outsider' Divide in the European Union." *International Migration Review* 29 (4):964–99, 1995.

van Houtum, Henk, and Anke Strüver. "Borders, Strangers, Doors and Bridges." *Space and Polity* 6 (2):141–6, 2002.

Walker, Neil. "Beyond Boundary Disputes and Basic Grids: Mapping the Global Disorder of Normative Orders." *International Journal of Constitutional Law* 6:378–96, 2008.

Walkom, Thomas "Trudeau Quietly Agrees to Share Info on Canadians with U.S." *The Star*, March 13, 2016.

Walzer, Michael. "The Moral Standing of States." *Philosophy and Public Affairs* 9:209–29, 1980.

Spheres of Justice: A Defense of Pluralism and Equality. New York: Basic Books, 1983.

Wells, H. G. *The Future in America: A Search After Realities.* Lexington, KY: Forgotten Books, 2014.

Wendt, Alexander. "Anarchy Is What States Make of It: The Social Construction of Power Politics." *International Organization* 46, no. 2 (Spring 1992): 391–425.

Whelan, Frederick G. "Democratic Theory and the Boundary Problem." In *Liberal Democracy*, edited by J. R. Pennock and J. W. Chapman. New York: New York University Press, 1983.

Williams, Bernard. *In the Beginning Was the Deed.* Princeton: Princeton University Press, 2005.

Wolin, Sheldon. "Fugitive Democracy." In *Democracy and Difference: Contesting the Boundaries of the Political*, edited by Seyla Benhabib, 31–45. Princeton: Princeton University Press, 1996.

Index

Abizadeh, Arash, 101, 198
Act of Supremacy, England, 36
Agamben, Giorgio, 64–5, 162, 218, 220
Ahern, Jayson, 53
American Recovery and Reinvestment Act
  (2009), 144
Amoore, Louise, 222
Anderson, Benedict, 42, 108
Anderson, Malcolm, 95
Ansel, Christopher, 91
arbitrary power, 166
Arendt, Hannah, 23–4, 63, 165, 188, 196,
  217
Aristotle, 27, 101, 218
Australia, 208–9
Aviation and Transportation Security Act
  (ATSA), 143

Barkakati, Nabajyoti, 190–1
Benhabib, Seyla, 122–24, 132
Benjamin, Walter, 64
Berlin, Isaiah, 76, 165
Bersin, Alan, 53
Beyond the Border Agreement
  (2011), US-Canada,
  22, 76, 81–4, 93, 175, 182–3
big data, 157–66, 221–24. *See also* data
Bigo, Didier, 40, 196
bilateralism, 206–13
biometrics, 58, 145–7, 155–7, 208–9.
  See also data
border, the
  attributes of, xiii
  defined, xi–xii
  estrangement at, xvi
  evolution of, 2–3, 141, 147–8
  frontier *vs.*, 10, 25–6, 29–30, 32–3, 35,
    43, 114–16
  heterogeneous inside, 11, 26, 41
  security after 9/11, 3 (*See also* border
    security)
  walling, 51–5
  zonal *vs.* linear, 10, 38

Border Enforcement of Security Team
  (BEST), 79–80
Border Patrol National Strategy
  2012-2016, United States, 60
border security, perimeter
  and beyond, new consciousness, 51–3
  center/periphery, 66–9
  distant self, 69–71
  evolution of, US 1986-2016, 51–3
  peripherality, security and borderlands,
    62–71
  walling, 9/11 first border patrol
    strategy, 51–3
  walling discontents, 53–5
  Zone of Heterogeneity, 58–60
  Zone of Surveillance, 56–8
  Zone of Vigilance, 60–2
border security, ports of entry
  Big Data and, 160–6
  classification, profiling, 151–2
  data, new security landscape, 147–50
  data and, 4, 6, 15–16
  data capture, biometrics, 145–7,
    155–7
  exit monitoring, 16–17
  politics of identification, 150–66
  predictive analytics, 152–3
  risk-based filtration and, 15
  security, 4–5, 140–5
  traveler programs, TSA
    Pre[check], 153–5
  trusted traveler programs, TSA
    Pre[check], 153–5
Bourdieu, Pierre, xvi, 164
Brown, Wendy, 2, 66
Buchanan, Allen, 95
Budapest Convention on
  Cyber-Crime, 214
bureaucracy
  data and, 160–63, 224
  rationalization, 6, 142,
    163–4, 165
Butler, Judith, 9–10, 71, 97

241

Made in the USA
Middletown, DE
17 January 2023

22348865R00149